RAMBLER
CORNWALL

Slow Travels Through a Salt-Licked Country

BY
ARUNDHATI BASU

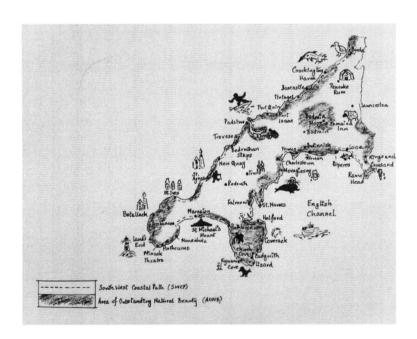

Illustrations by author

NEW YORK

Gaggling
Geese
PRESS

Illustrations by author
Cover design & logo by James, GoOnWrite.com
Formatting by Polgarus Studio

For Adi,

I climb hills knowing that you have my back.
(Those kicks in the back were much needed)

"I have an idea that some men are born out of their due place. Accident has cast them amid certain surroundings, but they have always a nostalgia for a home they know not. They are strangers in their birthplace, and the leafy lanes they have known from childhood or the populous streets in which they have played, remain but a place of passage… Perhaps it is this sense of strangeness that sends men far and wide in the search for something permanent, to which they may attach themselves."

Somerset Maugham, *The Moon and Sixpence*, 1919

Contents

Acknowledgements

Aha, the part where I pander to my love for making lists.

Starting the roll call of dedications with Tuktuk. Dear sweet boy, you were missed unbearably on all our Cornwall trips and still are.

I could not carry on without a special note for my parents. And Twisha's mother, who stood at a bus stop in Calcutta and told my father that I was meant to study arts.

To Daphne du Maurier, who introduced me to Cornwall, and all the writers from the past whose books fed my passion. Celia Fiennes, Alphonse Esquiros, Wilkie Collins, Lord Tennyson, Enid Blyton, Agatha Christie, Rosamunde Pilcher… And Anamika, who brought it all rushing back when she said on a summer's day in East London, "Mom didi, you have to go to Cornwall."

To my former newspaper editors, Samita, Seema, Pratyush, Paran. You shaped me.

Anuradha, Elan, Sayoni, and Paromita, your inputs regarding the cover were wholly appreciated. Special thanks going out, for James, for designing a beautiful cover; for Rachel, for editing the book and giving it direction; Jason of Polgarus Studios for formatting the book without cussing me aloud for innumerable changes. For my best friend, my husband, for being my rudder all through the desperation of writing. Privately printing a book is an eye-opening journey and it really takes a village.

To all the chippy owners and the hostelries and the lovely people of Cornwall. To Alastair and his kind, who chose to become insiders. You are my heroes.

And to you who picked this book up, probably spent a pretty penny on it, thank you for rescuing me from the fate of being that author who has not sold a book yet.

PROLOGUE

There are places in the old countryside in Cornwall where ancient sycamores, hazels and oaks cradle you in their boughs, where skeins of sunlight filter through with effort and the grounds are thick with wildflowers and brambles and bracken, and curling fronds of fern so ridiculously lush that you wonder if you have perchance stumbled into a naturalist's dream. On a drowsy noon in April, beneath powdery blue skies, I am pottering through just such a place with my husband, when the apple of my eyes huffs and says, "Hurry up, would you? I am growing older by the minute".

"I'll be sure to take care of those grey hairs," I say in reply. The quip doesn't sit well with my co-traveller. I carry on nonetheless with the process of squinting at gravestones smudged by the passage of the years. It comes easy to slip into the serene mood of our surroundings, a medieval church sat atop a hill, to wrap myself in the calm that clings to the place of prayer like ivy that grows wild and luscious on the barks of old trees. Having had my fill of reading epitaphs and carried on stubbornly despite the silent stares of an impatient husband, I vote that we get back on the pastoral path to the nearest fishing village of Polruan. And I hear Adi sigh.

"I am growing faint, you know," he adds, for effect.

"Right you are, you poor thing. With longing for a pub (and a pint) I suppose?" I ask.

Here I present my companion, dear reader, on my various travels through Cornwall. The one who nurses a strong opinion on my habit of dawdling and airs it through frowns and furrowed brows, enough to give one heartburn. It has been a few hours of trampling through coppiced woods, but his protests would persuade you to wonder if we have been indeed tramping through the countryside for days on end. In the same breath, I must vouch for it that I would have no other companion for my travels.

The act of travel as the act of life itself is a fair bit about the person you are on a journey with. Here I must draw upon the thoughts of a wise relative, from a conversation on love and loss, and the longing one feels for a loved one lost forever. I haven't managed to forget his words, despite the fact that my mind is as porous as a sieve. He had said: "It is the people in your life that bring meaning to it. You will find the most idyllic places empty and devoid of pleasure, without these very people in it." He followed it up with an example, which I shall leave out for the sake of brevity. It sounded a bit obvious to me in the beginning, but the more I let the thought flower and mature, the more it appealed to me.

The year I begin my story here, in 2017, Adi and I are to leave Blighty for a new transatlantic home. It is supposed to be a toss-up between New York City and New Jersey, but we decide to tackle that dilemma when we cross the pond. Before leaving the UK, we make a farewell trip to our beloved Cornwall with the longest holiday we have taken there. Ten days of walking and pub-hopping to mark our reluctant journey into quarters unknown to us. The mood is bittersweet. Yet I get ahead of myself. I suppose I should take you to the beginning of my infatuation with Cornwall, where it all really started, before it took roots so strong that I had to write a book on it.

INTRODUCTION

Calcutta to Cornwall

I was smitten by Cornwall long before I crossed the River Tamar into the southern reaches of Britain. It started with a Daphne du Maurier novel I found in the old library of the missionary school that I attended in Calcutta. A bookish, spectacled twelve-year-old, I was riveted by the faraway land that the author wrote of.

It was not *Rebecca*, no. It was a well-thumbed copy of *The King's General*. I had no idea at the time that it was du Maurier's first stab at a novel and that she wrote it up while she lived in Menabilly, an estate in Cornwall perhaps better known to you as Rebecca's Manderley. Menabilly, as it happens, has been the historic seat of the Rashleigh family since the late 1500s. Significant as their status is as one of the oldest landowning families in the West Country, it wavers in the face of powerful fiction, which tends to overpower the real. And so we find that we know the Rashleighs' Menabilly as Rebecca's Manderley.

Days after I had speed read *The King's General*, I was left brooding about the story. The novel is set around the real-life discovery of a skeleton in the 1800s by one of the Rashleighs of Menabilly. It was found walled up within a buttress of the building. The family passed on the bones of the story to du Maurier. The backdrop was the English Civil War that raged through England during the 17th century and the remains were possibly those of a young Grenville (another illustrious family name in these parts), a cavalier and Royalist supporter of King Charles I during the war. The poor fellow had had a fiendish end. But strange is the turn of the wheel of fortune. The discovery of his earthly remains inspired an author like du Maurier hundreds of years later to write a novel. Which in turn got a girl in glasses and pigtails (yours truly), thousands of miles away, to dream of another continent. And to travel years later to du Maurier's beloved Cornwall. Makes you wonder if life is nothing more than a series of reactions sparked off by a chance incident.

The *mystère* of Cornwall had spread itself thick and penetrated the farthest corners of my mind, and if du Maurier was my literary compass, Enid Blyton and Agatha Christie played solid supporting roles. Years of reading had established the duchy for me as a place thick with drama, where it was not unheard of that a king should be born in a castle perched upon a cliff on a stormy night; where, in clifftop boarding houses, young girls learned to make the transition to "good, sound women the world can lean on", and alongside, practised the art of perfecting lacrosse and midnight feasts; where, one would bumble into confounding mysteries (murders in Gothic mansions) until a detective with an egg-shaped head and waxed moustache arrived upon the scene; and, where amid the desolation of the moors, inns carried on with dubious dealings. It was a world rife with possibilities.

Of every piece of literature I read, it was du Maurier's singular passion for the duchy that reached out to me. The author had left London for "the tail of England, still aloof and rather splendidly detached". Enchanted by the history of its locals, essential figures in the narrative of its small coastal villages, du Maurier wove her novels out of the warp and weft of the stories she collected. I found the tales of ship wreckers, smugglers and vicars alluring. I had to see du Maurier's Cornwall in the flesh and blood. And in doing so, in following in her footsteps, I was richly rewarded.

It was a journey into a land that was unknown, and yet in some way, strangely enough it was a place known. In the way that one sees a place twice over before getting there in person: once through the eyes of another, and then again, through the workings of one's own mind's eye.

Adi and I started heavy and hard, as tourists do. Ticking off places furiously even before we had a proper lay of the land. Skimming through places but not really seeing them for what they were, like a reader guilty of skipping pages of a chunky novel to get to the end. Newly married, my husband and I had arrived in Britain on a glorious summer's day in June 2012. A month later we were on our first road trip to Cornwall.

We were both finding our feet in a relationship that had been stormy, from the time we crossed paths at a bar in Delhi. In the early period of courtship, our relationship was conducted over the vast chasm of distance and time. Adi was in North Carolina getting his master's degree in business studies. I was making my living as a journalist in Delhi. We met while he was in town, interning with a firm. In time, he left for the States. As those couples, who have survived the tumultuous business of a long-distance relationship, know well, we had to dig into the depths of our determination to get to the other side, to end up together. The fact that we were both pig-headed (still are in some ways) makes it a sort of a miracle that we survived the test of time.

After Adi and I were married, we relocated to the UK. Rambling through the West Country time and again, falling in love with the Cornish country and simultaneously with each other all over again, we were in the process of growing and evolving in the relationship. Cornwall was the metaphorical glue. I don't think we realised it at the time. Our consciousness was overwhelmed by the newness of our surroundings. Hindsight allows me to think back to the halcyon years and appreciate the fact that through our travels, we were learning to lower the barriers propped up by our individual egos. The Cornish landscape was inveigling its way into our hearts, while binding us cleverly to each other, and to it.

To further the cause of our common love, we squirrelled away the pounds, and though we occasionally hit the pubs on weekends with friends, we were careful about squandering money on noshing at posh places. As we saw a little more of Cornwall with each trip, we were receiving an education of the finest variety. We were learning to linger. We were learning to be spectators to the spontaneity of life in the countryside. To luxuriate in the pleasure of exchanging thoughts with strangers we would possibly never meet again. Our travel philosophy was evolving.

To slow down and see more was to become our mantra and stick with us for good. Instead of haring from one village to another in a car — as we were wont to do during the first few visits to Cornwall — we were content with tramping along its coastal paths, meandering through meadows, pausing for a chinwag with locals. What furthered the cause of all this walking (and the inevitable side-effect of Elvis legs) is our discovery of our next Cornish love. Doom Bar, Betty Stoggs, Alfie's Revenge, Potion 9… local ales that tempted us to toss off more than a couple of pints at the end of each punishingly long walk. The upshot of these happy endeavours was that we managed to forget for a brief while that we had 'em legs.

***

To tell you properly about why I am a dyed-in-the-wool lover of the Cornish landscape, to go beyond the literary connect, I should take you to Salalah, for I was born there. It is a city in the Sultanate of Oman, the country in the Arabian Peninsula known for its spectacular landscape, Bedouin tribesmen and a surprisingly tolerant rhetoric apropos its conservative Arabic neighbours. It was suitably progressive that a young Bengali couple from Calcutta should decide to make a go of it there through the '70s and the '80s. Ashish had a lucrative job as a civil engineer while Shanta had let slip her dreams of continuing a career of teaching Chemistry to high school students in Calcutta. To Ashish and Shanta, I was born in the '80s, in their adopted hometown of Salalah.

In the first decade of my life, all I knew was the vastness of the desert; the infinite ripples of dunes in the Rub' Al Khali, the immeasurable sea of sand that stretches across southern Arabia; the sea mist, which rolled in wraith-like during the *khareef* (the monsoons). If I cast my thoughts back in time, it is a hotch-potch of hazy memories. Camels dead in the desert, toes turned up, literally; me in a flowery frock standing at the top of a dune with my father, surveying the intimidating landscape around on a hot day; cars floating like dinky toys in flash floods that swept through town in the wake of torrential rains. These are mixed up with stories culled, of the Queen of Sheba travelling through the land for frankincense, tales of lost cities, and explorers of old adventuring through the Rub' Al Khali.

I was enamoured of seeing new places, of hearing stories narrated by people we met along the way. For me, the twain went hand in hand. It goes without saying that my incentives for travelling in the early years revolved around the accumulation of toys, indulgently disbursed by the lovely stewardesses on Gulf Air. Those I hoarded like a magpie.

When we moved to Calcutta, the once iconic city in the eastern quarter of India, I was miserable to be thrown into a mode of life that was not a patch on my delirious childhood in Oman. What also happened around this time is that our travels started drying up. I was introduced to the city instead. To its ugly and its charming parts simultaneously for it is the kind of place where you cannot have one without the other. I found the legacy of the past engaging as we explored its old nooks and corners. The sprawling botanical gardens founded by a colonel of the British East India Co. in the 18th century; nearby, the grounds of my father's 19th century engineering college replete with mossy ponds and weathered buildings; buildings that had survived the Raj. We spent time in colonial clubs that clung to the memories of an era long gone. The last mostly took place in winter when my cousins from London visited us. In Calcutta, I learnt to appreciate the beauty of buildings, weather-beaten but crammed with period architectural beauty. I learnt that the past plays a crucial role in holding a city together.

A journalism course took me to Delhi. I ended up living there, working with the leading dailies in town. I must confess that I enjoyed the liberty of being the architect of my own life. I shared a line-up of rental apartments for years with my mates, till one left for Bombay and the other got married. Then I had an apartment all to myself. At work, I was contented. I had my fair share of press junkets. These took me around Asia. They even allowed me a bite of Africa. But I had seen nothing that remotely came close to Cornwall. As had not Adi. It turned out that my then boyfriend, now husband, had had a nomadic upbringing. As an army child, Adi had spent the greater part of his young life moving from one remote part of India to another.

While Adi and I were dating, we happened to be in the UK together in the summer of 2011. I was in London for my cousin's wedding, and Adi having just secured a consultant's job with an operations management and analytics firm was living in Leicester at the time. I took advantage of every weekend for a month, and spent it with him travelling to Cumbria, Scotland, Wales. Seeing places together was a tonic much needed. I was away from my desk at the newspaper for over a month and never had time flown so quickly.

Cornwall did not happen then. We wanted to see it properly and time was scarce.

After we were married, when Adi finagled a project in the UK, I was thrilled. Sure, it was going to involve big changes, more so on the emotional front. Families, friends and a job apart, I had to leave behind a beloved family member at my in-laws'. A handsome Labrador called Tuktuk. He came into my life because of Adi and even though I knew him for a short period of six months, we were inseparable friends. It was heartbreaking to part ways with Tuktuk and I suppose, both Adi and I looked for ways to supplement this loss — by stalking dogs in our new home country. Professionally, I had parted ways with a full-time job of reporting for *The Telegraph India.* My mind was filled with doubts. I held onto my pen by the tenuous thread of freelancing, writing articles for magazines and newspapers. The discomfort of giving up a life I knew was however far outweighed by the reward of exploring new realms.

And I was just that bit closer to Cornwall.

A Lay of the Land

Nestled within the lap of the English Channel and the Celtic Sea, and bound by the Tamar on the east, Cornwall is over two hundred miles away from the country's capital. In this modern era, even with bridges spanning the broad Tamar, there is the happy illusion of its isolation from the world at large. To begin the task of acquainting you with the land, I should deconstruct the duchy that is the western extremity of Britain. This undertaking is knotty, more so, if you happen to be an *emmet* as the Cornish refer to the likes of you and me, who are outsiders. But with that very word, the note is struck. Of a place far removed, of fantastic remoteness.

Celtic tribes have inhabited Cornwall even before the Roman invasion of Britain dated 43AD. It might be no more than a longish sliver of land - there's just 1,376 square miles of it - yet its history harks back four thousand years. The Romans, doughty as they were, left *Cornouia* (as they called it) to its own devices. Perhaps the terrain was harsh for them to navigate. But as sound businessmen, they wanted tin from Cornwall to further their trading opportunities. The duchy hardly has any Roman forts to show off despite the rest of the country being speckled with palaces, baths, amphitheatres and walls, legacies of the Romans who had occupied the land for four hundred long years.

The first mention of the land has been found in the written records of a Greek historian called Diodorus Siculus, who referred to Cornwall as *Belerion*, or, Land's End. The name itself holds a clue about why the county has been left alone by everybody down the ages, from the Saxons to the Tudors. Its Celtic identity was reinforced by Athelstan, King of the Saxons, who ruled between 925-939 AD. He designated the river Tamar as the border between Cornwall and the rest of the country. The next turning point in its collective history was its designation as a duchy by King Edward III in the 14th century, who established that the title to it should belong traditionally to the eldest son of the reigning monarch of Britain, which still holds good. In present times, it belongs to Prince Charles.

Closely entangled with this independent stance of the duchy is the Cornish language. A derivative of Brythonic Gaelic was spoken in Cornwall, or *Kernow* as the Cornish call their land. By the late 1700s, Cornish was a dying language. The changes started insidiously, sometime during the 16th century with the Reformation of the English Church. In the mid-1500s the Protestant king, Edward VI, dispatched commissioners to Cornwall to enforce the use of Book of Common Prayer among the Cornish. It was the government's bid to replace the existent Latin liturgy. Records state that the king's men did not get a cordial reception in the south west. The Cornish dispatched the following statement to Edward VI:

"We, the Cornyshe men, whereof certain of us understande no Englyshe, utterly refuse thys newe Service."

And they rose up in arms to march to Exeter. Of the 6,000 who had set out for battle, barely a thousand survived, thus setting in motion the depletion of the Cornish population who spoke the native tongue. I have not heard the Cornish language in person though that's not unusual as hardly anyone speaks it. Yet, I hear vestiges of it in place names such as Tywardreath (house on the beach), Penzance (holy headland), Praze-an-Beeble (meadow of the pipes), Marazion (little market), Polgooth (goose pool). Richard Carew, a Cornish antiquary had noted in his Survey of Cornwall in the 1600s, *"By Tre Pol and Pen / Shall ye know all Cornishmen"*. That bit holds true till date as we come upon a litany of names that goes the same way.

The last fluent native speaker of Cornish lived more than two centuries ago. Dorothy Pentreath, a resident of a tiny fishing village called Paul, is said to have maintained the refrain, *"My ny vynnav kewsel Sowsnek!"* ("I will not speak English!") up until her passing in 1777. By that time, her people had started the process of adopting the English language, and after her death, Cornish as it was spoken is said to have been a thing of the past.

***

The horn-shaped peninsula that is Cornwall is trimmed by a jagged coastline made up of secret coves and harbours, often hidden from prying eyes by towering cliffs.

"The forlorn coast draws me to it," says Adi, when I ask him about why he feels impelled to return to it, again and again. Ever a man of few words, my husband surprises me when of his own accord, he adds: "I have seen the ruggedness of the Pacific West Coast. And I would have thought it was the epitome of wild beauty had I not seen the Cornish coast." He is waxing lyrical and I tell him that he stands in danger of being deemed a poetic soul. Maybe we all have bits of poetry stuck in the nooks of our soul, untapped and unused, and so it outs itself from time to time.

All along the 400-mile-long coast of Cornwall, we come upon small villages cobbled together with stone cottages. More about their higgledy-piggledy charm later, but for now let me tell you a bit about the locals. The Cornish are traditionally seafaring people who tend to stick to the old ways of their forefathers. They fish for a living – and it is not uncommon to spot fishermen in grimy yellow oilskins towing luggers behind them. Their ancestors fished for pilchards. Since the mid-20th century however, pilchard fishing has dwindled. Its closest in-demand relative is the sardine - and we know how this one's beloved of the British.

I find sardines intolerable. Yes, I will do penance for it one day, but for now I shall transfer all blame on my roots. I belong to a fish-eating community. Bengalis are renowned for their fish-a-day lifestyle. All my childhood, I have been stuffed with fried anchovies, catfish and whatnot. My only way to counter this routine was to export the said fish out of the windows when my mother left the dining table for the kitchen. Upon her return she would enquire about the whereabouts of the fish. This is when I mustered up courage and lied blatantly. "Why, I had it already." It took her time to wise up to this ritual.

To give you a better idea about this obsession with fish, I should tell you about a small incident from my wedding. On the morning of our wedding day, Adi's parents sent mine a massive fish as per a Bengali ritual. Something about it being a good omen. The fish came dressed as a bride. Now note the impatience of the Bengali. When it comes to fish that is to be deboned and cooked, the fresher, the better. In record time, I watched the buffing, gutting and chopping of it, before it was thrown into an aromatic curry. "The poor fish bride was chopped up as soon as that?" Adi was aghast.

That said, I could not have gone to Cornwall and been a stranger to seafood (which I must say I enjoyed, especially the fish pies).

Closely linked to Cornwall's seafaring history is its association with the dubious business of smuggling. Between the late 17th and early 19th centuries, smuggling had become a way of life in Cornwall, so much so that the Cornish called it "free trade"; those who took part in the exercise were referred to as "free traders". They were doing everything they could to get through a period when Britain was grappling with economic depression, having taken part in the American War of Independence. The result of the country's bid to retain its grip on its colonies was that taxes on items such as tea, tobacco, salt, brandy and gin, had shot up. The common man was reeling under the effect of hyperinflation. For the Cornish people, the imposition of high taxes on imported salt, which was said to be 40 times the original cost, was a bother. You see, quality salt was required for the preservation of pilchards, without which the fishermen faced ruin. They had to find a way out of this sorry state, and what better way than simply acquiring their salt directly from the source?

The geographical isolation of Cornwall from London meant that smuggling across the Channel was possible without immediate intervention from the authorities. Further, the abundance of sheltered coves all along the rugged coastline served the smugglers' purpose only too well. Smuggling became a way of life and it was not unheard of for vicars and teachers to be hand in glove with villagers who flouted the laws of the day with impunity.

***

We have talked about the villages that string around the coast, but what happens inland? Here we see open moors riddled with granitic intrusions, heavily wooded tidal creeks, white China-clay country and remnants of its mining heritage. And because prehistoric people were attracted to resources that the land generated, which in Cornwall's case revolved around tin and copper, we find traces of their former presence inland through ruins of stone circles, menhirs, barrows and monoliths. These are remarkably undisturbed spots and here you find that the land has stories to tell for those who want to learn of them.

A 19th-century Parisian called Alphonse Esquiros, travelling through Cornwall in the 1800s, had remarked on its three crops - "one that turns golden head on the surface of the soil, another that is gathered in the gloom of the mines, and the last that ripens at the bottom of the sea".

Of the three, mining has not survived the passage of time, but a legacy of it is the Cornish flag itself. In it, we have a white cross sticking out from a black backdrop, symbolizing white tin oozing from black rocks. The flag is also dedicated to one of the patron saints of the kingdom of *Kernow*, St. Piran. Legend says that the Irish saint discovered tin and therefore kickstarted a profession that has sustained generations of the Cornish, apart from bequeathing them with an adoration for the bottle. St. Piran is said to have lived by the drink for as long as two hundred years, and get this, he died by it too. He was so in his cups that he tumbled into a well.

This brings me to my next observation about saints and this ancient land, which is doolally as they come, caught up as it is in tales of druids, devils, piskies and goblins. Almost every other village is named for a saint. St. Michael's Mount and Padstow are examples of places named for its two other patron saints, St. Michael and St. Petroc. Of more you shall come by, as you join us on our rambles intermittently over a period of five years along the South West Coastal Path (a scenic route) in a land that is tucked away in the southwest corner of England, at once aloof and remote. But wait, I do not imply that it is stiff lipped. No, that would be terribly amiss of me. It is simply this that Cornwall is content to be left on its own, its identity palpably different from the rest of the country, so that if you do happen to call its folk English, it might baulk and withhold from you its most distinguished contribution to the world: cream teas.

Now, as you come with us to Cornwall of the many saints, do remember three things. You've got to bring your imagination — without it you might as well stay home. Secondly, do not venture too close to the edge of the headland. Rushes of winds could very well sweep you off the cliffs even before the solitary chough has yelped to announce his red-billed presence. Lastly, whatever you do not do, do guard your booty of fish and chips with your life from the swooping, cantankerous bandits, the seagulls. I will not be held responsible for the loss of national treasure.

HARING AROUND THE
WEST COUNTRY

I

The Victorian Gentleman's Inn

Upon the midnight hour we reach a country inn in Cornwall. It will be the first of many, but for now we find a neat Victorian outpost stood by itself amidst swathes of land. At night it appears to be significantly lonelier than I hope it does during the day. There is no other building to be spotted around us. But that is a matter of perception. A country person might not raise his brows. The sky above us is an upturned bowl of dark velvet dusted with stars that sparkle like their faraway lives depend upon the very act of sparkling.

Having arrived notoriously late, not the done thing especially when it comes to the countryside, we are picking our way through a Victorian garden in the wake of a distinctly displeased man. He leads the way with a candle in his hand, that curious brand of British politeness thwarting him from chucking the candle at our heads for arriving late. Imagine it if you will, a maze of topiaries and no lamps to splinter the darkness of the moonless night. A cat as dusky as the evening sky, eyes glimmering green, tails us faithfully. I should swoon at these somewhat gothic beginnings (this is what comes from reading way too many Radcliffes). But much as I adore the old, there is something to be said about being born into modernity. No tight corsets and hooped skirts to get in the way when all one needs is deep breaths and the use of the critical faculty called reason.

Since I am taking you to the beginning of our exploits in Cornwall, the year is 2012 and we are in the middle of a season of many firsts: 'tis the first summer holiday of our residence in the UK, and we are a month into setting up our first home together in Leicester.

Now, I should not be declaring to the world that we live in the most mediocre city the Midlands has to offer; put together by immigrants, curry, and much later, the worthy bones of Richard III. One does not bring up Leicester in a conversation if she can help it, for there's no quibble about it. It is no undiscovered gem. On the 'gram, there is an account which is titled, 'Leicester, It's Not Shit'. Succinct, if you will. But I shall call it home for a while—and its location at the heart of the country is providential to our cause of travelling. Nowhere is too far, the Outer Hebrides excepted.

The season is unfolding rapidly, as if summer like an amateur poker player cannot wait to show its full hand. Long sun-drenched days, eccentric friends, pints of bitters, meaty pasties; the note is struck for the firming up of a long-drawn obsession with the county west of the Tamar. We are aliens, yet curiously enough we feel at home. There are inescapable cultural differences, though nothing truly insurmountable. We are imbibing a new way of life. The most significant realisation on our part is this that things do not operate on a last-minute basis in this new land. When you grow up in a country where things are habitually dealt with at the eleventh hour, where procrastination is king, and everyone is punctually late for everything, you struggle with a radical way of thinking in which events are planned months in advance.

As it happens when you spend any amount of real time in a new country, you start the process of assimilating, giving into a new way of thinking. And with the passage of time, you do not know when this new way of life becomes as natural as breathing. It is the nature of travelling and living in places that you have not known before. The mind unfurls, soaking up pieces of information like a child thirsty for new words, and you realise it with a start one day that to go back to the way you were is the challenge.

Getting back to the July bank holiday weekend when we set out for Cornwall with great expectations, Adi and I. We are accompanied by a quartet of newly acquired friends. They are Adi's Indian colleagues with vastly different personalities, yet we enjoy each other's company. A couple, Ella and Firdous, and the other two die-hard "bachelors" or so they claim, Hitman and Hoonar.

Hitman has been delegated this unusual handle by the group not in the way of nefarious activities, but because the man is literally a hazard behind the wheel. Hoonar, for all his obsession of evading baths and patchworked jackets (which we have tried our best to nick and burn), is the original boho spirit.

I believe I should set the stage for why we turn up awfully late at the inn.

A party of six, we split into two rental cars and drive south of Leicester. Enroute during a half an hour break in Bath, Adi, ever the wise head in the group, suggests that we should probably have a gander at accommodations. Yes, we have gambled some. This might sound nowhere as tricky as Roman legionaries wading through rivers and marshy beds to reach Cornish grounds, but we have made a most "dangerous" presumption. We have set forth for our Cornish jaunt with no hotel bookings in place. "What audacity!" The knowing shall mutter.

In the shadow of Bath's grand buildings that have turned honey gold under the loving gaze of the morning sun, the six of us scan the Web for B&B options, on our laptops, eyebrows touching scalps at extortionate prices.

It takes us the better part of an hour – enough hemming and hawing thrown into the mixture - before we decide upon a night's stay at a boutique inn in North Cornwall. In the village of Port Isaac. We also settle upon the decision to book the next night's stay later. "One day at a time" is the not too bright thought running through our heads.

When there's no one to question a pack of fools, be sure of it, trouble is to be found sat around the corner. First things first, however, we have got to make it to the inn by evening.

"Let's leave it to no later than 9pm," says Adi. Best-laid plans.

Somewhere on the M5, the motorway between Bath and Port Isaac, the engine of the car I am sat in starts sputtering. Eventually it dies. At the wheel is Hitman, known for two things: risqué driving and amorous phone conversations, both activities often conducted simultaneously. "Why on earth are we making stops this early?" asks Firdous, appearing a few seconds later upon the scene, Hoonar and Adi in tow. They have been tailing us all along. Their faces mirror my own bewilderment. Hitman has no idea of what is going on here. Which is not unlike being on a plane flown by a clueless pilot.

Can any good come of such a situation, I ask you.

It takes us time to arrive at the unhappy conclusion, but we eventually arrive upon it - that our friend has kitted up the tank with the wrong fuel. Diesel has been subbed with petrol some time during the process of Hitman sweet talking one of his many girl friends on the phone. The prospect of being stuck on the motorway for hours and the fact that our errant driver is nonchalant about the whole affair, together fills me with a volley of emotions. Inside I am an infuriated dragon, belching fire. Outwardly I have the comportment of a cow. I have been waiting for a toilet break. Ella and I have been steadily emptying cans of ale in the last few hours. Eventually we scramble up the bushy slopes of the motorway for a wee. It is a scratchy affair and the result is that I am feeling wronged by the world at large. The holiday, I think darkly to myself, is showing signs of unravelling into a failure of epic proportions even before it has taken off.

***

An hour into waiting for the RAC Breakdown Unit, my beloved and I team up with our couple friends to drive to the inn in the other car. To keep a man waiting for us into the late hours of the night is horribly rude. Hitman and Hoonar are left behind to spend an extra couple of hours in the company of the stalled car. As they twiddle their fingers upon the busy motorway, we press on through narrow B-roads into the countryside.

Landlubbers as we are, there are a few seafaring approaches to Cornwall through its various estuaries, but we are not in the frame of mind (as you can well imagine). But for the sake of hypothesis, if we had followed in the footsteps of Esquiros, leapfrogging hundreds of years into the past, we might have sailed up the Hayle estuary via the Atlantic. On a steamer bound for

Saltash, we would have battled our way through tempestuous climes and thrilled at the sighting of the estuary, which in the words of the Parisian author, "has its source in the cold heaths in the north-east of the county, runs a distance of sixty miles, with a thousand coils and bends like a serpent, and falls into Plymouth Straits, displaying at its mouth all the majesty of a great river."

The Tamar is a broad river. Isambard Kingdom Brunel, the British engineer made famous through his audacious engineering feats — building bridges, viaducts, tunnels, ships and docks — commented on the girth of the Tamar in 1828: "Much too wide to be worth having a bridge." The incongruity of his belief must have struck him about 30 years later, when he worked on the Royal Albert Bridge that hugged the coast, connecting Plymouth (Devon) to Saltash (Cornwall). Our satnav takes us via the shortest route onto the Tamar Bridge, which runs parallel to Brunel's Royal Albert, and I wonder if I should quibble about this. Changing our course to drive on the Royal Albert, but we want to make good on time. The drive is going to take us an hour more and we are at the threshold of midnight.

How black the night is in the country! Not a person lurks outside in the villages we pass through. Neither do we spot a glimmer of light in any window. As a city person, I find it a bit unnerving. Ella, on the other hand, takes it upon herself to utter intermittent shrieks, declaring, "Ooooh, it is spooky!" A few more prolonged "oohs" and her husband whips his head around from the front passenger seat, asking her to put a lid on it. I am secretly relieved.

We pass by hamlets of whitewashed cottages and bunnies startled by the full beam of the car, as we skirt around invisible pastures held in by dark hedges. We are on a sojourn into the unknown, hurtling down lanes, it seems. "Hurtling" is illusory, however. The speedometer registers a sedate pace of 25 mph. On those B-roads, streamlined so that they can accommodate the passage of barely one car at a time, we are raiders of the lost ark on the quest for treasure. A bed for the night.

In a couple of hours that stretches as taut as eternity – have you noticed how time is a flexible entity when you're weary — we are in the fishing village of Port Isaac.

At the end of our journey, the car trundles up a country lane that deposits us outside an inn with a gravel driveway. The hotel with its impressive Victorian gabled facade is silhouetted against the dark sky and not a soul is to be spotted. It is late after all. The crunching of the gravel beneath our feet is exaggerated by the quiet of the night and once my eyes get used to the darkness, I can see the outline of a reception hall. Inside, for the most part, it is cast in shadows. A candle glows faintly upon the reception table, behind which is sat a man. He is none too thrilled at our intrusion. Face frozen into a mask, he informs us in bland monotones: "I will take you into the garden for the first room. From there you may make your way back to the main building for the other two rooms".

Here then is our own male Florence Nightingale leading the way, candle in hand, till we arrive at an iron gate. Outside it is a fountain with a stone cherub atop it. The figure is so alabaster white and otherworldly that my knees start knocking together right away. I watch as he punches a code into a keypad, the gate swings inwards and opens into a garden whose grandeur is perceptible even in the dark. Gardening must be the national passion given how the British have perfected the art. On any given Sunday, drive past a cottage in the countryside and you will invariably notice men and women pottering about their gardens with lawn mowers, bags of compost, hedge shears, secateurs. Picture those cottages, festooned with climbers, hollyhocks and hydrangeas; topiaries trimmed to military precision, little frogs and hedgehogs probably nestled in the shade of an army of shrubs and bushes. It is all as wholesome to the senses as the sight of a table laden with afternoon tea.

The garden room at the inn turns out to be a suite with a campy name, *The Love Shack*. Its solitary situation aimed at sparking connubial bliss. Lest the circumstantial pointers be not broad enough, the bed is sprinkled with oxblood rose petals. I roll my eyes and I think to myself, what an appropriate beginning. Having drunk deep and long of the brooding pages of a du

Maurier book, here I am in an unlit Victorian garden, which could have belonged in the 1800s.

We might as well be in the middle of nowhere.

None of us lily-livered four, Ella, Firdous, Adi or I, are in a hurry to lay claim to the shack. Daylight might transform the situation, who knows, but there's the innate fear of dark in our minds that humans are coded with, to contend with here. The kind of genetic coding that has been passed down by our primaeval ancestors, who lived in caves and associated darkness with the proliferation of nocturnal predators.

We wait up for Hitman and Hoonar inside the shed. The boys when they arrive, are visibly overcome by the vision of their lonesome quarters and the double bed trimmed with roses. We leave them to make peace with the situation and make our way back to the main building. This time though the cat stays behind, perched on the high walls outside the shack.

Inside the main building, we share a moment of delight. Our room is a cosy affair. Faded wallpaper and snug bed, with an ensuite bath. But what on earth? "The door does not lock!" I exclaim. Sod's Law. "This is not acceptable!" I say indignantly to Adi, who's too exhausted to care. All my hopes of him addressing the situation, namely, stomping down to the reception, suffers a quick death as he promptly burrows himself into bed. My husband is singularly devoted to the cause of sleep, and short of a few ghosts moaning in his ears, he will not be kept from his kip. Soon enough, tiny snores fill up the room.

Meanwhile, I obsess. A remote countryside inn, an unlockable door and a modest piece of luggage holding it in place, does nothing to calm my taut nerves. I lay awake for a while fighting sleep, waiting for the door to creak open. My only distraction is to reflect upon the drama of the day, to picture the glory of the evening sky. I have never seen as many stars in my life dusting the firmament; nature has put on a dazzling show, as if to pat away the troubles of the evening.

***

I must have drifted off willy-nilly for when I open my eyes, morning has dawned with a drumroll of liquid sunshine. The skies look freshly washed and daylight banishes all cowardly drivel of the dark hours from the mind. I feel as brave as a ghost hunter and strut into the garden with its sequestered shack, tut-tutting at my erstwhile frayed nerves. The garden has a duck pond, bushes, brambles, trellised blossoms; in its backdrop is the shimmering Celtic Sea. Why, it is almost a secret garden! Have I stepped into the pages of a book and time-travelled to a historic inn? High ceilings, floral wallpapers, compact bed, the works really, except for the odd matter of a jammed lock.

The inn having started life as a Victorian gentleman's residence, I imagine that a "gentleman" during its early years of existence would not feel very gentle about foibles such as these. He might be frowning invisibly even as we walk beneath its portals, who knows. For I gather that there's a ghost or two in residence at the inn, of which there are several worthy candidates. Maybe, the guardians of the property's secrets are in no hurry to leave them unguarded. How the years must have seeped through and settled comfortably in the stones of this building, how diverse the scenes of the many lives that have been played out within its old walls, for isn't a house more than just a shell for taking shelter?

While Adi takes his own sweet time in the bathroom – longer than my average morning toilette — I do a bit of reading up on my phone. The inn's wifi is ponderous, but I manage to gather the kind of history that adds ambience to my surroundings. The inn, it informs me, began life as a family house that was built by a man from the nearby village of Chapel Amble. I am curious about the man's story and how it melds with the building I find myself in. His name was Buscombe, and he appears to have been an enterprising fellow. Having crossed the seas and reached Bombay, India, he had made a tidy fortune from the stevedoring business. When Buscombe returned home to his native Cornwall, he was an accomplished figure. The gossip mills must have been overworked, I imagine, what with the addition of his Eurasian wife and a new moniker, Squire Hill. In these parts, where the villagers would have delved inwards for spiritual sustenance and looked askance at any suggestion of "vulgarity", by which I mean the flaunting of one's wealth, he would certainly have made tongues wag.

The Bombay-returned "squire" bought land in Port Isaac and constructed a grand residence for his wife and two children in the early 1800s. It was known as Tregenna in the early days. Buscombe's son, the heir apparent, however yearned to return to Bombay and set sail for the distant city. He met an untimely end during the voyage. Following this, Squire Hill's family stopped living at the inn (I wonder where they left for).

The ways in which houses change hands, passing from one family to another, make me think that it must be the natural order of things that nothing should last forever. In the early part of the 20th century, a wealthy London widow by the name of Mrs. Egerton-Jones, bought the house. The story goes that a certain Captain Allerdyce from London arrived at the property to court one of the widow's two daughters and ended up marrying Mrs. Egerton-Jones herself. But when she died, the captain moved bag and baggage to London and Buscombe's building was left empty again. But not for long because the house did boast of modern comforts (such as electricity). It was acquired by a local landowner. The building passed hands after him, and by the '70s, the erstwhile splendid Victorian gardens, greenhouse, and vinery, were reported to have gone to wrack and ruin. You would not know of its former state of déshabille if you sauntered into the gardens today. Its patch of green is worth a look in, conceived as it was as a "public garden" during the industrial revolution when privileged intellectuals did their bit to "gentrify" the not-so-privileged lot.

Without these historical references, the inn might just be another beautiful building in slate, where people pass each other like ships in the night. The present moment by itself is enchanted. A gay wedding is underway at the inn. All packed up and ready to go, we are as if seen off by this old house of Buscombe, with bright clusters of pink and purple hydrangeas blooming in the gardens on this lovely July morning, and elegantly dressed men and women waffling, flutes of bubbly in their hands, carefree chatter filling the air with a hum of happiness. And just like that, the strong Cornish sun has cast off the shadows of the previous night like a phantasmagorical trick conjured by the mind, leaving me with the invigorating thought that we are to come upon unknown quarters soon.

II

When the Road from Porth Quin Leads to Redruth

From when we leave the inn, the road is a sinuous rill, meandering through miles of soothing green countryside before it dips into the sheltered cove at Port Quin. There is just the sea and us, the morning we drive into the village. The tranquillity is punctuated only by a symphony of waves relentlessly slapping the rocks. The Cornish call it the singing of the shores. When fishermen needed to find their way home and land was obscured by a blanket of fog or intense darkness, they listened intently to the sound of the waves breaking upon shore. The shores sang to them, much like the setting sun beckons the wild geese to fly home before it disappears for the day.

Skirting barnacle-encrusted rockpools in the cove, we come upon a solitary red dinghy tilted on its side upon the small beach. Not a soul is to be seen. Even the gulls, the feisty, feathered residents of Cornwall's coastal villages, have given Port Quin a miss for more popular haunts.

How dramatic Port Quin's inlet is! Jagged pieces of volcanic rock radiate into the ocean like dark, thickened talons of some primordial sea creature. A smattering of fisherman's cellars stands upon the cliffs overlooking the cove. Let's say, you are the kind of human being who is an island unto yourself and we are travelling together. You will find yourself enticed by the lonesome posts of Port Quin. "Oh, for that cottage there upon the cliff," you might say to me, a tinge of wistfulness in your tone. For while habitation has crept into almost every village along the coast, Port Quin remains a hamlet, with not a single village store to serve it.

It is the village that died, they say.

Port Quin used to be a fishing village synonymous with pilchards. By now, you know that pilchards largely drove the economy in Cornwall. Like its counterparts along the coast, a large cross-section of the population in this village too lived off the haul of pilchards from the choppy waters off the coast.

Faced by the silence that envelops the village, except for the splashing of the waves, I find it easy to believe the story behind its desertion. In the 19th century, the men of the village went out fishing one night. They never returned. The staunch of faith reason that the fishermen had tempted fate by venturing out on the day of Sabbath. The women, unable to carry on with their harsh existence, and possibly to escape a place that was associated with deep sorrow, abandoned their houses. Not a soul was left in Port Quin.

The solitary nature of the hamlet invites speculation. Leaning against the hump of a rock in its deserted cove, I mull about them, the former inhabitants of Port Quin. Where did they leave for? Why did none of the descendants return to claim this photogenic little place?

The stop at Port Quin is a spontaneous call and I am glad for it. We are not to come upon another abandoned village like it ever again. A hint of what used to be, before the residents left it for good, is preserved in the way of its old fish cellars. Nostalgia, we know, is a precious commodity and so these cellars, where pilchards were once salted and pressed into barrels for shipping to Europe, have been repurposed as holiday lets. Naturally, they do not rent out cheap.

In Carolina Cellar, a two-bedroom stone cottage located atop the slipway, if you can find a booking for yourself (it runs full more often, than not), you are looking at spending over four hundred quid for a two-night stay. That is an estimate for the month of October — which is not even peak tourist season. But here's the thing. You know you are paying for history commingling with solitude, for waking up to a world that is blue. And if you have not slipped in your contact lenses yet, why it would be difficult to tell where the sea begins and where the heavens end.

Walks in Port Quin are filled with possibilities of stumbling upon smugglers' tunnels in dank old caves and coastal paths that take the walker through pastures and kissing gates to a folly that used to be the scene of drunken bashes in the mid-1800s. It belonged to no count or member of the nobility. It was the property of a businessman from Wadebridge who decided that his country den should be called Doyden Castle. His hedonistic den is up for grabs too, as a rental. I would like to peek inside this 'castle', but it being a holiday let, I have to let go of my curiosity, because the others have more on their mind. Also, we are into a different kind of travel these days, haring around places in a car because we have not yet stumbled upon the kind of joy that one derives from slowing down. With each consecutive trip we are to take into Cornwall, we will start leaning in favour of lengthy hikes.

I find that it is the indescribable allure of travelling. It makes you constantly re-evaluate things.

In St. Endellion within the meadows of a family-run strawberry farm, we sit on benches under the strong gaze of the noon sun. The grass is a startling shade of neon green, the sky freshly laundered. Sat outside, we devour crisp calamari, salads and paninis, the air invigorating, the sun baking us slowly but surely. Oh, how wonderful food tastes under the open skies! In front of our eyes, a handful of tots and dogs of various makes and sizes, run the length and breadth of the pastures, adding to the cheeriness of the July morning. Maybe we are all on the sets of a British seaside resort ad.

***

After we have had our fill of the farm's gustatory delights, we arrive at a port town in the spectacular Lizard Peninsula, Porthleven. It is the most southerly port in the UK. The town is furnished with charming stone houses; net lofts (garrets where fishermen traditionally hung fishing nets for mending); fishermen's cottages; a 19th-century harbour that is a safe haven for fishing boats; and the clock tower which looks like a church but is not – it is home to the town council and a snooker club.

It is fitting in the scheme of things that I give into the national tendency to waffle over a Sunday roast at a pub where the stone walls ooze the promise of stories, dark and disturbing. The imagination has the run of the place, for it has the kind of interiors that reek of tales of privateers, smugglers' tunnels and resident ghosts. *The Ship Inn* is the quintessential old British taproom, its timeworn character stamped all over the timbered bar and fireplace, flagstone floors, its cosy nooks and crannies. Documents date the pub back to the 18th century. Almost every inch of its walls and ceiling has been taken over by a farrago of beer mats and brass tankards, so when you are done with craning your neck to get an eyeful of the accents, you have all of five ales to choose from at the bar. It takes me no time to decide my tipple. It is my very first pint of Doom, the ale named for the infamous sandbank called the Doom Bar, off the town of Padstow, that has been the undoing of many a ship.

The Doom, in my fancy, is the perfectly titled drink, fit for a stormy day when the waves are said to rise spectacularly and crash against the windows of *The Ship Inn*. If it makes for a dramatic picture in the mind's eye, I am all for the spectacle it must be in the flesh and blood. It is a hot July's noon when we find a place in the pub's beer garden to rest our behinds. A gull perches itself strategically above us on a high stone wall, not unlike a splendid carving in stone. I wonder if we are playing a part that has been carried on since ancient times in this busy harbour town. People sitting outside the pub, albeit dressed differently, and mindlessly watching the goings-on.

Banter with friends apart, there is enough to keep my senses occupied. The gulls let loose discordant wails from time to time, the jowly fisherman shuffles down the path along the harbour, while a few yards away, people amble around the local fair, the stalls of which hug the harbour. But one significant difference crops up — old-timers must have had a more compelling view of ships wrecked off the coast nearby, having been caught in the south-westerly gales that this part of the country is well known for. Wrecks were a frequent occurrence in Mount's Bay. A survey study from c.1810 noted: "Within a very short space of time, not less than twelve vessels have been lost near, and within sight of, the inhabitants of Porthleven." This called for a safe harbour. It was indeed a necessity – and the harbour was built by French prisoners from the Napoleonic War over a period of 14 years. Courtesy of their sweat and toil, by the middle of the 19th century Porthleven had its protection from the sea in place. Thick sea walls that stand up to the lashings of the sea during relentless storms, sheltering boats and luggers from the fury of nature.

***

On the periphery of Porthleven, we stumble upon a vintage car fair. In a field, we join a merry crowd in a collective gawping at colourful retro cars. There's the Bond Bug, which is a British compact two-seater on three wheels, an odd tangerine-hued number which sticks out amongst the beauties on display. Of particular note, is a pink Cadillac synonymous with The King - as they call Elvis in Memphis. A steady stream of male admirers hovers around it, including the (besotted) husband and his friends. If we are to ask one and all, of all those who huddle around the Cadillac, about what they might want to win in a spontaneously organised raffle, your guess is as golden as mine. Adi and a friend take turns to sit inside the Cadi, tinkering with the dashboard, their glazed eyes not unlike that of children who cannot believe their fortunes at being handed a booty of their choicest candies.

A few yards away people queue up at food stalls with orderliness and patience, as is the British way. Teenagers and children are spread out on rugs and steadily overdosing on a diet of candy and popcorn. It is difficult not to fall prey to the general air of happiness all around.

To round off this tale, because our first holiday in Cornwall is not fated to be without a generous share of twists and turns, to our dismay we find no place to plonk our weary bodies. The sun can sap you of your vigour in the matter of a few hours. Naturally you find yourself grateful for whatever accommodation comes your way after having scampered around the coast. All our dreams at this point revolves around the availability of a hot shower, to be scrubbed and tubbed for bed.

This time around, we are sat in our cars in Penzance, yards away from the home of Maria Branwell, mother of the Bronte sisters. Once again, we are hunched over our laptops.

Rooms at the Falmouth University it is, bereft of students. Everyone has left for home for the summer holidays. The room is basic. We have a bed and an en-suite shower. All that we need really. It happens to be one of the most inexpensive places I have stayed in, in all my years of travel. It is midnight by the time we check in to our room, yet no pother, no crabby receptionists to contend with. Late into the night, by the time we dump our luggage in our respective rooms, we are ravenous. It has been a long day, and though we have not been short of food all through, hunger kicks in once we have settled upon our accommodation for the night. We set out in search of food and wind up in the old mining town of Redruth.

***

In the late 1600s, a British traveller called Celia Fiennes rode through Redruth on horseback. She described it as a "little market town" where "they carry all their things on horses backs, soe that of a market day which was Fryday you see a great number of horses little of size which they call Cornish Cavelys;". Fiennes made a quick stop in town to have her horse re-shoed by a shoesmith, who provided as fine a service as she was used to in London during the day. In an aside, she added that her equine was no match for the hardy horses of Redruth, who could trip along the cobbled roads in town without incurring injuries. This nugget from Fiennes' journal paints a picture of Redruth's former importance. The town boomed with business in the 18th century when the copper that was mined here was in great demand.

On some of our later explorations, we catch sight of the remnants of the tin and copper mines that still survive around Redruth. They are lonely outposts that have been left to the mercy of the elements. And they are crumbling away. Two hundred years ago, no one could have envisioned the abandonment of the mines that were a prime source of livelihood for the Cornish villager.

The British novelist and profligate, William Beckford, was in this part of copper mining country in the 1780s, somewhere around the Great Consolidated Mines that was a conglomeration of a number of mines. It was the largest single producer of copper in the county and had produced a record 442,493 tonnes of ore between the years 1819 and 1858. Of his experience at the mines, Beckford wrote: "At every step one stumbles upon ladders that lead into utter darkness or funnels that exhale warm copperous vapours. All around these openings the ore is piled up in heaps ready for purchasers. I saw it drawn reeking out of the mine by the help of a machine called a whim put in motion by mules, which in their turn are stimulated by impish children hanging over the poor brutes and flogging them without respite. The dismal scene of whims, suffering mules and hillocks of cinders, extends for miles…" Disconcerting scenes for a dilettante with a country estate and vast fortune to his name.

Another interesting account of the appearance of the ore itself is to be culled from the diaries of Fiennes who rode side-saddle on her horse through every county in England. We might find it strange today that a woman of her day could be bothered about such a rough profession such as mining was. But then, we are talking about an unusual woman in every way. Fiennes was a solo traveller, something that was almost unheard of in the 17th century. She was also unusually keen on studying mining, probably on account of the land she owned in Cheshire where the first known deposits of rock salt were found. In the landscape around Redruth, which she found "very bleake and full of mines", Fiennes stopped for a proper look at the ore. She depicts the ore as akin to tin, "only this looks blackish or rather a purple colour and the glistening part is yellow as the other was white…"

Passing through the beat market town a few years after Fiennes's journey, author Daniel Defoe dismissed it as "worthy of no consideration". One can attribute it to a difference in perspective, or, it could have been simply this that Redruth was about to undergo a significant change in status, starting the mid-1700s. From a town that had one main street, it was to swell in size to accommodate a growing population. When John Wesley, the proponent of

Methodism, arrived with his brother in Redruth in the late 1700s, it would have further drawn attention to the town. The Wesley brothers delivered a series of sermons at Gwennap Pit, an abandoned mine dig that was converted into an open-air amphitheatre.

In this village named for a stream that ran red from the extraction of ore, and which many a curious traveller passed through in the old days, we find the Redruth Kebab House. A tiny Turkish kebab joint representative of every other kebab house in the country, beloved of locals for post-pub visits. A rotating slab of meat, pockets of bread stuffed with slices of hand-carved meat and spices, fistfuls of spicy veg to accompany this meaty carnival, and then, your bare hands to bite into this juicy fest. No cutlery, no faff. Just a kind of no-nonsense popularity.

When our respective orders are ready, we fall upon boxes of kebabs and chips with singular focus, not an errant word slipping out of our mouths. In the background, pop hits play on a small television mounted on the wall. At a corner seat by the shop window, sat by himself is a gangly boy with a ginger mop of hair and freckled nose. There is enough booze in his system to make him slur as he registers our presence, his tone riddled with astonishment. How on earth have people managed to drive into his godforsaken town?

The actual words which issue forth from his mouth, while in the process of devouring a hefty kebab roll, goes thus: "Whatever are you folks doing in this shitty old mining town? No one comes to Redruth!"

III

King Arthur's Corner

Harry of Devon is a stickler for his holidays in Tintagel, a town in the northern part of Cornwall. Every summer he is to be seen on this rugged part of the coastline, cavorting in the cerulean waters of the Celtic Sea. He must be an old chap by now. When I set eyes on him first, he is paddling in the shallow waters near Merlin's Cave, a stick clamped in his jaws, no cares hanging about his beautiful blonde head.

I should slip it in right about now that the subject at hand is a golden retriever, who at the point of time is caught up in the tireless cycle of diving into the choppy waters and fetching sticks tossed in by his mistress. If I open this account of our time in Tintagel, chronicling an encounter with a retriever, it is because I like dogs more than I like humans. But then you already know about it. I find that I am in the right country for the British embrace dogs like no other race. And they are particularly chummy when one trots out a comment on their beloved companion. That's when any kind of barrier is swept aside for a proper natter about the dog's name, age, predilections, diet.

It is the second day of our weekend trip and the six of us have driven into the town of Tintagel, based on my hankering to clap eyes upon the ruins of an old castle. Our friends indulge me. They tease me good-naturedly about my tendency to do research on places I want to visit and then plan our travels. But they too gasp with pleasure when we end up at Tintagel Castle. Weathered by the passage of time, it is no ordinary fortress. King Arthur lived here, as goes the legend — if you place faith in the likes of them. For my part, I like a good story and will lend it the time of day.

In her book, *Vanishing Cornwall*, du Maurier pointed out the historical fact that towards the end of the 5th century A.D. there was a Christian warrior called Arthur who fought the Saxon kings. He might have been a Cornish chief. Du Maurier wrote: "Arthur is to Cornwall what Theseus is to Greece. His myth is everywhere…Not in Cornwall only but in Somerset and Wales, and across the Channel to Brittany, Arthur is a hero; a Celtic warrior, a Breton prince, a Cornish king."

The nearby market town of Camelford is believed to have been Camelot, Arthur's seat. In its vicinity is an ancient site called Slaughter Bridge. There a battle was fought between the Cornish and the Saxons, in which Arthur was supposed to have been fatally wounded. Recalling this association of Arthur with Camelot, there is a Victorian pile by the name of Hotel Camelot in Tintagel. It is an attractive landmark in town, once a sought-out destination for travellers in the Victorian and Edwardian eras.

Let me tell you a bit about the layout of the castle, as I have gathered from my visit to it. It is bifurcated. A part of it rests on the mainland. The other half is laid out on a promontory that retains a connection with the mainland through a neck of land, long lost to the sea. Flights of stairs, steep and crumbling, are hewed into the stony cliffs. Up these, I gingerly climb to the remnants of the structure that stands watch upon the mainland. They strike the senses as impressive and gaunt, at once. I look down the length of the steps I have slogged up, and almost involuntarily, I take a step back. One misstep and I might take a tumble into the sea. Let me rephrase that. To be precise, first I should be dashed against the rocks, then the wind should provide the finishing touches by sweeping battered ol' me into the cauldron of turbulent waters below.

To shake off the frisson of fear, I let my imagination wander around my immediate surroundings which resembles a courtyard. Neighing of horses. Patter of feet. People entering and leaving the castle premises. I can almost hear the sounds from medieval lives lived out here.

We descend the stairs and make our way to the other half of the castle. This part, as I mentioned already is built on a headland. I feel deep envy of those who lived here. The headland may easily be mistaken for an island. One hundred and forty-eight steps lead us to the top, leaving us breathless enough to make one wonder if we have been struggling up the highest peak in the world. We find ruins of what once was a great hall and an arched doorway, and I think we have reached some sort of paradise.

I cannot tell which I am more enchanted by. The spectacular location of the castle or the legend of Arthur. I am not alone in feeling this kind of fascination. There have been so many visitors before me who have felt the same.

Earl Richard, the younger brother of King Henry III was wooed by Arthur's birthplace. Unlike me however, the earl had the power to exchange three manors for the piece of land he came upon in 1233. The island of "Tyntagel" then would have been a world unto itself, somewhat detached from the rest of the world. Having acquired his heart's desire, Richard built a castle that spanned the two cliffs at Tintagel. The mainland clifftop had an outer bailey while the headland was home to an inner ward, a great hall, and some chambers. The bridge between the two cliffs is said to have had a drawbridge and gatehouse, now lost with the passage of time.

The Great Hall is the perfect spot for us to plop down and let our legs recuperate from the steep ascent involved in reaching both parts of the castle. I wonder how it might have looked when Earl Richard built it as a paean to Arthur. The earl was bred on tales of Arthur written by Geoffrey of Monmouth in *Historia Regum Britanniae* (*The History of the Kings of Britain*) in the 12th century. It is supposed that Richard might have been ambitious about Tintagel because he wanted to be a part of the story woven around Arthur and through it reach out to locals who believed in the existence of the legendary king. Could Richard have been a romantic, consumed by the literary works he read? Even his walled gardens — of which the walls remain on the exposed part of the plateau upon the cliffs — are speculated to be a kind of reference to the story of Tristan and Iseult that is intertwined with Arthur's.

Of all that survive of Richard's castle are ruins, of the great hall, the kitchens, and the lodgings. In the midst of these ruins, I have an odd photo op with my husband. Hitman asks us for a shot and what occurs to Adi is that it would be immensely funny to have no campy photos of him hugging me. Better, a picture of him pushing his newly wedded wife off the cliff. However wonky his sense of humour, it ends up strangely as a great addition to our photo album. Though later, it gains my mother-in-law "tsks" when she sees it and comments, "Poor you. The son has indeed inherited the father's awful sense of humour."

***

In his 12th-century annals on the kings of Britain, the Welsh cleric Geoffrey of Monmouth first listed Tintagel as the birthplace of Arthur, an illegitimate king born of an affair between a king and the daughter of a local ruler. Medieval folklore or fact? Really who knows, but there are many versions of the tale.

In Peter Ackroyd's *The Death of King Arthur*, a contemporary retelling of Sir Thomas Malory's 15th-century classic *Le Morte d'Arthur*, the legend of Arthur's conception begins on a stormy night. The Duke of Cornwall is said to have been lured away that night out of Tintagel Castle, on some false pretext. He was killed, and the lecherous king, Uther Pendragon, who had been eyeing the Duchess of Cornwall for some time, arrived in the castle to bed her in the guise of her dead husband. Merlin the magician had facilitated the king's wish. Out of this wild night was born Arthur. The Legend of the Round Table then grew around the medieval tales of King Arthur. And the Age of Chivalry revolved around the theme of rescue of maidens in trouble. While both might be folkloric, the castle is not. Its ruins are vertiginous, perched precariously upon cliffs that tower above the sea.

Tintagel has always belonged to Cornish kings. Based on their excavations, which have unearthed thick masonry walls and flagstone floors of slate, archaeologists point out to the elite presence of Dumnonian kings in Tintagel during the Dark Ages or the early medieval period.

Dumnonia is the Latinised name for a kingdom that existed in sub-Roman Britain between the late 4th and 8th centuries in present-day Devon, Cornwall, and parts of Somerset and Dorset. The palace of the Dumnonian royalty appears to have been luxurious. The Dumnonian people must have lived well, going by the recovery of fragments of amphorae which were known to have carted olive oil and wine from the Mediterranean countries, and of imported bowls, plates and painted French glasses, from which they drank imported wine.

By the early 7th century, the palace was in the process of being abandoned. The end was nigh, probably brought about by the outbreak of bubonic plague. The second time around, Tintagel was abandoned following the reign of Richard. The earl, in any case, hardly spent time at the castle, busy as he was on the religious front, conducting the serious business of crusades to the Holy Land.

Around the time that Cornwall was declared a duchy, in 1337, the castle was already in ruins. Edward the Black Prince set about renovating the buildings which would have suffered significant erosion.

The elements are severe in Tintagel and the bite of the wind invades my bones, even on a summery morning. It's blowing a hoolie out here and I feel like a figure made of straw in the face of it. It is an effective way of being reminded of your place in the vast scheme of things. Add to this the effects of coastal erosion and you know that the ruins have been whittled down to their present state by the relentlessness of natural forces at work.

The Black Prince too hardly lived in Tintagel. It was home to a small number of his staff. It does not come as a surprise then that by the 1600s the castle had been deserted. This time, for good.

Next came the Victorians, with their fascination for folklore and legend. Lord Alfred Tennyson put his own spin on the legend, and naturally after this, there was no stopping the inflow of tourists. A product of his age, novelist and poet Thomas Hardy was enamoured of the castle. He kept re-visiting it with his wife and in it he had the inspiration for a play titled *The Famous Tragedy of the Queen of Cornwall.*

How deeply the castle must have impressed him! Hardy described the stage for the play, "assumed to be the interior of the Great Hall of Tintagel Castle: that the floor is strewn with rushes: that there is an arch in the back-centre (a doorway or other opening may counterfeit this) through which the Atlantic is visible across an outer ward and over the ramparts of the strong-hold". The tragic story of Tristram and Iseult or Isolde was Hardy's motif for his play. Hardy's representation of Merlin as an "ageless, deathless" and "a phantasmal figure with a white wand" plays to the gallery.

I explore Merlin's Cave because how can one remain unmoved by legends surrounding the wily old wizard. Accompanied by Hoonar, who is enthusiastic about all eccentric ventures in life, I scamper down the boulders to the shingled beach. This little stretch is mostly populated by dogs who turn up here to play in the waters. It is where I meet Harry, the fluffy retriever from the neighbouring county of Devon. He has just had his legs operated, and is feeling jittery about tackling the boulders, points out his mistress. She reaches him and helps him negotiate the rocks. Soon after, we see him paddling in the waters with a big grin on his face.

The wizard's hangout is a deep-sea cavern, damp and so dark that I must switch on my phone flashlight to have a proper look in. The bed of the cave is sandy but the rest of it is all about volcanic rocks, through which the sea has worked its will and carved out this subterranean chamber. Merlin carried the infant Arthur through this cave, according to Tennyson's *Idylls of the King*:

> *"They found a naked child upon the sands*
> *Of dark Tintagil by the Cornish sea;*
> *And that was Arthur; and they fostered him*
> *Till he by miracle was approven King"*

We have gone a few feet, which is nothing compared to the full length of the cave – it spans a length of 330 feet - when the tide sweeps in. Merlin must have been in remarkable shape to have carried Arthur all the way through to the opening on the other side of the rocks, beneath the castle.

In my head, I am reliving my beloved childhood stories of Blyton's five getting caught in caves. The ledges, the friend and I fantasise, should serve as a larder, and that flat projection in the corner is where we may find shelter from the tidal water. We lack Timmy, who should have got busy sniffing out the strange smells in the cavernous interiors. We also fall short in the food department. The Five were never caught without a respectable assortment, tins of tomato sandwiches, canned peaches, chocolate squares, chunks of pineapple, and ginger beer.

By the time we get back to the low rocks that are strewn around the entrance to the cave, the waters have swollen. Swirling above our ankles, the frigid oceanic waters make me long for warmth.

Indelibly linked with this beach is another memory, another day, of meeting an enthusiastic creature, a springer spaniel called Jade. On the day in question, it is rainy and the waters are particularly choppy, but let that not be in the way of a spaniel who has set his heart on paddling into the icy waters and fetching his precious ball from the waters to his master.

Jade's human is a middle-aged man in shorts and a Stetson. I comment upon his throw which is powerful, when he kindly offers me the ball, and says, "Here, you have a go then."

"Oh no", I think, but take up the offer anyway. The mixture of dog drool and sea water is ghastly. It has made the ball gooey and slippery, which makes me only keener to get it off my hands, my eagerness at being rid of it more forceful than that of the dog waiting for it. I hurl the ball with all my strength. For some strange reason, the damned thing takes an oblique path and lands somewhere amongst the dark, slippery rocks jutting out from the waters.

It is a challenge for Jade to find the ball. The man eventually heads down, slipping and sliding over the mossy, slick boulders jutting out of the waters, and guides Jade in the direction of the ball, a bright yellow speck riding choppy grey waves. Later, when he has come back to where we are, he remarks: "Such a girly throw!"

I cannot even call it mansplaining. Truth be spoken, it was a pathetic toss.

The South West Coastal Path, that 630-mile iconic national trail that skims the cliffs all along the south west of England and runs almost all along the coast in Cornwall, passes by Tintagel too. It makes for some spectacular walks. I am tempted to take off my shoes and walk bare feet on the grass as I gaze at the Celtic Sea, hypnotised by its myriad of blues. Within minutes however, reality sets in as I feel something squish beneath my feet. I have murdered a leech lookalike without realizing it. I rub my feet against a large boulder to be rid of its remains when to my horror I spot a dozen more of the slimy suspects clung to the surface of it. The shoes are back on in triple the speed that it has taken to coax them off.

This little incident apart, I see why King Arthur was said to have been enamoured of the landscape. Along with Merlin the magician, Queen Guinevere, the handsome knight Lancelot, and the other knights who were part of the mythic round table. In the same breath, I cannot see why Earl Richard and the Black Prince could not be convinced to live in Tintagel's castle that rises from the top of the cliffs like a dream made concrete in stone. After all, how does one say nay to the eternal drama of nature unfolding before the eyes here, which (to channel Hardy) conjures "scenes, with their passions, hopes, and fears/ sunk into shade these thousand years".

Our legs shake immeasurably after the descent and we wind up in the afternoon at a pub, where we meet Harry again, with his human mum. "We cannot help coming back to this spot every summer. Harry loves it," she says, a trifle indulgently.

A few pints and chips get us back up on our feet and we expend this energy at nearby Trebarwith Strand. Shy of two miles from Tintagel, it is our introduction to the sandy and rocky loveliness of the coastline in Cornwall. First, we drive on roads intrinsic to the duchy. Superbly narrow lanes where to drive a car, a rented one at that, is to have your heart in your mouth. A single-track lane, an offshoot of the B3263, takes us into Trebarwith Strand where within the foot of a valley lies a hamlet, cliffs rising steeply on either side. We park our car atop the hamlet and find the place deserted, reinforcing the image of Cornwall's wonderful isolation.

There are all of four or five establishments. A café, a pub, a bucket-and-spade surf shop, toilets and a souvenir shop called 'Spriggans Hollow', selling holiday kitsch. In case, one is befuddled by the name, the proprietor has decided to eliminate all questions by putting up a board outside the shop. A picture of a wizened creature with pointy ears and gnarled features, the "Spriggan" in question, is followed by a one-line description: "Bodyguard to the little folk and keeper of fine things".

We find likewise references to the supernatural, most places we go. The faery folk are the celebrities here, which speaks volumes about the vivid imagination of the Cornish. In mock deference to the land's old wives' tales, Ella and I have already bought each other a "piskie" pendant in Tintagel. I still have it strung on a chain. The piskie, a Cornish take on the English pixie, is a playful elf-like thing supposed to bring one good luck. I might as well be in Blyton's Land of Topsy Turvy, in the enchanted world of elves, fairies, talking birds and whispering trees that mutter "wisha-wisha-wisha" in my ears.

Trebarwith has a mile-long stretch of powdery golden sands, which when the water sweeps in at high tide, is swallowed whole by the sea, but there are rich rewards when it secedes. We find plenty of rock pools coated with sea-snails, periwinkles, limpets, an abundance of mussels, and small alcoves to explore along the cliff edge. In the years to follow, we are to be acquainted with the British love for rockpooling, a great way to study aquatic wildlife. I have indulged in it later on during our travels through Looe, spotting starfish, cucumbers, blennies and butterfish, but without disturbing the lives of these bottom dwellers.

I am fascinated by rocks. It is derived from my father's obsession with studying rocks, having studied geology as a young man, before he pursued engineering. He would find Trebarwith entirely captivating, with its dark grey outcrops of volcanic rocks stacked one above the other by some unseen hand, with precision.

Off the beach and within the bay is a cliff stack exposed like a black hump upon the waters. Sea birds have colonised Gull Rock. We are sat on the cliffs above the hamlet beneath the afternoon sun for a fair while drinking in the beauty of the landscape before we take off for St. Ives. It will be a long day. We shall head south to St. Ives, then backtrack all the way up north to head home. A bit of poor planning there, we realise on hindsight.

But oh, the descent into St. Ives! It is picture-perfect. At the point where there is a dip in the road, the sea in a glorious shimmer of pale sparkling blue leaps up to meet our eyes, making me gasp with pleasure.

> *"As I was going to St. Ives,*
> *I met a man with seven wives…"*

Do you remember that old riddle? Only in our case, no kits, cats, sacks, just six of us in St. Ives where we walk the roads of a posh place filled with art galleries and cafés, brimming with Londoners. The town named after Saint Ia of Cornwall, conjectured to be an Irish princess from the 5-6th centuries, has been on the Londoner's map ever since the Great Western Railways in the latter half of the 19th century brought Victorian holidaymakers to St. Ives. It is a place built on the fishing trade as of old, but for some time now the economy in town has been thriving off the bustle of tourists.

The beach at St. Ives is spotted with stripy windbreaks (a curiously British seaside affair that I don't remember seeing anywhere else in Europe or North America), tots building sun castles and sunbathers spread out on striped deckchairs and rugs. Hitman, Hoonar, Adi and I wade into the waters. It is desperately cold despite the warm temperatures of a July noon. Numbed, we return to the beach to find a tiff brewing. Firdous looks mutinous and scowls away. Ella and he leave for home in one of the cars, a tad abruptly.

After I take a few photographs of the beach spilling into the turquoise-azure waters of the Celtic Sea from the clifftop, where I also pause to admire clusters of dark purplish black knight posing arrestingly against the blue backdrop, the rest of us pile into the other car. Hoonar takes over the wheel. At one point I doze off in the back, lulled by the sweet steady motion and wake up startled to hear Adi shout. We are saved from a near head-on collision. Hoonar has been driving calmly and steadily on the wrong side of the road.

On hindsight, when I have had time to parse the details of our first Cornish road trip, I see how it has been rounded off neatly. It began with a whimper on the motorways and almost ended with a bang on its dual carriageways. But I lived to tell the tale and one cannot simply ask for more.

IV

What's the Deal with Glamping in Late Autumn?

The first taste of Cornwall has been irresistible. Adi and I are drawn back to it in the autumn of the same year, when the two of us decide on glamping, one late October weekend. Nothing rings sensible about it. The subtext to this being a miserably cold camping trip concluded in the Isle of Wight, off the south coast of the country, a week before we go glamping. While I had vowed not to put myself through such an ordeal again, here we are. Not a fortnight has slipped by and we have booked ourselves a weekend stay in a yurt somewhere by the Atlantic Coast. In the Cornish hamlet of St. Genny's.

Actually, I should own up to it that it is my idea. I have undertaken an assignment to write a piece on glamping for a lifestyle magazine. "Why, why, do I do this to myself?" I ask of my husband as I wonder aloud during the drive. I have little foreknowledge of what glamping entails and absolutely zero idea of what it is like to glamp in the countryside in late autumn. Sleeping in a tent beneath the stars, with walls and a roof over our heads to protect us from the elements. It cannot get hairy, I tell myself.

However, I snap up the assignment because we have the urge to break away from the grind of daily life. I am trying to build a fledgling career as a freelancer, awfully trying when you have to push yourself every minute, work at procuring approvals from editors for story ideas, and try not to give into procrastination at every possible turn on the road. Adi is struggling at work with a difficult client. We need a break.

It's gone midnight when we reach the farm, home to our yurt. A five-hour long drive got over with, we cannot wait to slip into the cosy warmth of bed. The farmer, Chris Fellows, is surprisingly young in my books. I have been expecting an old man with a leathery face. He has been waiting up and welcomes us warmly despite the late hour. I cannot help but feel sheepish about the timing of our arrival. The farmer's companions are holding up well too. A portly beagle called Spencer and a gentle hound, a Weimaraner, with eyes of amber. He answers to the name Rufus.

We follow the three, Spencer leading the way as he sniffs his way through the field. The farmer informs us with an indulgent smile, "If you see him loitering in the dark, do not worry. Spencer is forever seeking sausages." No need to exact the imagination to see where Spencer gets his girth from. A steady dedication to scrounging around for food dropped, or most probably, offered by glampers who cannot resist his solemn dedication to the cause. Rufus offers us his loyal presence. With the stealth of a grey ghost, he pads alongside, in a gesture of camaraderie. Each time we meet dogs on our various travels, I am filled with longing for Tuktuk. I am never to see him again. The handsome Labrador, who I adopted as one of my soulmates, dies in his sleep a year later.

***

We pick our way through a meadow cloaked in dark. The midnight sky looks black velvet and is dusted with stars. I find the night skies in Cornwall remarkably rewarding. It makes me grateful that we are where we are. That we have made time to appreciate this and stepped beyond the weekend gig of hanging in city pubs. There is such a world of calm to be found in the country. The heart soars and glides to the tranquil rhythm. Nothing is contrived here.

In the beam of our torchlights, we spot a few yurts spread out at some distance from each other, in the field. It suits us. Our yurt is circular in shape, remaining true to the original nomadic affair that came up on the steppes of Central Asia thousands of years ago. Walls woven in latticed wood and covered with canvas surround us, topped by a lofty dome with a circular skylight dab in the middle. Beneath the skylight is strategically positioned a double bed with a slatted headboard in oak. The idea is to let the occupants of the yurt doze off while gazing at the night sky.

The immediate impression is of a profusion of maple-coloured wood within the yurt. It is spacious, and to my relief, it is toasty inside. Fire crackles in the flagstone hearth, fire pokers hanging behind on a wrought-iron stand. The farmer has kept the fire going. The eyes rove, quickly taking in the paraphernalia of bedside tables and floor rugs. The rest of the furniture includes a couple of armchairs, a dining table with chairs and a side cabinet kitted up with a dual-burner gas stove. The cabinet also contains an assortment of pots and pans, chopping board, plates and quarter plates, cutlery, coffee filter, a roll of kitchen paper towel, cheese grater, wine glasses and tea mugs. Basically, everything you need if you want to cook your own meals while on holiday.

The yurt has all the makings of a camping experience with a touch of luxury. Glamping. A portmanteau of the words "glamour" and "camping", a strain of hospitality that travellers have embraced with vigour. And I see its appeal now that we have had a taste of it. I have been there with camping — conversant with the specifics of scouting for a camp site, pitching tent, checking for wind cover, the works. But give me the creature comforts of home with the experience of camping — the wonderful ease of slipping into bed without having to make it, to walk into a cabin instead of propping up a tent – and I am an easy convert. Glamping's the call. Reassuringly, we are not insulated from nature.

Our research, before we booked the yurt, threw up a mindboggling roster of glamping getaways. We could have opted for a horse-drawn carriage, the horse being one of those shaggy beauties. Or, we could have gone down the route of any of these: a vintage camper van, an eco-pod, an airstream. There was also the option of hopping onto a roulette, a wooden gypsy caravan; a bell tent; the ubiquitous tipi. The yurt sounded simple and homey, and more significantly, it fit into our budget. Many a mickle makes a muckle. Money's a bit tight these days. Relocation has cost us dearly.

Modestly lit with the dim glow from lanterns, shadows flit within the yurt as the crackling fire in the log burner cements the mellow mood inside. I can make peace with the idea of leaving behind the conveniences of modernity, to live a day or two in the country in rusticity, without electricity or proper mobile network. To keep the fire going, we stick wood into the burner. I accomplish this task under the eagle eyes of the husband, who is regularly subjected to my bouts of clumsiness. The task of stoking the fire makes me feel grand, nothing less than a girl scout.

The bed is an icy block, a platform of misery, on which the warmth of the fire cannot reach us. I get up and jam on two pairs of woollen leggings (not an easy task by half) and the only other jumper I have for the weekend. Yet, I am nowhere near being snug.

Eventually, the fire dies out. The night feels infinitely long. Adi and I snuggle for warmth, staring through the skylight at the midnight blue of the sky. Slumber sweeps over us at some point, but all through, I feel the intense cold rise from the bed and seep into my bones. It is a state of half wakefulness from which I awaken fully when the sun's rays sneak in through the skylight and feather my face. For someone who resents waking in the early hours, I jump out of bed with alacrity. I need to thaw. Waking Adi, I scamper to the barn a few yards off, which houses the showering stalls. More than anything, I need to wash off the exhaustion of sleep deprivation. There is a kitchen and a communal table to share meals with fellow glampers. Understandably enough we have no company, seeing how freezing the countryside is already. I luxuriate in a long warm shower, letting it sluice off the miserable cold of the night from my bones.

A breakfast of tea and a day-old pain au chocolate in the yurt completes the process of waking up and we are ready to go meet the farmer. I want to interview him for the article I am working on.

Fellows is the first of the tribe of London workers, thirtysomethings who leave the city for greener pastures, who we meet during our travels in Cornwall. As a corporate worker, he had eventually had it with the frenetic pace of urban living. The list of things that he did not like about his erstwhile life was getting longer and he was ready for a change. With his wife and young daughter, he bought the 18-acre farm with its Cornish name, Pencuke, which means 'Swallow's End'. The Fellows family concentrates on organic produce.

"The simple life of a farmer suits me. It is hard work, but I have no regrets," says Fellows, when I question him about the massive leap he has taken. A quote from du Maurier surfaces in my mind. In her diary, the author had written about her decision to live in Cornwall. "Oh, these are my people, they really are. What have I to do with London? I shall live and die here in Cornwall and do my best to write about them. What's the use of being clever and witty? It's a heart that is the needful thing."

As the interview is wrapped up, he asks, "Did you sleep well though?" It has been lovely, I assure him. I know I am lying through my teeth here, because it is on us. I could have timed the trip better, in summer, when the yurt would have been a pleasure to bunk in. Plus, the farmer has been through and through a fine host.

The experience of being one with nature adds to the charm at the farm, he continues, warming up to the subject of my story. At Pencuke, there are no gimmicks that some glamping sites offer. Gold-panning, sport, crêpe making and fairytale themes are not on the menu. The emphasis is on a good old-fashioned return to nature, with certain material comforts in place. I see how it has been achieved. The yurt lacks electricity, as a deliberate measure. The point is to detach the self from a plethora of modern technological obsessions and engage with our loved ones at a more basic level. Chatting, playing board games and the like, cut the mustard. I inform our host that we appreciate the top-notch showering facility, for having walked bleary-eyed in the middle of the night to the loo at the Isle of Wight campsite, I know a good thing when I see it.

Fellows is keen that we should have a tour of his farm. "Oh no," I think, for the meadows are boggy. When the occasion demands wellies, it is natural that I should have a pair of city boots on. This translates into less of walking, more of sinking. I am intensely aware of pools of water squelching beneath my feet. Regardless, I plod on to meet the farm's livestock.

First up is a pair of Exmoor ponies, Alex and Jasper. They are nowhere in sight. The farmer peers into the distance, hollers out, and after a while, gives up on the two itinerant fellas. "They are in the habit of disappearing to explore the grounds by themselves," he tells us. Acres to plough through in soggy boots does not sound endearing and we leave the ponies to their rambles, instead making the acquaintance of a primitive breed of deer-like sheep called Castlemilk Moorits. Then, a few Portland sheep and large white British Lop pigs. Fellows also wants to introduce us to some visiting animals - his friend's horses are staying with him for some time.

For a while, I forget my wet-boot woes. The equines are a comely pair. Mouse, the male Shire cross is huge, handsome, and friendly. He sticks his white nose out of the paddock and nuzzles us. Ebony, a Welsh cob crossed with an Arab, on the other hand, is all about attitude. She won't meet us. To make good on her stance, Ebony stands with her back to us the entire time. We coax and cajole, but she stays unmoved. The world shall have to do with her beautifully shaped behind.

***

The sun is high in the sky when we leave St. Genny's, after I have washed the muck off my boots. A heartbeat away is stood Crackington Haven, a village by the Atlantic, where the ocean can be rough around its small, shingled cove.

We will return to Crackington Haven two years later and rent a whitewashed cottage with a friend in frigid March. It will be in Higher Crackington, but of this we do not dream. Right now, we dream of conquering climbs by the sea in beauteous Lizard.

Perched at the edge of a peninsula, Lizard Point is known for its white lighthouse and a former Victorian hotel that now serves as a youth hostel. Such an enviable location, you would think, with its own seascape at the most southerly point in mainland Britain. Herds of buxom Jersey cows enhancing the picture-perfect quality of the landscape. Yet, I am not convinced. I had thought I would be swept off my feet. Perhaps, I had set too much by my research on it.

My other memory of the Lizard is on the greyest of grey days, when the heavens open above our heads and let rip. Stormy climes, turbulent waves. They conspire to put you in mind of a cosy cottage with a roaring fire in its wood burner, and you burrowed into a wingback armchair, nose buried in a novel, a cup of tea at hand. It is the kind of soggy day when the sky merges with the sea in clammy shades of grey, so that a friend of ours, Bhavna, visiting Cornwall for the first time, keeps wondering aloud about it, "Now, is that the sea?" Each time we disappoint her till at one point near the dilapidated chimney stacks of some tin mine along the coast, she gets off from the car, and declares with the air of a victor: "I finally see the sea". On just such a day, Hoonar is camping at Lizard with his brother. We stop at their campsite to check in on them. Shivering in the sharp wind that drives the rain into slanting sheets so maniacal that my umbrella threatens to give up on me, I see the expression on his sibling's face. Misery's writ large on it. "He's decided that nothing should stop us. We should carry on as before," he says. Do I detect a touch of asperity in his tone? To be caught with a brother used to a Rastafarian mode of existence in a tent and no way to leave… I have known of lesser joys in life. We leave them to their devices on that perishing noon.

On the present noon, beneath clear blue skies, we find our way to Kynance Cove. The National Trust car park at the cove is off the A3083 that leads to Lizard Village and access to it is via a private road off the main Helston-Lizard route. Signages warn us against strong currents, swimming at low tide, and the presence of adders. Thankfully, on the open heaths above the cove, we are not presented with the opportunity of making any reptilian acquaintances.

The cliffs around Kynance Cove are tricky to negotiate. And what's better, they are sheer. I have to ingratiate myself with their steep nature, for my husband is insistent on charting the thinnest of trails that snake the slopes, and I manage to clamp down on an attack of the nerves. For the most part, we skirt the coastal path, trimmed with uneven edges of dark stone. Wild heath flowers spring up in dribs and drabs of purple. Below us is the cove. We stand for some time at this spot, staring at the vision that is unfolding before the eyes. From the crescent of the sandy beach, a profusion of devilishly dark rocks emerges and lumbers into the sea. Serpentine rocks, which up and close reveal subtle green and red marbled streaks. But from afar, they put me in mind of an ancient sea monster slumbering on a shimmering bed of lapis-blue waters. The water deepens to an inky blue around the rocks. The contrast is at once mesmerising.

The walk down to the cove itself is treacherous in stretches. Rough man-made steps lead down to a broad expanse of pebbles and boulders – it is a rough ride in inappropriate footwear. Even in sturdy shoes, we wobble as we cross a sea of pebbles, while little boys and girls play on the beach a few feet away. Our mission is to grab a tea break at the café that we have spotted from up above. I am thoroughly for the national practice of winding up long walks with teacakes and the life-affirming pot of tea.

When we reach the café, I choose a local dense cake for our repast. We have gathered a seat outside with a view of the cove. What a spectacular spot it is! White clouds billow in the sky above waters that graduate in hues from turquoise to azure. I break into my *hevva* cake and find it laden with the kind of rich taste that is cobbled together with a mix of flour, butter and lard. With each bite, I am partaking of a Cornish tradition that goes back to its long-lost days of pilchard fishing. The word "hevva" is derived from the cries of a man known as the "huer", who in the old days stood at a clifftop hut and scoured the seas for tell-tale signs of shoals of pilchard. Upon a sighting, he would cry out loud, the air ringing with the words "Hevva, hevva!" Hearing his signal, the waiting fishermen would set forth on their boats in the direction of the spot where the pilchards were seen by the huer. The women meanwhile would bake hevva cakes in anticipation of their men's arrival from sea. I can imagine how this cake might have revived the fishermen after their toils at sea. It is a hearty treat alright.

Hypnotised by the dream-like vision that unfolds before the eyes on this stretch of the south-west coastal path, I understand why Mr. Tennyson had a weakness for the landscape here. In the 1800s, the poet was on a walking tour of the cove with the poet and critic, Francis Turner Palgrave, and the Pre-Raphaelite sculptor, Thomas Woolner. The trio was joined by two artists of the Pre-Raphaelite school, William Holman Hunt and Valentine Cameron Prinsep. As they roamed together, Hunt observed Lord Tennyson in his slouched hat, rusty black suit, and coat, wandering among the rocks, followed by Palgrave. Hunt wrote: "…if by chance the poet escaped his eyes for a minute, the voice of Palgrave was heard above the sea and the wind calling "Tennyson, Tennyson"."

The Pre-Raphaelite school of artists with their return-to-nature philosophy must have been a curious bunch, examining the flora and fauna and the serpentine stones in the area in great detail, before they went on to reproduce impressions of their observations in their respective works. I envy them their plein-air inspiration. I would set up an easel here too, though I can imagine being blown off the cliffs along with my easel and supplies given the eternally windy nature of Kynance Cove.

Look at Hunt's gusty adventure when he perched himself upon one of the cliffs for two or three days and painted a lustrous watercolour of the island.

About his blustery experience, he wrote: "My drawing was on a block, of which the sun had gradually drawn up one corner; this warped surface did not seriously interfere with my progress until one day a sudden gust of wind compelled me to put my hand on brushes in danger of going to perdition, when, turning round on my saddle seat, I saw my nearly completed picture circling about among the gulls in the abyss below."

Did Hunt abandon his work to the elements? No, it is testament to the perseverance of an artist in the face of all odds that with the aid of a friend and that of his trusty umbrella, Hunt retrieved the errant piece of paper caught by a tuft of grass.

The tide is out the day we explore the nooks and crannies around the tall dark stacks, making our way past the hump of Asparagus Island, which in my eyes, does not resemble an asparagus in the least. On the other hand, there's wild asparagus growing on it. We climb dark rocks encrusted with barnacles and examine the caves lurking beneath the cliffs. They are too dark and damp for our comfort. Adi won't be persuaded to enter their maws. Abandoning thoughts of exploring any, we choose a spot upon a tall rock, rest our behinds on it and idle around. Somebody has dug up sand and created a mini pool on the beach. In the midst of it, is jammed a teeny-weeny Welsh flag with *Y Ddraig Goch*, the red dragon. A girl plays in the waters under the eagle-eyed supervision of her mother, and in the distance, a lone man in his boat, dressed in the yellow oilskins of the fisherman, dangles a rod into the choppy waters. From somewhere, a chough calls out.

The hours roll away at the cove. We are filled with the quiet joy of doing nothing in particular. And yet nature's drama is everything here. I see Tennyson's "glorious grass-green monsters of waves" and echo his sentiment that one can sit at the spot all day. One may not however be literally sat all day if only for the fact that nature turns wilder here by the minute. The tide sets in all too soon before you take note of it - and you find yourself wading through the ice-cold waters of the Atlantic to reach solid ground.

This is the starting point of a long love affair with Kynance Cove and we find over the course of the years that there is no turning away from it with just the one visit. We keep coming back every year, moths to its untamed beauty.

V

Great Expectations, Dashed

Expectations cranked up we speed in our four-wheel drive to Land's End.

Now would you look at the appellation, Land's End. There is a world of suggestion in those two words. We daydream about arriving at a spectacular landscape perched above the Atlantic. I have gone the extra mile, pictured myself clutching me heart, shedding a tear or two. That should give you an inkling about the hyperbolic path of my sentiments, on occasions. Land's End sounds like it should have a measure of drama. This climactic sounding place is at the extreme westerly end of Cornwall. Here most adventures begin and end, and proof of it is to be had in a group of cyclists we sight, kit up in clingy lycra and assembled at one point. They are probably starting their journey from Land's End and heading to John O' Groats, which is located near the tip of mainland Scotland. Or, it could be the other way around. Though if we are to be pernickety about facts, the actual northernmost point of Scotland is two miles from John O'Groats, at Dunnet Head. But John O'Groats being the traditionally acknowledged tip, we shall make peace with it, let the gaffe pass.

The point here is the end-to-end journey between Land's End and John O' Groats. It measures a distance spanning 874 miles between the signposts at these two landmarks. Britain is the epitome of a compact nation. If I felt it after making the transition from India to the UK, I feel it even more, now that I have hopped over to the other side of the pond. The journey between Land's End and John O' Groats, and vice-versa, is hallowed business. As one may expect, people have let their creativity go places while undertaking this route. Some have completed it on foot — have feet, will walk. Others have resorted to public buses, cars, motorcycles, unicycles, bicycles and tricycles, skateboards, horses and wheelchairs. You name it, chances are it has already been covered — and if not, you can set a new record.

I picture people — those with enough ambition — wracking their brains to leave their footprints in the annals of this feted route. Take John and Maud, your average British couple, living in a small cottage somewhere in Kent. John turns to his wife of many years, Maud, and wonders aloud, "Love, now that I have enough time at hand (having retired a few months ago), what do you say to the idea of biking around the country?"

Maud: "Absolutely not. I will not spend endless hours on a bike getting saddle sores (Maud is fond of her armchair). Who will look after Flopsy?"

Flopsy is their cat, doubling up as a convenient excuse for Maud to miss out on life events that call for exertion, involving the transference of her behind from the armchair to the world outside. The cat is *numero uno* in the family. Just as a mother uses her little tyke, Flopsy is Maud's trump card in weaselling out of hairy scenarios.

John thinks of a middle way. After a few days of slowly scouring the Internet for inspiration, he comes up with another suggestion: "What about the Land's End to John O' Groats route? Do you remember, we went to Land's End years ago? There was a dedication to a cyclist there that I could not forget, even though you do carry on about my poor memory. The chap had completed the circuit eight times over and died on the 9th attempt, on the way to John O' Groats. I have been curious about what made him travel the same route time and again."

Maud: "John, how badly do you want to get rid of me?"

John: "Oh darling, you won't go all sensible on me now, will you?"

Maud relents grudgingly after a week and adds that they might as well set a record of some kind. "All that work to no end, cannot be!" She comes up with a crazy-fangled notion of making a go for it on a motorised armchair fitted with a transparent plastic brolly. It's England after all, and in all probability, you never know when, it will be drizzling.

John and Maud might be figments of my imagination, but there are strange records out there. Of people who have hitchhiked between the two landmarks, not forgetting the ones who have opted for fighter jets, motorised supermarket trolleys and traction engines. You see, Maud has it sorted. Why not travel within the comfort of your armchair instead of pulling all sorts of physical stunts. Walking, running, biking… let the wily rascals go for it. Did I hear you snort? Okay, then picture a man in a bathtub on wheels. That did happen. Another fellow played golf all the way, putting away till he had completed the journey. No one could accuse either of them for lack of imagination. Certainly not you or I, nestled comfortably within our capacious sofas, passing judgement on the world at large.

Parking's free at Land's End because we have reached late in the day. The crowds have left. What joy, I think. This is around sunset, which in summer is late enough for the amusement arcade at the entrance to have shut shop. We stroll through the empty arcade, an overbearingly commercial claptrap. Gift shops and entertainment theatre aimed at children, who would therefore spend time with Wallace & Gromit and Shaun the Sheep than walk around the iconic location where land is said to end. I remark to Adi: "If I were two years old and I found this winning combination of fudge-y ice cream and games, who would give two hoots about whether land began or ended here?"

Sauntering, we come upon a whitewashed building. Bold letters, painted in black, shout its identity: PENWITH HOUSE, TEMPERANCE HOTEL, EST. 1860. The original building was a small outpost, a simple cottage when it was conceived of in the 1800s. How twee the word Temperance seems, yet it brings to life the campaign that swept through the UK during the 19th century. The call of the movement was that people temper down their alcohol intake. In course of time, it advocated complete prohibition. The attempt was to direct one's attention towards good coffee, cocoa, and books. Typical posters from the temperance years went along these lines: "Drinking leads to neglect of duty, moral degradation and crime"; "Lips that touch liquor shall not touch ours".

I do not think I would fight this strain of thought, except that a prohibition of any kind will make people rear up and demand the very product that has been banned from their lives. My husband shall vouch for it, as we are in the process of a dry month. Yessir, not a drop of alcohol with our meals.

As temperance halls, hotels, and inns sprang up all over Britain, in the year 1834, the *Preston Temperance Advocate* listed qualifications for establishments that aspired to be associated with temperance. For a Temperance House, Temperance Coffee House, or Temperance Hotel, the establishment needed to satisfy these points

- "A respectable eating house."

- "A respectable lodging house, to accommodate persons who object to stopping at public houses."

- "A place of casual accommodation, where persons can come to transact business, read the papers, or enjoy social intercourse, or where parties, societies and committees can meet for similar purposes."

- "… rather than let people go to the public houses … it is also recommended to supply various liquids which are pleasant to the taste … coffee, tea, milk, ginger beer, lemonade, peppermint water and raspberry vinegar. The latter are much in use, diluted with hot water, and sweetened."

Ironically enough Adi and I have worked our way through bottles of alcohol at one of these very temperance spots in the country. *The High Cross Coffee House* in Leicester was designed by a local architect in 1895 with elevated notions in mind. By 2012, it was a roaring pub, *The High Cross*, where we gathered for post-prandial drinks on weekends. Enough nights have been spent there on the bender. The railway-travel visionary Thomas Cook would have been mortified had he witnessed this change in the city he had adopted as his home. Cook had moved from Derbyshire to Leicester, where he promoted a lifestyle of temperance. Along with other members, he founded the Leicester Coffee and Cocoa Company Ltd. through which worthy establishment, 14 coffee and cocoa houses were set up in town as healthy alternatives to pubs. The High Cross Coffee House on Leicester's High Street was one of them.

The powers of temperance were moral and more potent than we can give them credit for. During a 15-mile walk from Market Harborough to Leicester one June day in 1841, on his way to attend a Temperance Society meeting, Cook conceived of the idea of railway travel. It was a business that revolutionised the concept of travel, yet to begin with, it was paired with temperance. Cook noted: "… what a glorious thing it would be if the newly developed powers of railways and locomotion could be made subservient to the promotion of temperance." Four-hundred odd passengers, all members of the Leicester Temperance Society, were transported in open tub-style carriages by the Midland Railway Company to a temperance meeting in Loughborough. Pomp and pageantry being the bedrock of British society, a band accompanied the travelling temperance practitioners.

In India, and particularly Calcutta where I hail from, we are only too well acquainted with the Brit's penchant for grandiosity. This goes back in time to the 17th century, when an English East India Company vessel sailing up the Hooghly encountered a Bengali washerman. They welcomed him on deck with bags of gold and precious things. The washerman, unaccustomed to such grand gestures in his daily life had simply gone on board, expecting a pile of unwashed clothes to launder.

I digress (terribly). But there's purpose here of injecting perspective into the story. To return to the *Temperance Hotel* of Land's End, the worthy little establishment came up in 1860 for the benefit of Victorian travellers. It offered hot and cold luncheons daily. Mr. W. Thomas was listed as its proprietor. Now, it surely provides those who stay there with adequate booze, for it offers accommodation in the shape of Penwith Studios to travellers. At its rear is a signpost drawn on the whitewashed walls of the house indicating it as "The First & Last House in Britain". It has been upgraded from the small cottage that it was in the 19th century to a larger version. In 2012, we stand in front of this extended affair of a cottage, bemused. I find its charm considerably depleted from the original version that I have spotted in books.

***

At Land's End, the cliffs are bare of vegetation, except for clumps of purple flowers and lichen. They swoop into the ocean, from which rises stacks of stone. There is that wonderful formation south of Land's End, the Enys Dodman Arch, a rock shaped elephantine by the elements in their playfulness. Beyond it rises an islet crowned by a jumbled assortment of granite stacks, resembling a cluster of siblings of varied sizes and shapes gathered together.

Further ahead, before our eyes meet the horizon and where the grey expanse of the sea surges into a grey sky seamlessly, there is a lighthouse sat upon a series of islets known as the Longships. It is an unremarkable lighthouse, yet how important it must have been to ships on stormy nights when the oceanic waves ran wild. We sight it on a relatively calm afternoon, but the Romantic artist, William Turner, had captured the turbulence of the ocean in his watercolour circa 1834. Titled *Longships Lighthouse, Land's End*, in the painting, everything is a blur. I wonder if Turner had watched the unabashed fury of the wild ocean as it went about its work of erasing all sharp lines and edges from the horizon, challenging the eyes to grope for form because all you discern in his work is the rough shape of a sea vessel, tossed about on the waves like putty; gashes of grey and thick white waves engulfing the lighthouse. In the backdrop, roughly visible, is the elephant-shaped arch.

During the mid-1800s, a little-known Victorian author sat upon the headland of Land's End and found himself enthralled by the scenery that unfurled before him. Baker Peter Smith wrote about the 'multicapsular curiosities of the region' in his book, *A Trip to the Far West*.

"I reached the Land's End and sat down on a protuberant block of granite, close to the precipice, overhanging the multitangular rocks which form an impenetrable barrier against the raging tides of the mighty waters," Smith gushed, observing alongside the Cornish choughs screaming above his head. He felt great admiration for its "multiplicious beauty" (and evidently, his editor had no quibbles with his obsession with the prefix "multi").

My thoughts upon reaching Land's End are less ebullient. I find resonance instead with the travel notes of Wilkie Collins. In his rambles on foot across the West Country in 1850, the writer had come upon this part of the country, the draw of which he likened for the tourist in Cornwall to that of Jerusalem for the pilgrim in the Holy Land, the "Ultima Thule" where all progress stops because it is what has been guiding the traveller all along in his journey.

"The Land's End! There is something in the very words that stirs us all. It was the name that struck us most, and was best remembered by us, as children, when we learnt our geography. It fills the minds of imaginative people with visions of barrenness and solitude, with dreams of some lonely promontory, far away by itself out in the sea," wrote Collins. A century and a half ago, he had distilled the crux of my crestfallen thoughts in his notes. Isn't it strange and quite wonderful to find a connect with a person who belonged in another time and place? Someone you haven't met nor will. Yet the thinnest thread of thought can form a link across the chasm of time.

I half believe that you are in danger of missing Land's End if you do not quiz your way to it. I also wholly believe that it could have done without the arcade, if only in pursuit of the kind of haunting loneliness that such an ancient landscape naturally demands. The pre-historic cliffs were formed when a mass of boiling granite forced its way through the surface. Proof of the strange fascination that it exudes lies in the steady draw of travellers to Land's End for thousands of years now. In the old days, it had evocative names like *Belerion*, or "the shining land". Its Cornish name was *Penn an Wlas*, which translated means the "end of land".

In a land steeped in myths and legends, it makes sense that the ancient people would have propagated the idea of Lyonesse, the lost kingdom of King Arthur. They firmly held to the thought that it was dissolved in the waves somewhere between Land's End and the Isles of Scilly on a stormy night. Lord Tennyson indulged the fancy in his Arthurian epic, *Idylls of the King*, in which he referred to Lyonesse as the "land of old upheaven from the abyss" fated to sink into a watery underworld, "Where fragments of forgotten peoples dwelt,/And the long mountains ended in a coast/Of ever-shifting sand, and far away/The phantom circle of a moaning sea".

Hundreds of thousands of people continue to throng the cliffs at Land's End and it is a given for all and sundry to head to the iconic fingerpost. No visit to this corner of the earth can be deemed complete without a windy photograph taken at the famous fingerpost that marks the distance in miles from Land's End to New York (3147) and to John O'Groats (874). On bespoke photos, they throw in a marker for the Isle of Scilly, which can be seen from where we are, on a clear day. But it is closer to sunset and we have to squint to see the silhouette of the isle as a faint smudge on the horizon.

Had we reached the post earlier, we would have shelled out ten quid for a customised photo in which our hometown – Leicester - would have been added to the sign. But for all our sins, for reaching late, we are delighted with the photo that a kind European woman takes of us. It is a mawkishly sentimental shot wherein my husband is looking at me, a besotted grin upon his face; mine's turned away with a coy smile upon it. Unashamedly campy. Certainly not pre-meditated. How it comes about is this. The woman says something funny and I cannot remember it for the life of me, but the outcome of it is that the photo takes on a mood its own. We look so windblown in it – almost instantly, I am transported to the bluster of that summer evening.

Land's End for me is a crucible of these cheesy memories, sprinkled with a dose of disappointment. There's price to be paid for a lively imagination I suppose. However, I do spot the dedication that John recollects in his conversation with Maud. Someone had remembered the efforts of the cyclist who had undertaken the journey between Land's End and John O'Groats—which normally takes a cyclist about 10-14 days—eight times over. On his 9th attempt enroute John O' Groats, the man had breathed his last. There is a stirring note about it for there is something to be said about the death of an adventurer who takes his leave of the world doing what he loves best.

There is the option of dialling up the craziness quotient at Land's End. Climb down its rocky cliffs. This however is exactly what they warn you against. It would be easy to dash your head against the rocks and exit this world speedily.

Nobody warned Fiennes against such a foolhardy venture in the late 1600s. Her account of her adventurous descent is filled with the poor grammar customary to her writing style, along with an essence of the views she beheld. Fiennes noted: "The Lands End terminates in a poynt or peak of great rocks which runs a good way into the sea, I clamber'd over them as farre as safety permitted me; there are abundance of rocks and sholes of stones stands up in the sea, a mile off some, and soe here and there some quite to the shore…" Having made all that effort, you would think she would have dipped her toes in the waters, but no Ms. Fiennes had had her share of adventure alright. She took off on her horse for Penzance.

We head in the other direction, and within 10 minutes find ourselves at Sennen Cove. A small fishing village with a long arc of sandy beach, which when we reach turns out to be the playground of surfers. We take a break at the cove, watch the waves wash ashore and recede as we munch on packed sandwiches. The impromptu picnic is improved upon by the view of the Atlantic in an idyllic place where the pace of life seems to have slowed down remarkably.

But continuing a few miles south of Land's End, something entirely out of the ordinary awaits us. A sight that Fiennes would have marvelled at, given her weakness for discovering unknown sights and places within her own land. The Minack Theatre in Porthcurno. In 2012, when we set eyes upon this open-air amphitheatre carved out of the cliffs, with a grand view of the vast ocean, the stage is set for our next experience at the theatre. At the present, it is a pitstop on our drives, but we are left marvelling and make our way back to it the upcoming year.

VI

Arabian Nights

My in-laws visit us every year. They like the slow pace of life in the English countryside. My father-in-law, a retired general of the Indian Army, has connections with Blighty. His father was educated at a school in the Cotswolds; subsequently, he attended the Royal Military College at Sandhurst, before serving as a King's commissioned Indian officer with the Cameron Highlanders (a Scottish infantry regiment) and the British Indian army. Also, as a reader, I think my father-in-law's imagination is stimulated by the landscape. My mother-in-law's great-grandfather studied in England. The in-laws had been over in 2012 just as we were settling in but had missed the bus to Cornwall. Hearing all about it, they express their interest in taking a peek at the West Country. We are only too keen.

A cottage is duly booked in the town of Tintagel, in the summer of 2013. It is a complete coincidence that when we bring them to Minack Theatre, we find out that Arabian Nights is to be staged shortly. How thrilling! We buy the tickets along with a sweatshirt for me because the breath of the sea is unaccountably chilly. Clouds brood over the ocean in black masses. But we have the abounding enthusiasm of the traveller.

I am amused to see my in-laws' reaction when they walk into Minack. It mirrors my astonishment at the sheer beauty of the spot. Even now, on my second visit, my eyes cannot fathom such loveliness as they behold.

Nothing prepares you for the reality of Minack because let's face it, nothing compares to the verisimilitude of seeing something in person as opposed to reading about it. If I am to attribute a baking metaphor to it, it is like tucking into a slice of luscious pie you have baked as opposed to merely fantasising about it. That moment that you sink your teeth into the pie is one of truth and beauty. Just as being sat at Minack Theatre, feeling the strong winds in your hair and surveying the vast ocean in front of you, is an experience of joy deeply felt.

If you catch a play here, you've bagged gold. We have Rowena Cade to thank for all of it.

A wealthy woman from Derbyshire, Cade arrived in Porthcurno after WWI and bought the Minack headland for a sum of £100. In her fondness for the stage lay the first stirrings of this grand vision of hers. In the late 1920s, *A Midsummer Night's Dream* was enacted by local dramatists at a meadow nearby. Soon they were on the hunt for a new venue, for a performance of *The Tempest*, and this search led Cade to the cliffs below Minack House, where she lived. To her mind, she had found the perfect spot. As a word, I think 'perfect' is overrated. What is perfect for one, might not work for another. But one look at Minack Theatre, and you and I, we would agree unanimously on the fact that Ms. Cade had hit the high notes of perfection.

Along with her gardener, Cade dug into the cliffs and moved granite boulders to carve out the lower terraces of the theatre. They worked through the end of 1931 into the next year and fashioned a basic stage and seating area. It took them about six months to accomplish this, which itself speaks volumes about the backbreaking work they must have put in. Cade herself fetched sand from the beach at Porthcurno, lugged beams from the shoreline all the way up to the theatre, and worked with cement, using the tip of a screwdriver to decorate surfaces with Celtic designs. Photos reveal a frail woman with a shock of white hair. But don't be misled by appearances. She was an all-weather worker, carrying on with improvements to the theatre into her 80s.

"And though she be but little, she is fierce." The oft-quoted Shakespearean line keeps coming back to me when I think of Cade. She managed to bring her vision to fruition by the summer of 1932, when the first performance was held on the gully above Minack Rock, lit by car headlights attached to batteries.

In all my travels, I have not seen the likes of Minack Theatre. I have marvelled at the sight of the ancient amphitheaters of Europe, in Verona, Rome, Tarragona, the handiwork of ambitious Romans who had left traces of their engineering marvels everywhere they had gone. Cade must have been inspired by their enterprising architecture. What she put together runs along the lines of a Roman amphitheatre.

The most spectacular amphitheatre I have been to, would be the 2nd century AD theatre in Tarragona, a small Catalonian town on the Costa Daurada in Spain. Overlooking the Balearic Sea, the theatre was built from the underlying bedrock. Yet a stretch of beach appears there as sentry between the ampthitheatre and the sea. By comparison, Minack Theatre is undoubtedly smaller in scale, but in my book it scores a notch above Tarragona by virtue of its location. At Minack, the semi-circular ring of seats that have been hewn out of granite cliffs have a ringside view of the Atlantic. Right on top, below a rambling affair of a garden sprinkled with sub-tropical blooms and succulents, we are sat on hyperreal artificial turf, Adi, his parents and I, watching *Arabian Nights* staged by a bunch of drama students. The sprightly souls have put together a scene redolent of an eastern bazaar, undeterred by gusts of wind and rain clouds gathering above our heads. Plays are rarely cancelled in this theatre. Slowly, the characters start appearing and Scheherazade and Shahryar take to their unusual stage upon the ocean.

The various scenes unfold, drawing us into the myriad layers of the enactment, but there are moments when I cannot help but stare at the ocean, the cliffs surrounding us, and the tail of land that tapers below the stage into the ocean in piles of stones and boulders. I store this landscape in the mind's eye, to be taken out at leisure on days when *ennui* has the mind in its grips, to invigorate the cells and to take inspiration from the story of a wildly romantic theatre brought to life by one woman's relentless passion.

SLOW DOWN, SEE MORE

VII

A Winter's Weekend

I suspect that we are eased into the philosophy of travelling slow by the fact that in 2014 we trip down to Cornwall towards the end of winter, when the days are yet to lengthen. Unwittingly it is a lesson learnt about the art of staying still, to enjoy the peace and quiet of a cottage. Where all one should do is stoke up a good fire, settle into a cushy armchair, kick back one's feet with a good book, and nod off into the cosiness of said cottage.

By this time, we have moved apartments from Leicester to Northampton, the town of cobblers. The move has been occasioned by a change of client for Adi. Making Northampton our base is easier for him. It takes care of the daily drive from Leicester. Also, we find Northampton more to our liking. It is quieter and has a homey vibe about it. I am relieved about the change. I have unwittingly gathered a stalker during the last few months of our life in Leicester, the owner of a sandwich shop to whom I had applied for a part-time job. The man has been sending me lengthy emails with harassing content and filling my head with disturbing details of his personal life. At nights, I lay on bed awake. Terrified. What if he shows up at our doorstep? I manage to block the man virtually and the relocation is a happy coincidence. I am liberated. I no longer need to fret about unwelcome meetings.

In Northampton I have made friends of my own, which includes the village grocer, runners at the sprawling park where I go jogging, the woman who tosses up delicious noodles at her mobile cart in the town's ancient market square. Adi and I have a bunch of friends with whom we party every other weekend at the Wetherspoons in town.

Yet there is an underlying tension to the fabric of our lives. That we might have to leave the UK and go back to India at short notice. Our residence in the country is sponsored by Adi's firm and his projects are time bound. So, we end up travelling furiously. In an effort to see as much as one can, we return to Cornwall twice a year, reserving the rest of our weekends for little jaunts to the Cotswolds and Wales. For longer trips, we head to the North. To Cumbria, the Pennines, the isles off Scotland. But this uncertainty that hovers around the prospect of leaving the country is a constant undertone to our tramping holidays.

On Fridays, unless we are sat in the local pub with a bunch of friends, we have movie nights at home with Hoonar. On one of these, we wonder where we should head for an upcoming bank holiday weekend in March. The toss-up is between the Lake District and Cornwall. Adi and I lean heavily in favour of the latter. Badgered, Hoonar gives in. Booking a cottage is a lark. It is off-peak season. We get a two-bed cottage for a wonderfully low price and I cannot wait to walk through its doors.

Here I must put in a word about the British tradition of bed and breakfast accommodations, which are reasonably priced and significantly lesser than the ones we find across the pond. It makes me wonder about this vast difference - because British cottage rentals and B&Bs offer an atmospheric escape. The rooms are not overtly decorated, but in an old-fashioned manner, which points to a long tradition of hosting travellers in basic inns, with a room or two perched above the village pub. It has carried over into the modern day. You can still stay at an inn, climb its steepish wooden stairs and find yourself in a small room, compact and comfy. No frills, no fancies. It's just what the doctor ordered.

We start with B&Bs in 2011 on our holiday in the UK. A year into our residence in the country, we are into booking cottages. We like the freedom they offer in terms of having our own kitchen, where we can codge up a few meals. It creates the feeling of being home away from home.

The cottage we have rented this time around is located in a small village in Bude, in the north of Cornwall. Crackington Haven. The village is part of the UK countryside, designated for conservation as Areas of Outstanding Natural Beauty (AONB). Sweeps of historic villages, gorges and coastline, old woodlands, flowery meadows, narrow lanes, the vast downs and the moors are all encompassed within the AONB.

***

Often enough, when we are out hunting the location of our cottage rentals in the British countryside, we have to go beyond the postcode-fed satnav and rely on good old-fashioned directions from the cottage owners. The satnav can take one down unnecessarily narrow lanes and rough roads. We would rather rely on the landmarks listed out by the owner through email. "Cross the turnstile", "look out for a fork in the road", and some such time-honoured pieces of instruction carry us through till we reach the cottage in Crackington Haven and find ourselves in a snug little affair, one of its nooks stuffed with books and board games. "We are all set," I remark to my companions. They look mighty pleased too.

Having done a grocery run before reaching the cottage, we have our holiday breakfast needs taken care of. It is cosy to cook inside. To rustle up a breakfast of eggs, sausages, toast, to slather our toasts liberally with creamy country butter. After the first of such relaxed breakfasts, Hoomar, Adi and I decide to tackle the village on foot. It is a hamlet really, served as it is by the one post office that looks long in the tooth and doubles up as a convenience store.

We start to walk down Mill Ball Hill, a narrow valley road that waddles past farms and pastures, a Methodist church, tiny pockets of cottages, and eventually swoops into a cove. Whoever talks about places by the sea having relatively mild temperatures should get a solid knock on the noggin. By the time, we reached the beach in little over half an hour, we are frozen. The wind is sharp, and the day typically English, leached of colour, hints of sea mist curling around the cliffs.

"I need coffee. What about that inn there?" I say to my fellow walkers. The *Coombe Barton Inn* offers us refuge from the biting cold, with cake and coffee. As with most inns in the country, it is historic, built three hundred years ago as the home to the manager of the local slate quarries. When we have had coffee and warmed ourselves thoroughly, we leave the inn reluctantly. Like ducks, we bury our necks into our thick coats and cross the valley road to the beach. A gale has picked up while we have been inside. But we persist in the face of it and explore the shingly cove, sheer dark cliffs towering over us. The beach is all pebbles, with rockpools on the fringes where folds of slate and sandstone begin the journey of creeping towards the sea.

The coast looks thoroughly inhospitable. It is the perfect backdrop for a spot of Nordic noir. The rocks, I imagine, would have been treacherous to vessels that sailed into the port that once existed here. Slate quarried on the beach was exported. Meanwhile coal and lime were brought in at Crackington Haven. I for one prefer the tranquil state I find it in. It also looks like it would have been a haven for smuggling given the secretive nature of its location, but of that I know nothing. I can merely speculate. We climb the cliffs for the purpose of rambling, but the frigid coastal air gets so intolerable in a while that we hurry back to the cottage, as fast as our feet will carry us, to get a fire going and warm our very souls.

When we have had a few board games in the cottage and thawed out enough, we feel peckish. A quick drive takes us into Tintagel nearby, where we walk around the village, familiar to us by now. We end up in *Pengenna Pasties*, each choosing a massive home-made pasty to chow down. Mine is cheese and chives encased in flaky, butter pastry dough, and it fills me up as thoroughly it was meant to do when it was eaten by tin miners on duty in the underbelly of the earth. The pasty, rhyming as it does with "nasty", is a piece of humble pie, a crescent pastry crimped at the edges, traditionally stuffed with meats and flavoured with gravy. As it turns out, and I am fascinated by this bit of detail, the crimped edges in the old days were marked with monograms of initials to indicate the miner it was meant for. The ropey edges had a purpose

- they served as handles, which could be disposed of after. The miner's hands being smothered in arsenic-laden dust. Even the crust of the pasty is thick, designed to survive a drop down a mine shaft.

As usual to the British landscape, there are stories associated with the pasty too. My pick of the lot is the one about the devil, who it is said, refused to cross the River Tamar into Cornwall. He had heard that the Cornish women were adept at turning anything that lived into a filling, and naturally he did not want to end up inside a Cornish pasty. Who would blame the devil?

The first day goes by in a fuzz of intermittent walking, playing board games, and consuming pasties. The second starts with flying kites. Hoonar has decided that we should make the most of our winter break and he has grand designs. There is a bright blue kite nestled in the boot of the car. He unfurls it with pride. On a day that has improved upon the previous one with the sun peeking through thatches of clouds in bursts, we walk back to the cliffs by the beach, where it is still blowing a hoolie, and trudge up them. Walking a fair stretch of the South West Coastal Path towards the village of Boscastle, we stop along a slope that rolls into the sea. Hoonar and Adi want to launch the kite. They take turns with a proper run down the slopes each time.

"Don't you go tumbling down," I say, before I settle on a patch of heather with a book. I carry one everywhere. Who knows when one is caught unawares by the whimsies of kite-runners, who shall not be budged from their mission. I look up from time to time to check that the boys have not run off into the horizon. As the kite grows smaller and smaller, my patience begins to wear thin. It is cold and I am craving the comforts of the cottage, thinking of a cuppa and snuggling with a throw in one of its worn-down armchairs. I inform Adi about my intentions and make my way back to the cottage.

It is me-time. I take full advantage of it, wool-gathering and wandering up the valley road, stopping by the gates of a pasture to meet a field full of young calves, their ears tagged with pieces of yellow plastic. Another brief stop is at a farm, where a curious horse neighs at me from his slice of paddock. I like conversing with livestock on these rural escapades. The horse, his body swaddled in a faded blanket, listens, and to my fancy, he nods. As if he understands everything I have to say. Next, I examine the small church more thoroughly, but find the door locked. The narrow lanes are bereft of people. The only semblance of humanity is a lone glove sticking out of the tall, yellowed grasses that fringe the lane. The cottage is awfully quiet too. I read for a while, have a cup of tea, and find the quietness of it pressing down on my senses. Is it because I am not used to the deafening silence of the countryside?

I am ready for my co-travellers to materialise. But they arrive much later. The rest of our time in Crackington Haven is whiled away in as tranquil a manner, rambling along the coastal paths till our hearts have had their fill, eating pub food and drinking house wines, chatting late into the nights on subjects esoteric and trivial, till it eventually rolls to a cosy end.

When we exchange notes during the long drive home, we agree on one thing. Curiously enough, this has been a most refreshing holiday, filled with the goodness of the bracing coastal air, plenty of walks, cakes and cocoa, and hanging around the cottage with board games. The perfect recharge for the weekend.

VIII

Smuggler's Top

By 2014, we are more at peace. The worry about an abrupt move has abated somewhat, though at the same time, work is frantic for Adi. He has started travelling to Belgium. I join him and live for a while in a small town called Mechelen in Flanders. It is followed by a longish stint in Brussels. Though I have immensely enjoyed travelling solo during the weekdays through Belgium, and on weekends, explored charming provincial towns with Adi, I have missed the routine of life in Northampton. When we return home, we catch up with the gang at the local pubs on weekends. Sometimes, we leg it to London.

Of our group, Sandy and Bhavna, a couple we are fond of suggest that we embark on a Cornish trip together, during an evening of harried rounds of poker at their place.

So, when spring is well-nigh, we return to the duchy. This time with our new mates. We book a cottage at a farm in Launceston, a market town located near the duchy's border with Devon. Upon reaching the postcode and entering the gates, to our utter astonishment, we spot a German Shepherd gambolling in a bathtub in the sprawling gardens adjoining the cottage. A woman comes forward, introducing herself as the landlady. She puts the strange scene that we witness in perspective. "Zack is a great lover of baths and he is fond of his bathtub, especially on sunny days," she says. Why and how a dog has his own bathtub is another matter of course. And who am I to question the ways of a dog lover really. In the past, I have been known to throw a pirate-themed birthday party for Tuktuk, complete with sparklers and cupcakes. Nonetheless

I cannot help thinking that it is an interesting note to start the holiday on. For in the past, I have participated in the dragging of an extremely reluctant and smelly Labrador, to the bath. Here we have a dog, who is keen on baths. Wonders will never cease.

Staying on a farm has its advantages. In the evenings, when we settle down in the garden with our drinks and barbecue meats in the grill outdoors, we have an audience we have not accounted for. A herd of curious cows. They moo, they linger, looking for treats, then they leave as abruptly without so much as a by-your-leave.

Since Bhavna and Sandy have not visited Cornwall before, we volunteer to be their guides. We hike along the coastal paths of Tintagel; with pleasure we watch their reactions at finding themselves surrounded by the dark, wild beauty of Kynance Cove; introduce them to the tasty kebabs at Redruth; and the holiday is rescued from being relegated to a bag of repeats by the happy chance of us coming upon the fishing village of Polperro.

I think nothing of the surprises that such a village can hold. It will be a pretty settlement, surely as the rest of them, seeing as it is located within the AONB, but could it offer more? I have a passing knowledge of smuggling in this part of the country – gleaned from reading Daphne's books — but not a farthing more. We do not know the specifics of where these dubious activities thrived along the Cornish coast. Polperro is the first of the prominent candidates on our travels. In fact, we realise that we have reached the king of the string of former smuggling villages. Parking is at the edge of the village in the hamlet of Crumplehorn, which is said to have derived its name from the livestock that roamed the countryside. Picture sheep/cows with long, curled (maybe crumpled) horns. Our attention is engaged by a mill house, stood at the top of the village of Polperro. The *Crumplehorn Inn* comprises a whitewashed clutch of farmhouses, topped with roofs of slate, walls thick with lashings of dark ivy. The visual element is elevated by the presence of an old water wheel. The Domesday Book, which is Britain's oldest existing public record, mentions the property. It dates back to the

14th century and started life as a corn mill and farm, known as Killigarth Mill, and later, Crumplehorn Farm.

A couple of 17th century Cornish antiquaries, Richard Carew and John Norden, wrote favourably of their visits to Killigarth. Carew noted: "It yeeldeth a large viewe of the South coast, and was itselfe, in Sir Williams time, much visited, through his frank invitings". Once again devastating spellings aside, we get an idea of the popularity of the establishment since the early days.

I am intrigued by the inn's 18th century role as the spiritual home of smugglers and privateers. And as the actual home of Zephaniah Job, the hero of Polperro, who single-handedly organised the finances of a rag-tag bunch of contraband dealers from the village. The Smuggler's Banker, as Job was known, was a clever man with a finger in every pie. He served as financial advisor, accountant, and a banker who issued his own bank notes, not only to the smugglers but to the local gentry as well. Job was in charge of the pilchard export trade in Polperro, while also streamlining the business of smuggling, and hiring lawyers in Cornwall and London to attend to court cases concerning the smugglers. He arranged money for those stuck in prison. All this apart, Job was a coal importer, a seed, corn and timber merchant, and had leased a few lime kilns. His entrepreneurial skills did not end there. The man sold linen, sourced from Ireland, in neighbouring Looe.

I want to meet Job, if only to take tips from the man who wore so many hats yet had the time to leave behind calligraphic records of his business dealings for posterity. And here's ol' me, trying to keep my head above water, in mastering the one profession I chose in this life.

***

Steep cliffs rise on either side of the road that winds into Polperro, past stone houses, barns overgrown with ivy and the village hall. They are bordered by sprigs of early spring wildflowers and a brook that ribbons through the village, passing beneath small stone and wooden bridges. A compact milk float appears, ferrying people to and fro. The vivid-red electric car in the old days carried fresh milk to the village and was most probably drawn by a horse. The converted float trundles along the lanes of Polperro, with a fresh cargo of passengers. In its wake, we follow the road that starts shrinking into Fore Street, once we have crossed pasty shops and ice cream parlours, art galleries, and attractive cottages advertising B&B vacancies. A line-up of commercial establishments, more art galleries, shops touting Bavarian cuckoo clocks, folkloric piskies, and leather goods, takes us past *The Buccaneer* restaurant, its name a reminder of the village's privateering past.

A parrot-green vintage Chevrolet pick-up truck is lodged in the alley, cradled by houses on both sides. It barely fits and we have to sidle past. The warren of narrow streets is explanation enough for the traffic-free policy of the village. It also means that you can truly amble, take in the ambience, peep into atmospheric cottages that turn up with evocative names. *Gulls Cry, The Cuddy, Smugglers Cottage, Talland House,…* I bask in the leisurely stroll and give into the pleasure of not being nosed on by errant cars. We stall in front of *The Smallest Shop* in Kernow, which looks not unlike a rabbit hutch; we browse canvases in galleries and move at a remarkably slow pace.

Breaking for afternoon tea is a rite of passage in England and we do so at a 16th-century timber-framed cottage that looks straight out of the pages of a fairy tale. Everything within the whitewashed walls of *The House on the Props* looks ancient. True to its name, it is propped up on stilts athwart a gushing stream that spills into the inner harbour, and beyond it, empties into the sea. The dark wooden beams repurposed from an 18th-century old ship are strung with various nautical references, and signages above the wooden till instruct us to eat cake — lots of it. We are on the job.

Within a few minutes of the order having been placed, a few slices of cake are brought over by the woman tending to the bar. There's cream tea and scones for the boys, and we girls stick to hunks of creamy walnut, carrot, and fruit cakes. In between, we gather from the woman that the house is reputed to be haunted. Now, who does not love a good ghost story?

Turns out, the ghost has a name, Crushana Northcott. She is a former resident of *The House on the Props*, known to show up on a rocking chair positioned along its windows, with her gaze trained seawards.

Now, how can I leave you with the suggestion of a haunting and no backstory for the resident ghost?

Northcott was quite the trooper, as the story goes. She is said to have warned smugglers of the presence of the authorities by placing a doll, dressed in the garb of a customs officer, at her shop window. Goes to show that the people of Polperro were an ingenious lot, who had a handle on circumventing the revenue men and looking after their own. Somewhere along the way, tragedy befell Northcott. She lost her young son to a random accident upon the cliffs and her husband never returned home from sea.

Of the bulk of smuggling villages on the southern coast, Polperro is the busiest today. Yet, in no way does it detract from its appeal. The village has more than its fair share of pubs and restaurants. I count more than a dozen. A far cry from the 1500s, when English antiquary and poet, John Leland, passing by the village, described "Poulpier/Poulpirrhe/Poulpyrre" as "symple and poore".

A gallimaufry of fishermen's cottages climbs above the inner harbour, which is the hot spot in the village. The network of twisting alleys and streets disgorges visitors on a stone bridge above an inner harbour. At high tide, the inner harbour is filled with water, and when the waters secede, it is transformed into a river of mud, dotted with small fishing boats lying on their sides, all askew. The cottages on the eastern part of the harbour, known as The Warren, are a line-up of period properties dating back to the 16th century. Mostly fishermen's cottages, their whitewashed fronts and window frames are painted in hues of blues and greens. One of them belonged to a beloved resident of Polperro, Dr. Jonathan Couch. A 18th-century naturalist, historian and village doctor; also the forefather of Daphne du Maurier's Q, Sir Arthur Quiller-Couch. Dr. Couch's book, *The History of Polperro*, published posthumously, is a vast repository of information about the village as it used to be. Such as the fact that The Warren is called so probably because "it was a rabbit reserve when the owner of Killigarth lived there".

**

That Polperro is a working fishing village to this day like a few others on the coast, is emphasised by the fishy odours that hang around the inner harbour like an aura; it is reeking near the small fish shop, which advertises line-caught mackerel and cod and what not. I am hardly alone in not warming up to the "perfume" of Polperro, though no self-respecting Bengali from Calcutta would ever complain of it, the Bengali's olfactory senses flowering at the obvious presence of seafood.

"Polstink" is a nickname that Polperro acquired at some point of time. Now, it might have been coined by some "jealous" neighbouring village in the past, but you can hardly dismiss notes from the diary of John Wesley. The Methodist preacher got the full malodorous effect of it when he visited the village in 1768 and walked into his lodgings. What did he find? A room piled high with pilchards and conger eels. No dithering on his part then, when a friend offered him alternate lodgings.

If you are looking for a different perspective, ask a seagull. The gull mafia must find the stench aromatic, hovering as they do along the inner harbour, perching themselves upon the walls and adding to the scenery as easily as mizzle goes with skies leached of colour. I almost mistake a big gull, sat upon the walls adjacent a cobalt blue ceramic urn, for an art installation and a testament to Polperro's artistic leanings.

We escape the fishy smell for a while by perching ourselves atop the beer garden at *The Three Pilchards*, with pints of Doom Bar. The pub is one of those heritage suspects with an old fireplace and wooden beams, the kinds where the carpet should be layered over with years and years of spilled pints – possibly dating from the 16th century when it was built by a pair of Italian brothers who exported pilchards to their homeland. Rumour has it that the other passion of the village was conducted within its premises by a landlord, who offered faithful customers contraband booty at the bar.

Local morality that revolved around smuggling was non-existent in the duchy. The necessity to cobble together a decent living far outweighed any prickling of conscience among villagers. During my research, I come upon notes by a disapproving witness at the scene. Wesley. He branded it "an accursed thing" and noted that in the village "wellnigh one and all bought or sold uncustomed goods." I wonder if he had the opportunity to look down his nose at the benefactor of the village, Job, but since the man arrived in Polperro only in the 1770s, chances of that are dim.

The museum of smuggling and fishing in The Warren is a treasure house of information for the curious traveller. It furnishes one further with photographic accounts of Polperro's free-trading past. One of the most charged stories it tells is that of "Battling Billy". The timeline is the 18th century when a small-pox epidemic swept through the locality. The dead used to be buried at night. Using the hearse as a convenient mode of transport, the landlord of a local inn, Billy, conveyed kegs of brandy inland from the shores. He was proved right in his surmise that it would pass detection till a cargo was unloaded by daylight. When revenue officers arrived at the scene, Billy is said to have broken into a gallop on his horse and declared: "If they shoot me dead, my body will drive the load to Polperro." And that's what happened. Billy was shot through the neck. His lifeless body, it is said, was sprawled across the horse and continued through the cobbled streets of Polperro.

Quixotic tales swirling in our minds, we weave our way through pubs and cottages down the winding street, in the ghostly footsteps of smugglers and fishermen lugging their carts laden with fish or hidden goodies, to the outer harbour. The scene of many a drama, when braving inclement weather, smugglers would have arrived in the cove under the cover of night, to load and unload ships.

We exchange smugglers and officers for artists. In a small studio, we come upon a headful of titian curls bent with deep concentration on a canvas. The artist turns around and greets us. Her name is Gina. As we chat, for time is not a harried commodity in this part of the country, it transpires that she paints Polperro over and over again. Originally an outsider to the village, hers is the story of one who became an insider.

Later, Adi and I both agree upon it that the contentment of Gina's choice is mirrored in her soothing personality. What is life if it is not about listening to and acting upon the calls of our heart?

***

On another occasion, a few years down the line, when Adi and I are on one of our walks in Polperro, we spend time around its rugged coastline that lends a ready hand to the colourful stories that abound around the illegitimate trade. The shores are wild and rocky, the beach small and sandy, but given to disappear quickly under incursions of the sea water. I spot a cave on the beach. The tide is yet to set in. And I want to have a go at it. Adi, already paranoid about exploring dark and damp caverns, baulks when he hears the story of the smuggler who died within while trying to escape the revenue men. "Naturally,

Willy old boy lives in it now. People have heard his shrieks now and again," I say, with a straight face. The nail is driven into the coffin of our cave explorations. Wild horses shall not drag my husband in there.

We climb the rocks above the cave instead. It feels good to fantasise about buying up the old boarded-up building perched on the cliffs. The *Old Net Loft*. What a crescentic view it has of the tidal pool beneath, and that of the wooded hills swooping into the valley that is dotted with centuries-old stone cottages. The net loft must even now withstand the worst of gales as it has for a couple of hundred years at the least. Couch left notes on these storms that assailed the harbour: "The noise of the wind as it roars up the coomb, the hoarse rumbling of the angry sea, the shouts of the fishermen engaged in securing their boats, and the screams of the women and children, carrying the tidings of the latest disaster…". It sounds awfully threatening and gloomy. As for our location at the net loft and fantasising about it as a residence, I realise that it would be a mighty pickle to be caught in it during a storm.

All this mooning over an abandoned pilchard loft means that we miss the signs of the tide sweeping in. By the time we descend, the waters have reached waist level and holding hands, we try not to slip upon the rocks as we wade back to the quay. The freezing waters wake us up from our daydreams in a jiffy.

We find a bench on the quay to gather our wits before cracking on. The plaque on the bench recalls a woman who has exchanged her earthly life for another, but her heart it says, her heart is still in Polperro.

For entirely different reasons, my husband's heart too is in Polperro. He says that it is the only time and place that he has seen me driving in an empty parking lot (adjacent to a field that is home to an angry bull) like a complete tool, shrieking, "Here bull, I am comin' for ya!" Don't ask me why. Even I do not know the rhyme or reason to my strange ways.

IX

Nelson's Hometown

It is gone midnight when we drive into the fishing town of Looe, on an Easter bank holiday weekend in 2016. It is one of my treasured memories from our various breaks in Cornwall, which may have to do with the fact that we are to spend five long days here. It may also be the company, for we are travelling in a group of six. Hoonar is the only common quotient to our other road trips. The other faces have changed. This time around we are in the company of Adi's colleagues, a couple, Chandra and Praya, and a girl called Parul. I have been recently been on a holiday to Sardinia with Parul and found in her an adventurous co-traveller.

Four miles from Polperro, we arrive in Looe in two cars. The town is deserted as we coast by a stone bridge. Within minutes, the car is grumbling up a hill. The road narrows, winding through a line-up of whitewashed cottages, and a couple of hairpin bends later, the car groans up the steep incline with the enthusiasm of an ancient biddy. And we find ourselves in front of the cottage we have rented for the break.

A similar path was charted 165 years ago by Wilkie Collins and his artist friend Henry Brandling, when they embarked upon a walking tour of Cornwall in the summer of the year 1850. The two friends arrived in Looe late at night and passed the same stone bridge as us, beneath "dark night-clouds" among "the whistling music of the wind" as observed by Collins in his book *Rambles Beyond Railways.* Like them, we get an eyeful of the town that is tucked within a valley, from our cliffside rental property. Hopping off the car, we stretch out limbs worn out by the inactivity of a long drive and note the quaint prettiness of it.

The village is festooned with strings of fairy lights. The solitude enveloping the town that has gone to sleep is a balm for the senses. The salty tang in the night air assures us that the sea is our neighbour. Given my boundless reserves of enthusiasm, I would normally take off to explore our surroundings, but the pall of darkness combined with a body drained of all energy, drives me indoors. Tomorrow shall arrive soon enough.

The boys leave in the search for parking spots. I don't envy them. We have seen first-hand how narrow the streets are, not to mention, the sharp dip; I join the others in calling dibs on the rooms. We have no fair chambermaid or landlady to welcome us, as Collins and Brandling. It is the 21st century after all. We find instructions to let ourselves in, in an email from the landlady. The cottage is commodious, and even though it is Victorian with its canted bay windows and roofs of slate, the interiors have been renovated to a modern sensibility. I would have preferred a dated look – but I am chuffed at the thought of the holiday that is yet to kick off and the cottage with its homey interiors sets the appropriate tone.

The next morning, the first of our four days in town, dawns gloomy and grey. This being the UK, it's nothing we are not used to. The view from the bay windows makes me feel like a great gull, staring at the town below meditatively. The windows open to a frontal view of town and fine angular views of the English Channel, which seems to merge into the sky seamlessly. Stone cottages with roofs of slate, stained mossy green, trail down the hill upon which we are perched. Beyond them, is a waterway busy with small fishing boats. This is River Looe, which empties into the sea and splits the town into East Looe (where we are) and West Looe. Further, beyond the river, West Looe with its plethora of cottages climbs a hill. Skeletal trees in its backdrop join bare branches to create a canvas of bleak barrenness along the horizon. I am stood at the window for long, head popped out, to breathe better the salty air and admire the sight.

In a while, when everyone is ready to step out, we troop down and step outside. I tip my head back for a daylight view of the cottage and find before me a property painted in pastel blues. It looks distinctly Victorian. Set back high above a narrow road, the stone plaque on the granite walls identifies the cottage as *Sunnybank*. The path that dips below the cottage is paved by granite walls, out of the crevices of which hang comely sprigs of wild plants and clumps of wisteria. As we skip down the road, I think aloud, "Hah, the climb back up shall be precious".

A few twists and turns past some whitewashed cottages and granite barn conversions and we are downhill, smack in front of a 16th-century Tudor building that served as guildhall and gaol between the 16th and the 19th century. The old cannon on the gabled porch, the timber-framed roof and mullioned windows look ancient. Nowadays there is no magistrate inside the guildhall, looking down his long nose at the disorderly, waggling his fingers and passing judgement. There are no dodgy fellows either lodged inside the old gaol, but there are historical objects instead to be found on display. Antiquated weights and measures used for fair trade, prehistoric animal remains, a whipping contraption known as the cat o'nine tails, bottled antidotes to witchcraft, pilchard presses. Vestiges of past eras and a mix of strange paraphernalia to boggle the mind. These local museums are modest in size, housing artefacts in a few rooms, but how they engage the imagination, tickling it with stories of life as it would have been in old Cornwall. They are the town's antiquated storytellers.

From the time of Edward I when it had its roots, Looe has aged well I think, as we wander through town. Its streets are teeming with bakeries, their windows laden with delightful cakes that we fall prey to eventually, shops sell sweeties, angling shops offer everything one needs for a shark fishing trip, counting in clothing, binoculars, clocks and barometers, while pasty shops have pasties on display; pasties that are larger than my fist. Bacon, cheese and leek; potato and leek; onion and pickle; steak and stilton. Life is pasty-some in Looe. You could lunch like a miner and feel rum about it (I would keep that bottle of indigestion pills handy).

We give into the pasties, alluring as they are, and after we have walked off this breakfast of champions, we linger around the river. Hopping across it, we take a look at West Looe and arrive at the conclusion that East Looe is decidedly our jam. We make our way back to the arched stone bridge linking West to East Looe, its stone troughs brimming with profusions of fuchsia and white petunias.

Spanning the shallow river flooded with a fleet of picturesque fishing boats, the bridge is the perfect perch from which we admire the town, stretched out in front of the eyes. On either side, wooded hills rise high. "…here and there a cottage peeps out among the trees, the winding path that leads to it being now lost to sight in the thick foliage, now visible again as a thin serpentine line of soft grey," observed Collins. He was stood where I am now. We are separated by the wall of time, but given his descriptions, I find that on the surface not much has changed in Looe. Houses continue to straggle towards the sea, the streets still are narrow mazes to lose yourself in, and the hills with their bounty of houses, as of old, join the harbour that opens into the English Channel. The river remains dry for the best part of the day, but when tidal waters stream in through the inlet, the fishing boats bob as if in approval of a full-bodied estuary.

Another day, when the sun shines intermittently, we loiter around East Looe beach. We have access from the hill on which our cottage is propped. Down it, steep steps carved into the cliffs take us past a terrace and onto an expanse of sand. At one end of this beach are black jagged rocks protruding into the sea and trapping sea water within rockpools, encrusted with barnacles and seaweed. Past the west end of the beach runs the Banjo Pier, the first of its kind in the world, and built by a local engineer in the 19th century.

The pier is a favourite with anglers, but blustery conditions have rendered it empty. The girls and I decide on a spot of walking. We carry on to the bridge and cross over to West Looe. On the South West Coastal Path that runs parallel to the river, and along the harbour walls, we stop at a life-like statue of a one-eyed seal plonked on the rocks. He has a prime view of the lifeboat station and that of the fishing boats bobbing on the river.

By this point, and before I carry on any further, I should clear up any confusions regarding the title of the chapter. Looe is not the hometown of Horatio Nelson. The hero of Britain was born in Norfolk and has as little to do with Looe as I have to do with Marmite. Looe belongs to Nelson the seal, the beloved local we do not get to meet. The scarred bull seal lived on the rocks near the harbour entrance for over 25 years, breathing his last in 2003. Nelson's diet was taken care of by the kind fishermen and townspeople of Looe, who affectionately refer to him as the "grand old man of the sea". In the scheme of things, it is befitting that the people of Looe commissioned a life-size bronze sculpture to remember their flippered friend by.

So, here is sat Nelson, the one-eyed rock star of Looe, flippers akimbo, sunning his bronzed body for good upon the rocks in town.

Familiar by now with the coastal path that swerves up above the harbour into West Looe, we make our way to the deserted Hannafore Beach. Since we have timed it right, for it is low tide, a dark shingle beach is stretched before our eyes. Sea water is trapped in the rockpools, where when we look carefully, we spot starfish, sponges, sea-squirts and spider crabs. We take care not to disturb these marine inhabitants as we slip and slide over slabs of blueish-black slates that are stacked dramatically along the shore.

Across the waters is a verdure hump of land jutting out from the English Channel. Looe Island. Thick woods, a couple of beaches tucked into quiet coves, remnants of a medieval chapel, colonies of birds, and a remarkable lack of roads, commercial establishments, and cars, mark the island today. But it must have been a centre of pilgrimage in the early days when it was known as *Enys Lann-Managh*, Cornish for "island of the monk's enclosure".

Joseph of Arimathea is said to have visited the island with his young nephew, Jesus. There are speculations too that Looe Island could have been *Ictis*, the Roman port of tin trading during the 5th century when Phoenicians traded with Cornwall – the belief somewhat cemented by the discovery of coins and artefacts on the island, dating back to Roman times. St. Michael's Mount is a close rival for this ancient tin trading centre status, if you are to go by the Greek historian of old, Diodorus Siculus. But there can be no quibbles about the fact that Looe Island was a base for smugglers who hid their contraband booties in the caves here before ferrying them to the mainland, when the coast was free of the watchful presence of revenue men. This naturally led to HM Customs establishing a house upon the island as a lookout point for bootleggers.

The skies grow ashen even as done with skipping across the slates and boulders, we are sat awhile on the rocks. When the waters begin swirling in, we scuttle before the ocean reclaims the beach.

It's cream tea o'clock.

While the rest of the country breaks for its sacred afternoon tea, which author Henry James declared to be an "eternity of pleasure", in the southwest of England, you cease all activities in order to make time for cream tea. In other words, an afternoon repast of scones, clotted cream and jam, to accompany the must-have cuppa. There is a serious debate in these parts about what goes first on the scone. I have asked for "advice" in the tearooms of Cornwall and that of Devon, only to be informed in no-nonsense tones that while in Cornwall, the jam Is the first layer, then clotted cream; in Devon, it Is cream first, followed by the jam. Such "grave" matters are not to be messed with and it is best to toe the line. After all, I do not want to lock horns with irate locals.

***

East Looe with its bustling nature is such a contrast when we have crossed back over from West Looe that it takes me a few ticks to recalibrate the senses. I achieve this with scones and tea in a quaint tea shop in the company of my friends. Adi and the boys have joined us for tea.

In between our chatter, I glance at the busy thoroughfare of East Looe and struggle to think that the town was once so sparsely populated that both East and West Looe were deemed part of the "rotten boroughs". In the 18th century, a place with a meagre number of voters was declared to be "rotten", a word that could signify either corrupt or declining, or both, because if you think of it, a small electorate means that it is easy for votes to be swayed. Just to give you an idea about how small the numbers were in this part of the world, East Looe at the time had a few hundred houses and all of 38 registered voters. Together, the two halves of Looe returned two members of parliament, until the Great Reform Act of the 19th century. The numbers have swelled in modern-day Looe. According to a census from 2011, it has about five thousand plus residents.

Post tea, Adi and I part ways with the rest of the gang for a couple of hours. We want to nose around town and go about it at a relaxed pace. Don't you just love a good amble? We peep into shops that sell enough sweets to sustain whole armies of children; we browse nautical-themed souvenirs, the kinds that you find hanging around in every port town worth its salt; and, press our noses against bakery windows, lusting at the wholesome sight of rustic loaves of bread. Faffing about, we spot the narrowest of alleys that appears to have squeezed itself between houses, mossed-up steps winding up. What lies around the corner? The mood of exploration is terribly addictive, enough for me to stomach the darkening of the husband's eyebrows – a visceral reaction of his to stairs.

We leg it uphill. Now wait, does that signage mention a bookshop up the road? Thoughts of rummaging around it transforms me into a goat and I scurry on. This does not go down well with Adi, but he knows a lost cause when it is staring him in the eye, and what's worse, this cause is up a steep road. Adi's dilemma is that he wants to execute an about-turn and go downhill, but can he really abandon me at this point. The thought of me in a bookshop strikes my poor husband, who already has towers of books at home to contend with, with fresh terror. Every time a house move comes up, the thought of fessing up the extra bucks to have a hefty collection of books carted, strikes him with fresh intensity. Naturally, this means that I do not have to urge him at all. No need for a "come with" here.

Inside the *Old Hall Bookshop*, I am treated to second-hand books and rare editions. Wooden shelves lined with dusty book jackets are spread out across two floors of a converted chapel. In case, it please the visitor to while away time inside, there are cosy chairs to sink into and lose oneself in between the yellowed pages of well-loved editions.

I am enveloped in the musty smell of second-hand books and nostalgia. This would be my go-to scent in the whole world – it transports me to summer holidays as a child when I would rush to borrow well-thumbed Enid Blytons from a senior at school. Within the hallowed walls of the erstwhile chapel, I inhale the scent of the pages before moving on to inscribed flyleaves. It is a fine-tuned process that will resonate with someone somewhere who picks up a book and sniffs its pages, then proceeds to flip through them, to check for inscriptions.

I pick up an Anne Radcliffe. The lady who is sat at the till is enthused at my choice and is content to hold forth on the genre of the Gothic novel. Now Radcliffe might not be a popular author – Jane Austen poked fun at her in *Northanger Abbey*, if you will – but I find her books immersive. Radcliffe infused her tales with the supernatural effortlessly. And as it turns out, the bookshop woman has written books on Radcliffe. "Fancy that!" I say to Adi, who is sinfully bored. Having bagged a few old editions, I leave the premises without feeling short-changed. No visit to a bookshop can be deemed complete without books bought and stowed into the tote.

Meandering through Looe is not without its pleasures. This is heightened by the fact that recreational eating here is an art. When we are peckish, there's enough to choose from. There are crepes to be tried, pasty samplings, ice creams, coffee, cream tea, beer at the local pubs along with pies and nibbles. Our favourite go-to in town is a restaurant which serves the best Thai I have ever eaten. Seagulls sit atop chimneys, alert to the possibilities of tasty bits and bobs dropped by grubby children. There's colour at every bend. Wee children waddle on with ice cream cones, at a street corner teens wolf down large pasties, leather-clad bikers stroll through alleys and young girls and boys crab in the waters of the estuary. The roads are narrow enough to discourage people from driving into these pinched stretches that meander past period stone properties till they spill into the harbour. The layout is purely quirky. In his book *Rambles Beyond Railways*, Collins remarked: "There is no such thing as a straight street in the place. No martinet of an architect has been here, to drill the old stone houses into regimental regularity."

The other aspect of the old port town that I cannot help noticing is its fondness for fishing and shark angling. Looe is the headquarter of the Shark Angling Club of Britain, which operates on a policy of catch and release. A historical centre for pilchard fishing, shark angling, and smuggling, we find that its maritime legacies hold good, especially through the laminated press cuttings and photographs that adorn the walls of its historic pubs and inns. On our second day in town, the six of us stop at the *Smugglers Cott* for a spot of lunch. It used to be Looe's smuggling haunt, a 15th-century property that was later restored using beams and timbers salvaged from a galleon, the *Spanish Armada*. Tales of smuggling have been passed down the generations in Looe too, word of mouth. At the 16th century pub, *The Jolly Sailor Inn*, also constructed from the salvaged parts of a ship, one of the landladies is known to have hid a contraband keg beneath her petticoats during a sudden raid. The woman calmly knitted away while her quarters were searched by revenue officers. No wonder that the government of the time was losing 20 per cent of the excise duty to smuggling.

Lunch within the medieval *Smugglers Cott* is delightful. The catch-of-the-day list is extensive. They have bass sole, ling from Eddystone (reefs in the English Channel), coalfish, John Dory, pollock and bay scallops, and some Indian grub too. Lamb *roganjosh*, chicken *jalfrezi*, and chicken *korma*. We settle on grilled fish and fish pies. What would the Cornish be without their pies?

I scour the pub wall with its collection of black and white photographs. They document stories of shark anglers and their thrilling oceanic adventures. My pick of the lot is that of a female angler posing next to the massive carcass of a shark strung up for measurement. Joyce Yallop, a grandmother in her 60s, had netted a 500-lb mako shark in May 1971 and left her mark in the annals of British shark angling. It harks back to a time, the '40s and '50s, when sharks were hauled up for weighing and crowds thronged the quay to watch the offloading of catches in the evening. Shark angling had become a national passion, when the rich and famous wanting a share of the pie, often landed up at the quay with picnic hampers of lobsters and Champers to take on angling expeditions. All of this is somewhat difficult to picture now, what with the multitudes interested in the more pedestrian pleasures of sunbathing, grabbing ice cream, or crabbing.

I feel like a magpie, mooching around the entertaining alleys in town, gathering stories from locals and photographs. Apart from exploring the nearby villages of Polperro, Mevagissey and Fowey, we luxuriate in the solitude of our cottage too, scarfing down cakes from the local confectioners and solving jigsaw puzzles. On our last night in Looe, we idle on the beach, silvered waves lapping the shore beneath a night sky riddled with stars. I find myself thinking of a time when smugglers would have unloaded their contraband goods here. The scene plays out in my head. The silhouette of a ship as it pulls into the shallow waters, a few hundred men on board and moored at some distance from the shore. Small boats are dispatched to the beach with booties of brandy and gin, men scurrying nimbly with their goods under the cover of night. And to the fervent mind unbidden comes Rudyard Kipling's smuggler's song.

If you wake at midnight, and hear a horse's feet,
Don't go drawing back the blind, or looking in the street,
Them that ask no questions isn't told a lie.
Watch the wall my darling while the Gentlemen go by.

X

In Fowey and Mevagissey

Time has a habit of standing still in Cornwall. Its towns and villages retain an air of simplicity that feels wholesome. This is how it must have been in the old days you think, as you repeatedly hear stories of fishing and smuggling that go hand in hand with the cobbled lanes that meander through Cornwall's hilly outposts. Now, if you will come with me to Fowey, it is a town on the southern coast with a natural harbour, once an important trading post in the thick of the smuggling scene.

The year is 1835 and the scene is a beach in Fowey. A couple of coastguards stationed on a hill nearby, espies the arrival of what they believe to be a contingency of smugglers, a significant number of them being boatswain (bosun). Having asked for reinforcements, the coastguards along with their newly arrived colleagues, engage in a tussle with the suspected smugglers. They end up arresting about five of the lot, though one of their team is rendered unconscious. Soon, they have help from a revenue cutter, which captures contraband brandy to the tune of 484 gallons. In court, the case is dismissed. The defence argues that the clubs used by the smugglers are actually walking sticks. Since one cannot be put behind bars for possessing walking sticks, the jury excuses them, and to cement this acquittal, the vicar of Fowey attests to the innocence of one of the accused. The others are redeemed in a similar manner through statements of their good character, issued by local farmers.

The incident makes it obvious that lawbreakers, privateers, and pirates were in vogue in this medieval town. Licensed to engage in maritime warfare, privateers had been authorised by the Crown to operate in the waters during the 14th and 15th centuries, as part of the Hundred Years' War (essentially a struggle for domination between the English and French royal dynasties, over the throne of France). The title conferred upon the privateers speaks volumes about the public's esteem for these individuals, for they called them the "Gallants of Fowey". The story should be incomplete without the mention of the woman who came to the aid of the gallants in the year 1475, when French marauders raided town.

In town, there is a listed building, *Place House*. To be fair, it is more of a castle than a house with its many turrets and towers. The lady of the manor was Dame Elizabeth Treffry. For six long weeks, she held off marauders. She is also said to have poured molten lead over their heads, from her tower.

Later, when a peace treaty with France was signed, the privateers received the raw end of the bargain - as you suspect was wont to happen. Their ships were seized, and several pirates hanged.

We do not chance upon privateers. Neither do we stumble upon gutsy ladies in towers waiting to tip buckets of hot lead over mischief mongers, but Fowey has *je ne sais quoi.* It is described to perfection by the English poet, Sir John Betjeman. "On a still evening out of season, with the sound of boats crossing the harbour, the creak of rowlocks, the occasional shouts over the water, the street lights shining on old slate walls and wet fuchsia hedges and shriveled hydrangeas, the Victorian stained glass shining out from an Evangelical evensong in the much-restored church, it is still like an Academy picture of the nineteen hundreds… It is a haunted town made for sailors and pedestrians."

From the time our group of six steps out of the large car park that is situated on a hill above town, and pootle downhill, we are captivated. The towers of St. Fimbarrus Church and Place House stand head and shoulder above a sea of grey slate roofs and chimneys. The hill dips sharply to reveal a view of the blue waters of the estuary that flow by Fowey, and beyond it, green hills undulate gently, the slopes divvied up into patches of pastures.

The town is a sight for sore eyes, a canvas designed by an artist who was in a generous mood, so he threw in coves, old-fashioned country cottages trailing up and down its steep lanes, brooding churches and bijou establishments. The boutiques of Fowey are elegant, but oh, how the brows touch the scalp when our eyes alight on the price tags. It is obvious that Fowey, along with the neighbouring villages of Bodinnick-by-Fowey and Polruan-by-Fowey, has always been well-heeled, as home to master mariners and wealthy shipping merchants. We trawl the length and breadth of it, mooching around bookshops, sighing over ornaments in shops — Adi conveniently turning a deaf ear to said sighs.

Everywhere we go in Fowey, Daphne du Maurier looms large. The town is awash with references to the writer, and we amble around, following this breadcrumb trail of sorts. Near St. Fimbarras Church — the medieval church dedicated to the memory of an Irish bishop called St. Fin Barr who is said to have passed built a small church in Fowey in the 6th century before heading to Rome — there's a bookshop, *Bookends of Fowey*. I lose the plot here when I come upon the antiquated works of authors, authors who wrote extensively on Cornwall and produced fascinating literature revolving around its smuggling past. There is plenty on du Maurier to sate the soul. It is all Adi can do to tear me away, by being clever and dangling the carrot that we should be off to see where du Maurier lived instead of languishing in the corner of a bookshop. I manage to leave the shop without going off the rails, over the acquisition of nearly every edition of Daphne's that I lay my eyes upon. I have no compunctions about buying different editions of the same title.

We make our way to Readymoney Cove, a sheltered beach nearby. Sat at the head of the beach is a former coach house where Daphne had sought refuge during WWII to sort out her messed-up life. The story goes that before she winded up in Fowey, she was living in Hertfordshire with a couple, who had taken her in while her husband was away at war. Daphne is rumoured to have been caught in an embrace with the husband of her hostess. She rented Readymoney Cottage in the early 1940s. The beach in front of the cottage must have been of great cheer to the author, for when we arrive here afoot, on a sunny noon, it is bustling with a battalion of children and dogs.

Eventually when she wanted a change from the cottage, du Maurier rented the nearby grand estate of Menabilly, built by the Rashleighs, who owned Readymoney Cottage as well. Menabilly, which is difficult for any literature lover to forget, especially the haunting words, "Last night I dreamt I went to Manderley again…" The way to the estate is barred today, not for any sinister reason, but that it is private property.

It is a sparkling summer's day and it shall not be complete without ice creams. Back in the town centre of Fowey, we arm ourselves with cones. It feels deliciously slow as we head to Fowey's harbour, licking ice cream and casting daydreams upon the waters of the green estuary shimmering in the midday sun. The old harbour is where boats arrived once, to unload their cargo of fish and china clay at the jetty. Dangling our legs from its brick walls, we watch the machinations of an ancient town – bold gulls keening and swooping across the estuary, as tugboats chug by. And I think of young du Maurier. For we are perched opposite another cottage of hers. This one is a whitewashed affair called *Ferryside*, sat squat across the river. When the author's family bought it in the 1920s, it was called *Swiss Cottage*; it was here that she had penned her first novel, *The Loving Spirit,* and noted in her diary a touch fervently: "All I want is to be at Fowey. Nothing and no one else."

***

On day four of our Easter's break, we swing into the other fishing villages on this part of the coast in a bid to see life as it is today in these former smuggling haunts. Do locals continue to cling to the traditional ways of living or have they swapped old-world for modish? We head to Mevagissey and catch breakfast at a café that looks like the kind of place the locals frequent. The fluffy omelette I am served is reassuring. We have arrived at a worthy joint. That, and a serving of chips, crisp on the outside, soft on the inside. How often do I have chips for breakfast? I carry on scarfing a hillock of chips, and after, it is a surprise that I can manage to waddle up the streets of Mevagissey. In a few minutes we find out that there are sharp switchbacks to take us uphill, and further on, into pastoral land. This seems to do the trick — of taking the edge off my immodest first meal of the day.

Named after two Irish saints, St. Meva and St. Issey, the village is unpretentious. A network of slender streets tapers up and down it, past boutiques, pubs, second-hand bookshops, and cafés. The streets are wrapped around legacies of Meva's fishing heritage — small cob and slate cottages, which look as if they have been assembled in a higgledy-piggledy manner. I imagine the interiors. Low wooden beams, small windows allowing the sun to pipe in, in measured amounts, lace curtains, stone fireplace, plump sofas. Cosy and simple. If I had been a resident in one of these cottages, a few hundred years ago, I would have watched horses pulling carts and swaying down the lanes of Meva. But in the present day, you have day-trippers like us on foot, and a few cars, which most probably belong to the village people because they are so very tiny.

In a musty shop brimming with camping junk and odd ends, yellowed compasses, rusted lanterns and war memorabilia, we meet a grumpy silver-haired man sat behind the till. He trots out a reluctant "hello" upon our entrance into his man cave. But who should follow soon in our heels, but a pasty lover. An English Cocker Spaniel, wet from a frolic in the waters, patters into the shop with a pasty in his mouth, looking solemn and ready to go about business.

In a world where business chains are lording it increasingly over smaller players in the market, it is reassuring to see family-owned businesses thrive in Mevagissey. The greengrocers putting together a neat assortment of veg in wooden carts; chippies selling fish-and-chips, which is but an institution of coastal Britain; and the sweet shop owner offering sweeties of every kind: gobstoppers, fruit pastilles, liquorice, lemon sherbets. In their individual ways, they are all organic to the village. Some folks still make their living from the sea, following in the footsteps of their fishermen fathers and forefathers. Even electricity was borne on the backbone of pilchards to these parts. The oil extracted from the fish lent electricity to the villages and Mevagissey was one of the first in the duchy to be powered up.

If the fishermen were known to have ramped up things on the money front by indulge in bouts of smuggling formerly, today they net catches of mackerel, bream, pollack, wrasse and garfish, and earn the extra quid by turning into guides for tourists, taking them out fishing, or out on the open seas, hunting sharks.

Our descent into the harbour area is made pleasurable by the aromas of fried fish and spuds frying in the chippies. Humans and gulls hover around the chippy in equal measures. Under the glorious midday sun, rows of families are sat on the quay of the inner harbour, heads bowed deep in takeaway boxes, stuffing themselves with their choice of batter-fried cod, plaice, or haddock, doused in vinegar and salt, accompanied by fair portions of chips and mushy peas. The familiar gulls come knocking, but there's no worry. We can tell. These folks are warriors who will wage wars for their deep-fried booty – plus, they are used to the fish-and-chips-poaching, winged mafia.

When I am able to tear my eyes away from this drama, staged effortlessly by humans and birds, and also feel the presence of the mountain of chips in my belly, I know I can look away from the chippy. Transfer my attention to admiration of the working harbour instead. The inner harbour has a fleet of fishing boats and sail boats laid askew on its silted, mossy bed. The quays have heritage designation, built as they were in the late 1700s when Parliament allowed the former medieval harbour to be developed to the standards befitting a port town. The outer harbour came later, in the late 1800s, only to be rebuilt because of the ravages wrought upon it by a blizzard; reminders of the visceral power of the sea.

In the backdrop of the harbour are strings of cottages perched upon the hills, formerly quarters of boatbuilders, fishermen, coopers. There are pilchard cellars too, most of them supposedly linked with the sea. I spot the local museum housed within an 18th century building on the harbour front and am surprised by the lack of entrance fees. Adi and the others opt for soaking sun by the outer harbour, at the end of which rests a small white lighthouse.

Praya, a kindred history buff comes with, to browse the museum. We walk to the harbour-front building, but not before I pause to catch a photograph of which I am inordinately fond. The backdrop in the photo is atmospheric. That of the inner harbour with its fleet of boats and plastic fish boxes plopped on the quay. In the forefront is a burly man, one of his legs raised in the air and in the process of bending over a young lad, as if to deliver a solid thwack. Behind them is a courting couple, the boy sat upon a bench, the girl standing and leaning over, to deliver a kiss.

The museum is built into the cliffs. Its beams are ancient, as repurposed wood from smugglers' vessels. It is chilly inside and the place smells of old books. Once the boatbuilder's yard, an aura of tranquillity envelopes the building. There is no docent. We are to rely on our own senses. Read write-ups accompanying the objects on display, if we are the curious sorts. Which we are. So, we spend hours inside, looking at the traditional Cornish kitchen, its interiors dark and shouldered by great beams of oak. The 19th century cast-iron kitchen range manufactured in Truro. The clome oven that appears ancient. This kind of oven was built traditionally dome-shaped to fit into chimney walls and it was heated by burning furze or blackthorn within its cavity. When red hot, the ashes were raked out, and tins of breads and pasties were placed inside. Following which, the door to the oven was sealed with hot ash to prevent draughts from seeping in.

The trappings of another age and time are before us, in every way possible. A butter churn, barley thresher, a cider press, weighing scales, an antiquated mangle, rusted household tools which I have never heard of before, such as a sugar nipper - tongs used to cut into whole conical sugar loaves because sugar did not always come so in ready-to-sprinkle granulated form, as we have in the modern age. The recreation of a Cornish kitchen is a telling record of the progress humans have made in time. Modernity has made it easier to live life on a day-to-day basis, but on the other hand, has it also paved the way for us to mope at leisure?

The museum is small, but it is a veritable capsule of time. Archives of photos paint a picture of life in Mevagissey since the early days. There are highlights of its achievements: I come across the photo showcasing the banquet that was held in 1896 on account of the village being the first to generate electricity, and fascinated, I read the toast: "Our town, its industries and its possibilities"; then, an official one-pound bank note framed on the wall; interesting notes on former residents, ceramic artists, and eccentric milkmen such as Cyril Furse, who was acknowledged as the fastest milkman in the west, for delivering milk on a Norton bike; Andrew Pears, the local soap maker who touched our lives across oceans, with the invention of a transparent bar of soap. The fact that we are in the village where Pears was born, thrills me to no end. It is an unexpected bonus to come upon a piece of my growing years in Calcutta, thousands and thousands of miles away in this Cornish village. The memory of the dull orange Pears bar resting on a wet soap dish in the bathroom washes over me in an unaccountably nostalgic moment.

The pieces on Mevagissey come together during my slow progress through the museum, like the jagged pieces of a puzzle that do not make any impression on their own, but assembled, make sense. The end result of this tootling around Mevagissey is that my appetite works itself up, gunning for a big pasty. Alternatively, fried fish. You know which it might be. I will peg it on peer pressure, all those people dipping into their boxes of fish and chips, and the wicked aroma wafting out of the chippy, mixed with the salty notes of the sea. You either cope or you capitulate.

That tang of vinegar, the lingering notes of fried cod and potatoes… surely you can smell it?

XI

Sailing on the Fal

The year 2016 has started well enough. We have been travelling a fair bit to Spain, Italy and France. Small weekend escapes booked via cut-price tickets on EasyJet and the dubious Ryanair that one can only remember for its bumpy landings and the relief of exiting the plane in one piece. All this joy is tempered by the news that we have to relocate a year later, perhaps to North America. My heart sinks at the thought of not being in this land that I have grown to love so. Adi has mixed emotions, having studied at Wake Forest in North Carolina. But surprisingly, he says that he is loath to leave the country that has been our first home together.

The last evening in the month of June has turned unaccountably sloppy, the damp cold of it press-ganging us into running down a pier. The moment has a noir tinge to it, rain pelting down on our sorry heads. The object of our breathless toil is a 50-ft high yacht moored at the marina, in the harbour town of Falmouth. The cold is intensifying with the downpour and our collective focus is bent on the mission of conjuring up the blessed yacht in our blurred lines of vision.

A trio of our friends, Ella and Firdous, and Adi's former boss, Dhiren, has booked us a weekend holiday with them aboard a yacht in Cornwall, the point of it being to make merry and celebrate my husband's birthday on the first of July. This shall be a test of our sea legs, particularly mine, because I am not a water baby. As I grew up and learnt certain skills, it seems that I have managed to forget the most important and life-affirming skill of all, swimming. In my mind's eye, I see your incredulous expression, and the mouthing of the words,

"Is that even possible?" That said, if only I had charged a dime for every time I heard it. I could have bought my dream house in Cornwall.

But mine is not to question the occasion. It is Adi's birthday weekend. Far be it from me to spoil the occasion with fears of a watery grave and basically all kinds of water-related disasters coalesced into one gigantic nightmare.

At the end of what feels like a long run that has done nothing towards warming us up, we find the yacht. Relieved, we scurry down the stairs of the yacht and enter a living area. The first impression is of wood panelling all around. Properly buffed, the reddish-brown of the wood is rich and offset by a wraparound leather sofa in soft shades of cream. On a dreary night as this, we can do with the woody glossiness of the interiors. The proprietor of the yacht, Cyprian Heckstall, shows us around, explaining the workings of the boat to five people, none of whom have any foreknowledge of sailing vessels. The tiny but well-kitted galley kitchen has pots and pans in which we can cobble up a basic breakfast. Or, if we are ambitious, cook ramen. Part of his orientation includes a host of don'ts. Somewhere, I feel sorry for Mr. Heckstall at handing over his prized possession to a pack of strangers. It cannot be easy.

Left to our own devices with a welcome bottle of wine, the rest of the evening begins with snuggling in the spacious saloon. Fortified by red wine and idle chatter, a halo of goodness envelopes me. When I get up to change into my pyjamas and have a quick look at the loo, my excitement has toned down several notches. Not because Adi and I have a double bedroom in which the bed takes up the entire space, leaving a slice of space at its foot for us to squeeze into. The game-changer is a tiny cubicle adjacent to our bedroom. This shall be our combined bathroom. On the left-hand side of the entrance to the cubicle is a shower head, adjacent to it and barely a step away, a basin. Half a step to the right-hand side of the basin is a Lavac toilet, a genre of vacuum toilet highly favoured by sailors since the '60s. How? Do not ask. The cranking mechanism atop the pot has to be yanked a couple of times, a pause of a few seconds thrown in. You also have to count the number of cranks to flush out the waste completely and effectively.

I refuse to drink further.

At the end of the night, our friends head to the wing on the other end of the saloon. I am surprised that the yacht has space to accommodate five people. We just about fit the bill in terms of numbers. No wonder, the loo is an itty-bitty hutch. There had to be some of compromise.

The bed is comfortable. In a state of transition between half-wakefulness and the netherworld of dreams, I am convinced that we have floated down the river. Soon to be disgorged into the sea. I do fall asleep at some point, to the lulling motion of the boat.

Early the next morning, I know that there is no way we are bathing in the if-I-put-my-arms-out-and-jump-I-shall-get-stuck kinda cubicle. We hop off the yacht onto the pier and turn back for a look at our bobbing residence. Having arrived in the darkness of a sodden evening, we have not even had a proper look at it. Why, it is a beautiful white yacht shining proudly under the bright gaze of the sun! And, sparkling clean. Must be the effect of last night's cloudburst. We carry on to the shower stalls, which are neatly lined up in the foyer of the marina's office. Right above it is a public house by the name, *Upper Deck*. It is not your spit-and-sawdust affair. The pub looks spanking new. We stop here for a spot of breakfast, and ah, how a cuppa wakes us up properly, to the view of rows and rows of resting boats, topsails tucked away.

***

Falmouth is a seaside town on the south coast of Cornwall with enviable views of the River Fal and a plethora of pubs that buzz with youth. It is a university town, so that's a given. But before we explore the libation scene out in town, we decide to take the day by the horns. Brilliant blue skies can change in a few blinks, so how can we miss out on the siren calls of the liquid sunshine?

We decide to take our yacht out for a spin. Or we let Heckstall and his mate – who is straight out of a du Maurier novel, with his ginger hair putting me in mind of the smuggler of old – acquaint us with the rules of sailing. First, we help them rig up the yacht. Releasing the sails from their fetters, takes more than a few minutes. By the time we are ready to sail, dark clouds have sneaked in on us. Not a surprise if you are used to the whimsical weather in the British Isles. The sun might have put on its cap, but it's still there. All's good. Time to don the worn-out life jackets that Heckstall hands out. They are bulky, but I am not fussed about fashion. One needs peace of mind when the thought of hitting the river bottom and becoming one with it is a constant thought throbbing at the back of the mind. As it happens, one of our friends does almost tip us over during his all too brief moment of playing skipper.

Each of us gets to play master-commander of the yacht in turns, which is thrilling because we are sailing from one of the deepest natural harbours in the world that has served time as the base of the U.S. Navy during WWII. A feather in our caps. Then the wind picks up on the Penryn. While my hair refuses to stay out of the way of my eyes, the river water bubbles like potion in a cauldron. The tide is in and a yachting race is underway in the distance. Sailors are braving the gust, tilted at alarming angles towards the river as they speed past pastel houses propped up on Flushing, a smallish village along the river, and opposite Falmouth. Before the start of the 16th century the charming rows of houses would not have existed. Instead, a heartbeat away from Falmouth, there stood the town of Penryn, where rumours flew thick in the air, of coaches drawn by headless horses that appeared before Christmas every year. You dared not look at them or you would perish. As for Falmouth, only a manor stood here, before any of the other houses came up in town. It belonged to the Killigrew family, a powerful, local clan. I find the name Maurier-esque. It turns out that two of the Killigrew wives were pirates during the reign of Elizabeth I. These doughty women stashed stolen goods in Arwenack House. Aristocracy would have been a useful front for their clandestine affairs. Oh, the stories that must reside within the walls of the manor.

From two small hamlets, Smithicke and Pennycomequick, which were divided by a creek and stood on opposing shores, was born Falmouth, the modern version of which I am sailing through. The town was a heavyweight port of the British Empire for the better part of two centuries. Midway through the 17th century to the 19th, it served as a Royal Mail packet station where post and important shipments were handled for the British Empire and Europe. It became powerful enough to overtake the importance of Penryn, which was formerly the big town in its vicinity.

I do not espy Arwenack House or whatever remains of it, but from the densely wooded land owned by the Killigrews of Falmouth, emerges the impressive bastions of a castle. "Pendennis Castle," points out Mr. Heckstall. "Henry VIII had it built when he realised the importance of the natural harbour we have here," he adds, acting the part of a tour guide in bursts. If Cornwall has stories to tell, she has storytellers to pass them through.

By now, we are in the part of the Fal estuary known as Carrick Roads. Almost opposite Pendennis Castle is another circular castle on a headland that is home to the charming village of St. Mawes. Both castles were part of a larger scheme of Henry VIII to reinforce the country's defence mechanism along the coast of England. With their circular bastions, they retain an air of artillery might, which must have been the general idea behind building them.

Even though the wind is icy, permeating layers of clothing, I do not offer resistance when the wheel is offered to me. The job description comes with the addendum that I do not tip us over. My concentration is intense, centred around the wheel, and I must confess that I have never felt more apprehensive yet more engrossed. Lives are on the line, skipper.

"There she sails with the most serene look on her face," says Mr. Heckstall. He might be mightily amused by the amateur's earnestness, but I follow his directions to the tee, steering us slowly back into harbour. The fact that I have been gripping the wheel with all my strength for some time now, means that my arm muscles are bunched up in protest. I feel the measure of them as I let go of the wheel. A rush of adrenalin and subliminal fear is replaced by exhilaration. Jelly legs, too. After a couple of hours of sailing, the sight of shore is welcome. From the safety of land, I can reflect on an observation once made by actor Morgan Freeman. "If you live a life of make-believe, your life isn't worth anything until you do something that does challenge your reality. And to me, sailing the open ocean is a real challenge, because it's life or death."

The Penryn is certainly not be the open ocean, but maybe I have lived a little.

The day cannot be left to end there. We arrive at the unanimous decision to venture into town. Wind up the day with a few pints. Falmouth town has the infectious vibe of a city. There is historic architecture to captivate the senses on Quay Street; behold a flight of granite steps, numbering 111 and named Jacob's Ladder after a businessman who had them built to connect his various properties in town; at Arwenack Street, Regency-era architecture rubs shoulders with the symmetrical Georgian style; on Church Street is an interesting theatre, formerly a 19th century polytechnic society converted into a cinema called the Polytechnic Picture Hall, and now, simply known as Poly; finally, there's the quay, lined by the quay custom house and a smattering of pubs.

At the quay, international news would have reached the country at one time, through the passage of small and swift-sailing ships. Today, no one needs to wait by the old quay to get news from around the world. Technology has brought more news than we can handle in a day, at the click of a button on our multi-faceted modern-day gadgets.

Through the *opes* of Falmouth we sight the glimmering waters, before trudging up to a pub on Trevethan Hill. I picture inebriated sailors walking the paths in the past, heading home bleary-eyed, having indulged in a brawl or two. Black eyes, ruddy cheeks, torn lips. We gather chairs in the pub's garden and join a handful of people watching the Euro 2016 quarter final. Germany is playing Italy, the two European football superpowers locking horns in Bordeaux. All eyes are trained on the large screen in the pub and the evening passes in a pleasant haze of beer, pot pies and chips, till matters heat up on the field. It is a penalty shootout that shall determine the winner of this match. I love me a good penalty shootout and it is impossible not to join in on the eruptions of cheer at the end of the evening, spiced up by mutterings of "bollocks" and "sod it".

There is enough drama both on and off the screen. Onscreen, we watch Germany catch the match with a penalty win, and that legend of a goalkeeper, Gianluigi Buffon, shed heart-rending tears. After, we get back to the yacht to prepare for an early start the next day. The plan is drive back to Northampton, and on the way, swing through the Roseland Peninsula.

XII

Tropically Yours: The Roseland Peninsula

Had we time on our hands, we would have moseyed along the portion of the South West Coastal Path that stretches from Falmouth to the string of villages on the Roseland Heritage Coast. This path is the UK's treasure trove of natural beauty, as I have mentioned before. A national trail, it starts at Minehead in Somerset, then it catches the coast all along Devon and Cornwall and winds up only at Poole Harbour in Dorset. Six hundred and thirty miles of superb walking path along the coast that would on the whole take a month of brisk walking. Realistically, however, if you are the kind of person who likes to amble and luxuriate in the rugged beauty of the villages that fall along the way, most of them tucked into scenic little coves, the trail could be accomplished in two. Even this number might be declared as ambitious by those who believe in the concept of slow travel.

From Falmouth, a car ferry transports us to St. Mawes, on a Sunday when the sun plays peek-a-boo through swathes of white clouds that have the run of the skies. Had we walked from St. Mawes to Portloe, it would have taken us the better part of 7 hours, not counting in the necessary coffee and loo breaks. Covering 22 miles between the two villages would call for a night's rest in Portscatho. Having worked a meagre number of miles of the Roseland Peninsula, I can vouch for it that every cell in my body tingled with pleasure at the time. But for now, our aim is to start the drive back to Northampton by the end of the day. It is imperative that we stick to the journey on four wheels. Our two sets of legs can work their magic another time.

The ferry costs us a mere six quid and saves us a whole lot of time. While on the brief passage across the moody green waters of the Fal, we turn back for a lingering look at Falmouth. The thick cover of woods corralling the slipway; the solitary boat bobbing on the waters, the few stone cottages stationed above the slipway; and in the backdrop, a blue sky smothered by billowing clouds. It is a scene to hold the gaze alright.

The country's second-most important port is behind us now with its cluster of houses trailing along the windswept slopes. I feel deep contentment. We have lived on the Fal and sailed across it. In a way, it has been home, even though for a short span of time.

Off the ferry, we get onto the A-road that winds into St. Mawes. We are in that part of Cornwall now, which is screened from the biting gusts experienced along the Atlantic coastline. The deal with countryside driving in these quarters is that you are flanked by tall hedges, trees joining boughs to arch above the roads in leafy canopies, till you feel like you have been transported to a subtropical paradise where exotic plants thrive because, baby, the balmy microclimate is just hunky dory for them. The lush environment cocoons the senses. Verdure valleys make up the bulk of the Roseland Heritage Coast, its fair share of rambling estates, gardens, and old creeks putting me in mind of the smuggler's leafy refuge.

***

Passing through the village of St. Just in Roseland, I spot stone pines, their umbrella shaped heads standing sentry above a few cottages. The hamlet is home to a 13th century church, an antiquated edifice placed strategically at the mouth of a lushly wooded creek, St. Just Pool. This is the church that moved Betjeman to observe that it was during his lifetime the most beautiful church on earth for many. It still is Mr. Betjeman.

Another admirer of St. Just's church was Henry Vollam Morton, a British travel writer of repute. In his book, *In Search of England*, published in 1927, Mr. Morton wrote: "I have blundered into a Garden of Eden that cannot be described in pen or paint. There is a degree of beauty that flies so high that no net of words or snare of colour can hope to capture it, and of this order is the beauty of St Just-in-Roseland."

Two miles into the drive from St. Just in Roseland, we find ourselves in St. Mawes, the road dipping into a valley and offering up a view cobbled together by descending slate roofs and whitewashed houses. In the backdrop is the serenely blue Percuil river, and further beyond it, dark woods swell, abutting pastures that look like they have been quilted together by a deft hand. We revel in the patchworked scenery of fertile and fallow land that unfolds before us as the car descends into the village, marvelling at the way it introduces itself to the newcomer. "This is just the beginning," it promises. We are tantalised.

Wild yellow flowers and shrubs together with lilac blossoms straggle along the pavements, making way for hydrangeas, country benches and red telephone booths. Thick foliage of alder, ash, birch, horse chestnut, Spanish chestnut, Cornish elm, English Elm, silver and spruce firs, larch, Scotch lime, English and Turkey oak, poplars, sycamores, and what have you, abounds in this part of the country. Cottages are screened by carefully shaped hedgerows. The hedges gain in height, grown as they are upon dry stone walls, out of the cracks and crannies of which spring wildflowers. It is quickly turning out to be a horticulturalist's delight—entire villages sculpted as if out of plants.

***

Horticulture is an artistic genre that works with nature, and which, I have little handle on. Naturally I admire those who are blessed with green fingers. Of note in this part of Cornwall, is the erstwhile Treseder family of Truro, which is single-handedly responsible for the cornucopia of greenery that coats the Roseland Peninsula.

In the mid-1800s, a nursery, the first of its kind in Cornwall, was started by James Treseder. The mantle of the business passed on to his son, John, who returned home from Australia at the turn of the century, kitted up with a proper knowhow of cultivating tropical plants. John brought with him seeds foreign to Cornish land. These gifts would change the landscape around for good. From records, we know of the *Trachycarpus fortunei*, known more commonly as the "windmill palm", distinct for its palmate dark-green leaves that fan out from a squat trunk; of *Gunnera manicata*, "dinosaur food", because its gigantic, puckered leaves recall the Triassic period reptiles that roamed the earth, by virtue of their size; the *Drymis Winteri*, "winter's bark", which is ornamental, but for its original use as scurvy cure during the 16th century, when it was discovered by a ship captain and contemporary of Sir Francis Drake.

John's legacy has been sustained by the temperate climate of south Cornwall. Fascinated by his legacy, I end up researching the Treseders and come upon a book written by Suzanne Treseder, a descendant of John's. In *A Passion for Plants: The Treseders of Truro*, she writes of the family's entrenchment in the practice of horticulture, over a period of 150 years. Six generations of Treseders have been nurserymen. That's one green family, ain't it? To continue with John's story, he leased land from the rector of St. Just Church when he chanced upon it. It suited him fine, this sheltered piece of land that was not private property. The tranquillity of the spot must have got to him. What happy coincidence then that the plants agreed with his judgement. They thrived in the humid temperatures typical to the peninsula.

In Suzanne's book, we have fond recollections from John's granddaughter, Marie Louise Treseder, who started working at the Truro nursery when she was 12 years old. She recreates a cosy picture of picnics when pasties were unboxed, and kettles brought to boil over a smoky fire. Marie Louise's memories of time spent around the church went thus: "The smell there was quite unique - the Mexican Incense Plant - Eupatorium of which there were large bushes. We could stand under the giant Tree Ferns. We looked forward to the times when the Fig and Medlars were ripe and there was also a delicious Box Apple tree." I imagine this picture alongside the brooding beauty of the creek, the solitary church enveloped within the sub-tropical lushness of foreign plants, and I think that the Treseders did alright. They had their own piece of bespoke paradise.

In a catalogue for the nursery, published circa 1902, John captured the *raison d'etre* behind his style of horticulture. "In these days of travel, when it is so easy comparatively to visit scenes which are altogether distinct from anything English, we naturally wish to produce in the home garden that reminds us of what we have seen in other regions."

In my mind, he is a visionary in the truest sense of the term.

***

People are pounding the pavement along a stretch of shingle beach in St. Mawes. This is Summer Beach, one of the three beaches in the village. A couple of kayakers have stopped for a break. To behold this idyllic scene playing out before the eyes, it is difficult to imagine the life of smugglers who operated from St. Mawes. The name of Robert Long, a 17th century smuggler, is associated with the village. What hardships drove him to risk his life and trade in contraband goods, I wonder. Did the authorities hang him somewhere along the road that we are on?

We're driving along the Percuil, the charm of which is unruffled by the blotted-out sun. If anything, the masses of frothy clouds suffuse the scenery with the kind of flamboyance it surely cannot have done without. Soon the road narrows. Almost as if it has been squished to fit in between rows of whitewashed houses. We skirt *The Idle Rocks*, a boutique hotel where we are to grab lunch this noon. But first, most importantly, the parking of the car. We find a lush lot, remarkably green as car parks go. On the way, we spot a plethora of dogs of various sizes and breeds, out for a saunter with their humans. A Pom scurries behind the mistress, a wooden basket dangling from her wrist, a couple of Springer Spaniels wait outside an ice cream shop with quivering noses, wagging tails, and a young Lab pup prances along to the harbour, his rhythm synced to that of his old man.

Before breaking for lunch, we walk along the harbour from which narrow streets veer upwards. The houses are not uniformly traditional. They are a mix of the old and the new and certainly look like they belong to a bunch of prosperous residents, who must have chosen the village for its retiring nature. There are no hordes of tourists to contend with in St. Mawes. Fishing boats bob at their moorings along the harbour, while other boats, large and small, are taken out for a swing in the river by expert boatsmen. In the background of this comely picture is the densely wooded St. Anthony's Headland. Once a protector of the coastline, a few minutes from the village centre is St. Mawes Castle. The coastal artillery fort was built by Henry VIII along with Pendennis Castle of Falmouth, as part of his fortification plans against invasions from France and the Pope.

When we are finally sat at *The Idle Rocks*, located enviably on the waterfront, I feel contentment and contemplation steal upon me, stoked by the beauty of the scenery before the eyes, the gentle lapping of waves at the harbour. I wonder, did the Celtic saint St. Maudez, feel the same when he came upon this small settlement that was subsequently named for him? He would have doubly delighted in the view, had he sat at a table like mine, laden with locally foraged produce. Grilled mackerel garnished with capers, roast sirloin paired with mashed potatoes and Yorkshire pudding, and crisped chips, are served up with gourmet precision. The dessert is a version of strawberry coulis, artfully decorated with splotches of red sauce, lashings of silky cream, tangy straw-like shards and sprigs of basil.

A herring gull has arrived to partake of this feast. We watch it hop over to the next table for nibbles, but it's out of luck. The table has just been cleared. At most times, dear gull, you will find that timing is everything.

At St. Mawes, we part ways with our friends, who have decided on an early start to London. Truth be told, I am looking forward to the two of us pottering about with no worries of delaying the others. Ambitious to see more, we are Portloe-bound.

***

On the way, we find Portscatho. The drive, though short, is incredibly lush. Lime green meadows are thrown up on the horizon and the A-road weaves through hamlets of hedgerows and canopied trees. In the distance, the spire of a church shoots for the skies. It is one of the many joys of driving around the British countryside – to come upon lofty spires and a countryside textured with brown ploughed land and pastures, velvety green.

In the few shakes of a lamb's tail, we are in the village of Gerrans, adjoining Portscatho. The church spire we had spotted from afar belongs to this old settlement which has been named after a Celtic saint, St. Gereint. No surprises there. Almost every other village in Cornwall seems to have been discovered or founded by some Celtic saint. The Norman church with its fine octagonal spire was a marker for fishermen out on the seas in the old days. For all its unassuming look, Gerrans had its share of adventure during the 18th century. The smugglers of Portscatho hung out at Gerrans' bay, conducting "free trade", for the smooth functioning of which they had scouts positioned on the hills along the coast to warn them of incoming revenue cutters.

It is difficult not to fall for these lovely old villages that seem content to be cut off from the world. In the Roseland Peninsula, the tropical surroundings enhance their comeliness. I remark to Adi: "You know, I can see us in a place like this." All the while, I am taking notes for the distant future when I dream of getting back to Cornwall with Adi and starting a bed & breakfast in this part of the country. This feeling is strengthened as we carry on and the road continues down a hill to unfurl several shades of blue on the horizon. The sea and the sky vie for beauty. But the sea wins this round.

In Portscatho, we are relieved to locate a parking spot for our car in the heart of the village. People in wetsuits make their way to the beach to bathe and I shiver at the prospect. It is unaccountably chilly even though summer has peaked. We decide to do our way of beating the nip in the air – with ice cream cones from a village shop — and have a gander at the small galleries, where local artists have displayed canvases splashed with colours of a coastal life. When we have had our fill of the tiny village, we end up dawdling at the beach, its slipway decorated by a cluster of boats that lie upturned, their colours bright under a brief spell of sunshine.

Farewell Portscatho of the small harbour, your boats yellow and blue and orange, your houses pristine and whitewashed, your window trims painted in comely pastels.

***

Portloe is unspoilt. Portloe is tranquil. Portloe is a revelation.

If I were a woman of fewer words, I would leave it there. But that not being the case by any stretch of the imagination, I better start at the beginning. With its name itself. I confess to an infatuation of sorts with "Portloe", for there's a ring to it. The old Cornish word for the place is *Port Logh,* meaning cove pool. I see how evocative the name is when we stumble upon a narrow path trailing down the cliffs upon which we have parked our car. At one point we stop for a bird's eye view of the village, nestled below in a quiet cove.

Rugged cliffs rise above the cove and whitewashed houses with roofs of slate hug the slopes. An occasional figurehead of a maid juts from the walls of a cottage, peering into the distance. Perchance she is waiting for the return of the ship she once belonged to. Nearby, an epitaph on a tablet of stone recalls Douglas S. Barton, who lived between the years 1919 and 2011, and has now "gone to explore the universe". I like the sound of it. Maybe I could nick it for my epitaph.

During our descent, nobody shows up. But then, I notice a woman reading in the quiet of her clifftop terrace. Someday, maybe I too shall be sat on my own terrace, watching day trippers pass by and give them a shout. We stop awhile to absorb the view of the cerulean sea and the startling green of the grass-covered cliffs. The glorious sunshine envelopes the landscape in a loving embrace. The stark whiteness of the cottages is redeemed by bright pops of colour. The mullioned window frames are painted yellow and blue. Half-shed bulbs of purple allium and sprigs of white wildflowers gather around our feet – and I say to Adi, "This must be what paradise looks like". Those who say that paradise is overrated have not come by the portals of Portloe.

In the naturally protected harbour, atop the slipway is located a 17th-century inn, *The Lugger*. Within its whitewashed walls, one of its landlords carried on a business that was common to these parts. He smuggled French brandy. But his name was unusual, Black Dunstan. It is not surprising that in the late 1800s, the landlord of the evocative name was apprehended and hanged. This dark past notwithstanding, the inn wears an elegant air. When we grab a seat on its sun-drenched terrace that has an open view of the harbour, we find that a cup of cappuccino is capable of delivering the joy that a bottle of bubbly customarily brings. It must be the effect of our sublime surroundings.

Time for us to undertake the coastal path in the direction of Portholland. We set off with just such a noble intent. But before tackling them cliffs, we wander around the fishing village that is full of old-world charm, the kind you see in shows on the telly. A string of granite cottages climbs down the narrow winding streets into the harbour, which is small but fetching. Hushed peace reigns over it. We sight somebody standing on the pebbled shores, lost in thought, his gaze trained seaward.

What a different sight the harbour would have been in its heyday when pilchard fishing kept the village abuzz. Nowadays, a small fleet of fishing boats carry on with the tradition. Tall piles of lobster and crab pots lie in a corner of the quayside.

You cannot deny the intimate air the village courts with its remarkable lack of commercial development, the houses probably left to their own devices since they were built in the 18th century. It is a curiosity, but in this modern age where we are showered with choices for every possible object under the sun, I have a soft spot for the adherence to the past. Portloe has all of two watering holes – *The Lugger* and *The Ship Inn* – where you also sit for a meal.

Trudging up the grassy slopes above the harbour, we find ourselves on the cliffs of the Roseland Peninsula again. Gusts of wind ruffle sweeps of droopy bluebells and our hair. We are on the coastal path to Pendower Beach. Just a matter of three or four odd miles, we think, hardly realising that the steepish stretches thrown in shall slow us down. The entire path is unfenced, which seems right to me. The Norwegians have a word for it. *Allmansrätten.* It means the right to roam, a right that has been exercised since ancient times. There is something liberating about exploring the wild outdoors, in connecting with nature, without the notion of boundaries. In the mid 19th century, the Norwegian playwright and poet, Henrik Ibsen, had come up with a term to describe this kind of "open-air living". He called it *friluftsliv.*

The path forks into two, one trail leading inland. The other continues along the coast, thick vegetation and furze paving the way. We stick to the coastal path and stop time and again to gawp at the inky blue sea below, fingers of land radiating into the waters like the giant claws of some prehistoric monster. The dark jagged silhouette of Gull Rock lies ahead, and far behind us, Portloe with its clutch of whitewashed cottages. Crunched for time, we have barely gone a mile when we realise that we have to turn back. Even this paltry stretch, deceptively so, has taken us the better part of an hour, what with the number of climbs thrown in.

No one is around. This gives me courage to let my voice ring through the early evening air and I sing my heart out till we come upon a bend in the path.

There on a bench, hidden from plain sight by overgrown foliage, is sat an old woman. Mortified, I tell myself, "she's hard of hearing". A furtive look and I see a small smile playing upon her lips. That's it. I pick up my pace and disappear downhill as quickly as the feet can manage.

We grab a seat on a ledge of rock jutting out above the sea. Soon, we shall be wrenched away from this landscape, but for now it is ours. The Atlantic spread out below us, the wind blowing strong, and the imagination transported to a moonless night when I would have peered and spotted silhouettes of free traders at work. And wondered if I might claim a share of their loot of French brandy, it being the kind of contraband that smugglers stored in cellars of farmhouses. After all, the scene was serious here on the Roseland Peninsula.

In lieu of this scenario, our eyes settle upon a more sedate picture. A man is fishing from his perch upon an arm of the cliffs that swoops down to meet the shore. On the slopes above him is a woman busy doing nothing. *Il dolce far niente*. It makes for a charming picture, and if I had my brushes and colours, this would have been my subject for the day.

I visit Portloe often in my mind's eye when I need a pick-me-up. I feel the wind in my hair, the solitude of the hills, and I think wistfully, oh give me a room in one of 'em stone cottages and I will never want for anything ever again.

THE LAST
LOVING LOOK

XIII

A Byre and A Cornish Farmer

The year we are to leave the UK has arrived, far too soon. It is the spring of 2017 and our hearts are wrenched at the thought of leaving the country. Adi's job profile is going to take us somewhere in North America. New York, New Jersey…it will all be truly new. The upheaval calls for a loving farewell to our favourite part of the country. We are loath to say adieu, but one has got to do what one has to. To make the most of this break, we book a place to stay in the wooded valleys of Lostwithiel for ten days. In our minds, it is bound to be an epic journey, the most special of all our travels through the years in Cornwall.

The weekend starts on a cheerful note in the early hours of the morning when we set off from Northampton in a rented car. Up and about by 4am, we leave home an hour later and stop for coffee at a Café Nero that's surprisingly open at the crack of dawn, in a small village in the Cotswolds. The chill in the air wakes me up with a jolt. Back on the road with our cups of coffee, we are greeted by a sight that turns up every spring without fail, when the British farmlands are transformed into carpets of bright yellow with the blooming of countless rapeseed flowers. We hop off the car and loiter in the fields, steeping our senses in the beauty of it.

I am witnessing dawn. Shockingly early by my standards. Now only if my father had witnessed such an event in person. All my growing years, he has expressed disapproval at my prolonged sleeping hours. It was a daily practice for him, and this he took great pleasure in, to press wet hands on my eyelids every morning. He insisted that I reminded him of Kumbhakarna, a man-eater or a *rakshasa* from the epic *Ramayana*. For the sake of getting to the point, I will have you know that Kumbhakarna used to sleep for six months at a stretch. Yeah, as you can tell, my father was into hyperboles.

After five hours of driving, we reach a big cottage perched at the top of a hilly road. I ring the burnished copper bell at the door, feeling it in my bones that this is not it. A man in a cashmere jumper opens the door and confirms my thoughts. We are at the wrong place. He gives us directions following which we turn around and carry on down the hill. At the end of a five-minute drive however, a farm shows up. The One.

Five hours on the road and we are hard pressed to put up our feet, unwind with chilled bottles of beer that we have picked up along the way. We enter our holiday nest. It is a former byre (British for cowshed), a detached one-bedroom affair with low ceilings and a far cry from the ramshackle barn it must have been back in the day. I like the open layout. Adjoining an open kitchen with flagstone floors is a living room kitted up with a telly, some books and board games stacked neatly into shelves. Off these, a corridor leads to the end of the byre, where a cosy little bedroom awaits, complete with an ensuite bathroom.

The frontal view from the byre is of pastures, upon which a flock of Shropshire sheep carry on with their ruminations. It should be a bucolic sight to wake up to every morning. I look at Adi, a wide grin on my face and say, "Our own pastoral retreat for more than a week. Bite that!"

Adi heads off to park the car. Meanwhile, I crack on with the job of loading the refrigerator with our haul of groceries. Suddenly I hear snuffles behind me. Simultaneously Adi's voice floats in from outside, "Don't get scared baby. Someone's behind you." I turn around and almost tumble over a prancing Border Collie. Eyes covered in black patches, she skitters up and down the living room with excessive energy, tongue hanging out. Can one be scared of such a merry creature? This is my first encounter with Meg the (slightly mangy) collie. And she does not leave me alone till she has had her fill of belly rubs.

Adi returns with our farmer host, Ed, who apologises for Meg's intrusion and declares that he shall get her out of my hair pronto. A very curious Jack Russell Terrier patters in next, through the open door. "Meet Gizzie", says Ed. The terrier is more measured. Having sniffed us thoroughly, she decides that Adi and I might be left supervision-free.

When the trio leave and we have settled down in the cottage, we discover to our delight that a cream tea has been laid out for us as a welcome note. It is the perfect start to our Cornish spring holiday. We layer the fresh scones liberally with strawberry and blackberry preserves, and clotted cream, ravishing them in the matter of a few minutes. Then steaming cups of tea. Let's not underestimate the reviving power of the afternoon tea.

We are on the higher reaches of the 12th century town of Lostwithiel. Immediately outside the farm two lanes diverge, fringed by fronds of fern and tall trees, strips of grass running through the middle of the tarmac. The woods are ancient and verdure, and they open up to the view of pastures terraced in an undulating manner across slopes that gradually meld into the horizon. Squat wooden signs point the way to the *Higher Demesnes*, *The Mill*, *The Barn* and *The Hayloft*, the sprinkling of names adding to the rural loveliness of our surroundings. The lane that dips in favour of Lostwithiel throws up a cottage or two along the way. A medieval stone bridge spans the river Fowey and leads to rows of white and pastel-coloured cottages, interspersed by antiquated stone cottages with Georgian windows. A stone church rises high above town.

Lostwithiel, with the name that means "the tail-end of the woodland", is a historic stannary town. Here in the old days, tin was brought for quality check and stamped, and taxes paid from the coinage to the crown. If tin brought wealth to the town, ironically enough, it is tin that divested it of its importance as the county capital in the 13th century. Rubble from the mines silted up the river that runs through the valley. Trade dried up as vessels could no longer find their way into town.

High on a hill above Lostwithiel is sat Restormel Castle, once home to the Norman lords who had founded the town. We spot its giant circular shell keep one evening. From the outside, you cannot tell that the fortress is in ruins. Its inner chambers are quite in tatters. Yet I imagine that it would have been a luxurious home. One of its former occupants was the 14th-century Edward of Woodstock, better known as the Black Prince on account of having imposed unspeakable cruelty upon the French during the Hundred Years War.

For the most part, people tend to pass through Lostwithiel on their way to Truro and Fowey, as we have in the past. But walking around its quiet lanes, we find it to be a good place to go antiquing, to while the hours pleasurably.

***

On the outskirts of this historic town that is filled with memories of civil war brutalities and destruction, Ed lives in a rambling farmhouse, a few steps from the byre, with his vet wife, Nicki. The couple have a menagerie. A tabby cat that likes to stretch itself flat on the guest bed and luxuriate in the fact that Ed's son and the girlfriend have just vacated the quarters, and the energetic canines, Meg and Gizzie. Meg being a Border Collie does her share of chores, rounding up sheep assiduously, after which every morning and noon she rests outside the pastures she guards. Gizzie, Ed informs us, has been rescued from a family where she was bullied by her Jack Russell brothers. She had started exhibiting signs of aggression. But, seeing as she is now, you would not suspect her troubled past.

The flock of Shropshire sheep at the farm are straight out of a nursery rhyme book. With their black faces, white woolly bodies and black legs, they are a study in contrast. A 1929 heritage description of this breed of sheep states that it should tick off on all these counts. "Alert, attractive, indicating breeding and quality, with stylish carriage and a symmetrical form, showing the true characteristics of the Shropshire." I do not know if our woolly neighbours satisfy all the above-mentioned traits, but they certainly possess dignity in spades.

***

134

The first afternoon when we get back to the byre, we meet up with Ed. He has offered to show us around the farm — if we are keen. I jump at the kind overture. Adi and I meander along the slopes of the farm with Ed, curious about his livestock. The first day of our stay, while barbecuing meat outside, we had spotted Ed feeding a lamb, its cute little body sheathed in grey wool, its face and legs evenly black. Ed had informed us then that the effort was not to domesticate him. "His mother refused him milk. I am his de facto mum," he had said. The lamb, meanwhile, tugged on a bottle of milk from his hands, an infant eager for nourishment.

One morning I heard its faint bleating. Following the trail of the sounds, I found him in Ed's backyard. When I patted him on the head, he was so utterly content that I was struck by the oddness of the situation. I have only ever chased sheep before this, in an attempt to befriend the nonchalant creatures. I have also never succeeded in getting close enough to pet one. So, shortly before we leave the farm at the end of our trip, we watch with pleasure as Ed tries and gets the little fellow to join his flock that has nine acres of land for its grazing and pooping needs.

For now, the leisurely meandering with Ed around the farm offers us insights into the changing scene in the countryside and the future of farming. Walking us to a newly-birthed sheep's pen, the wind whistling in our ears, Ed' story could be a prototype of other farmers in the duchy. His father owned a huge farm and a herd of 200 cattle. The time came when dairy farming began to lose steam. This was aggravated by the sorry matter of inflation and the fact that the new generation was keen to follow other professions. "Plus, all my conversation was going to be centered around cows, you know," says Ed. His son and daughter, it turns out, have carved out their own niche in life. The son is a communications press officer with a cricket board and the daughter is a psychologist.

Gradually, Ed sold his father's farm and purchased the present farmhouse with his wife. Here, they lead a pastoral life with their animal family.

By this time, we have reached the pen. An ewe stands still, staring at us with beady eyes, possibly reproaching us for invading her privacy. She is recovering from the birthing of two lambs, one of whom is the bottle-fed character we have had the pleasure of meeting. After a few seconds, the ewe decides she has had enough of us. She does an about-turn, her ample buttocks in our faces, and returns to the business of licking clean the chosen lamb that is the apple of her eye. The red trails of placenta snaking out from her rear make for an uncomfortable sight. The placenta we are informed, is not snipped off in animals as with humans. "Animals have their own ways of dealing with it. They are known to consume the placenta, if they are wary of predators around their young ones," Ed informs us.

Nature might be red of tooth and claw, as Lord Tennyson had observed in the cantos of *In Memoriam*, but she does equip her creatures with the necessary tools for survival. We are fascinated with these little inroads into rural life. As people who live in the city, we are really so insulated from the way nature works. The bee colonies are next in queue of our studies, and we notice that they thrill Ed. He speaks with passion when it comes to the wooden boxes that house his precious bees. They are stood in a row at the end of a small pasture with patches of berries, rhubarb, and leek growing around the edges. Shivering in the face of the cold winds that assail us, all I can think of is the warmth of the byre. But I am also engaged, by Ed's thoughts on the intelligence of bees. "For example", he remarks, "they are canny enough to figure out ways of stinging you — even through a beekeeper's suit. I have been stung a few times". There are swollen patches on his arms, he adds, to show for his beloved hobby.

When it is time to make our way back to the byre, the wind at its blustery best, we find ourselves temptingly close to the herd of Shropshires. I am hard pressed not to give chase. As if to tease us, a couple of frisky lambs with faces so black that we can barely spot their eyes, stop and stare, then gambol off in the direction of the grazing elders.

But the winner in Ed's coterie is Meg. Every day, before we leave the cottage and after we return, we are used to Meg waiting by the pastures. She squeals, whines and croons as we indulge in conversations with her. "Meg the Madonna", as Ed calls her with a cheeky grin, has a fairly unladylike comportment. Having identified Adi as Belly Rub Guy, she has a routine in place when she spots him. She starts with crooning, lays back and raises her hind leg, and within a brief second or two, has all four legs up in the air, splayed out for her quota of rubs. If you do meet her, carry a big batch of belly rubs for her, will you?

XIV

The Hall Walk

On the first morning of our current holiday, we embark on a long walk through Daphne country. We drive to Fowey, from where we take the ferry to the fishing village of Bodinnick-by-Fowey, which stands right across Fowey.

The Hall Walk is a route beloved of locals and a circular one at that, spanning a length of 4 miles. It is not a particularly arduous walk unless one's a confirmed couch potato, though we encounter a few steep stretches.

When we get off the ferry at Bodinnick-by-Fowey, we find ourselves outside Ferryside. Du Maurier's first home in Cornwall. The whitewashed cottage is built into the cliffs and trimmed with neat blue pipings. Originally designed as a boatyard in the 1800s, the du Maurier family had bought it as a rundown establishment in the mid 1920s. At Ferryside, du Maurier discarded the trappings of city life, of its oddities and pretensions. She would go boating and riding, living the carefree life of a country person. Beneath the small window of a room, supposed to have been her study-bedroom, I spot a jutting figurehead that is symbolic of her first work. It is said to have belonged to the wreck of a 19th century schooner named Jane Slade. Daphne came across it during her walks in Pont Creek. The figurehead, she discovered, was inspired by a real figure called Jane Slade, once the only female shipbuilder in the neighbouring village of Polruan.

As we climb above Ferryside and turn back for a look at the estuary, I wonder about the view that the young Daphne must have had. Even beneath the shadow of an overcast sky, the waters of the estuary gleam green with the wily beauty of the enchantress.

The author's son lives in Ferryside now. Thoughts of knocking on his door has occurred to me. Suitably alarmed, my husband takes bigger strides past the cottage. He knows that such ideas, once they take root in my head, carry the risk of being acted upon.

The moment of inspiration has passed. We lumber up the lane by *The Old Ferry Inn* that stands right across Ferryside. The inn is historic, dating back to the 17th century, along with rows of traditional fishermen and shipmen's cottages queuing up next to it. This is what charms me about the countryside in Britain. Everything exudes age. Every building, preserved remarkably well, is a repository of stories.

Our walks in the English countryside have attuned us to the ways of the land. Directions received from locals in rural areas are crucial. It reminds me of times when places were not mapped out on that practical thing called the satnav and that getting from point A to point B depended upon the goodwill of the person one met. Landmarks then are all-important. As we climb up the hill, we notice that our phones have stopped working. The network is dodgy.

We keep a careful eye out for directions received from a local passing by. Time has eaten into the memories of the exact landmarks here, so indulge me if you will. They go along these (hypothetical) lines: Walk towards the Old School House, carry on past the right lane there by the pub, followed by the gate of the churchyard. Then cross Two-Turn Lane, which goes past the sheep in their grassy knoll of heaven… you get the drift. These old-school directions fit right into the small ancient villages we find ourselves in. It is impossible to escape the feeling that we are caught in a time-bubble.

Once we make it past the stellar signposts into the woods, we strike gold.

Upon Penleath Point, we find a granite pillar inscribed with the letter Q. The cliffs clad in lush grass slope down to the sea, and beyond it is laid out the harbour of Fowey like a painting ridden with piers, tiny sail boats, and stone cottages tumbling into the waters. This tall monolith where we are stood, is where Sir Arthur Quiller-Couch would have stopped frequently during the Hall Walk and admired the view. He was a man of letters who lived in Fowey and went by the *nom de guerre* Q.

I am right excited to find it. So, I loiter. The memorial remembers the notable writer who had described the harbour as a fair one, "where vessels picturesquely rigg'd/Obligingly repair".

As it happens, Q had claimed it for his own too. "The harbour is not mine at all:/I make it so – What odds? /And gulls unwitting on my wall/Serve me for garden-gods."

Penleath Point, so beloved of Q, had royal admirers too. King Charles I had been entranced by the view of Fowey from this point in 1644, during the English Civil War. The king was staying with the Mohuns of erstwhile Hall Manor, which lends the walk its name. Cornwall was known for its Royalist sentiments at the time. At Penleath Point, Charles I was the target of a musket shot fired by parliamentary troops from Fowey, and while the king was saved, the shot killed a fisherman.

A cache of stories culled from just one place… the history buff in me is giddy for more.

The path carries on through woods and muddy farmland, kissing gates and stiles, till we descend into a hamlet called Pont. With its handful of cottages and muddy green creek, Pont is a place forgotten. A small wooden bridge spans the weed-laden waters of the estuary and a disused mill stands in solitude across the bridge. Who can imagine such a tranquil spot as the location of an important quay? But this was a place where once barges sailed in with their consignments of coal and limestone, timber and fresh produce.

We soak in the solitude of it, and oh, it is just so green. It is the kind of place where I would verily find myself a spot by the creek and daydream with a book in my hand. But we press on. Up a hill that climbs above the creek. It leads us to the 14th century church of St. Wyllow's with its square tower, the path framed by curling fronds of fern and wildflowers. This is du Maurier's Lanoc Church in *The Loving Spirit*.

St. Wyllow's, named for an Irish hermit who was murdered by a kinsman and is said to have managed to reach the spot where the church stands, his head tucked under his arm, is a serene place. Willy-nilly I find myself slipping into an older world order where faith would have been all-encompassing. Church bells sound the hour and we walk among its old gravestones. Just like du Maurier would have done when looking for the grave of Jane Slade.

Most of the tablets have turned green, coated with algae. Time has dulled the inscriptions on some. No wonder I cannot spot Slade's resting place. There are graves of a few unfortunate ones who had died of sweating sickness during the 15th century, others of the Victorians, and some of soldiers who had served during WWII.

As we pause to read the epigraphs, gathering the tranquillity like a comforting cloak about our shoulders, I think of du Maurier again. For she had arrived here on an early morning in July 1932 in a boat. She must have trod the same path as I, but she in a fine dress to marry her beau, a girl who roamed the hills and found herself nearer to the peace of god "among the wild things in the woods and fields, or on the rocks by the water's edge".

***

Leaving St. Wyllow's behind, we cross fields where sheep and cattle are slow munching the hours away (not being a part of the rat race must be liberating). In the distance, rolling hills meet arable pastures neatly, as if knit together by some deft hand. The country lane joins up with the road that meanders through the parish of Llanteglos-by-Fowey and into a sleepy little village called Polruan. This road being the only one in the place, do you then call it the "main road" or just "the road"? Deep thoughts as it may invite, let me take you down this very road that swoops as a serpentine affair through the village and at the end of its course opens up to the view of riverine waters shimmering in the bay, under the waning afternoon sun.

At first glance, Polruan is all cosy charm. Rows of stone cottages with crooked chimneys straggle down both sides of the street. It is the kind of place where you expect to come upon the Arcadian existence of a bunch of fishermen and their families. Names on signboards, *Sea Shell Cottage, Singing Kettle, Crumpets Café,* latch onto the imagination and add character to the village. The pasties displayed in the window of the café get me, and to assuage my gluttonous thoughts, I bag a couple for later.

A cursory survey throws up a couple of pubs by way of refreshment in the village. This should speak volumes of the size of it - and also highlight the cornerstone of any village in England. In the tiniest of hamlets, one finds a pub, short for public house where the village gathers and has continued to do since times immemorial.

Famished, we make our way into *The Russell Inn,* the first pub we see along the way, stationed as it is at the mouth of an alley that climbs up a hill. No time is wasted in ordering up pints of ales and fish & chips. It is the kind of lunch long-distance walkers will do anything for: forfeit an entire fortune for the pleasure of a deep-fried meal soused in vinegar and salt. As for us, it is our ticket to contentment and an encounter that is to last a long time in our minds.

The interiors are cool and dark with black wooden beams and floors of flagstone, as an old pub is wont to be, stone fireplace, solid wooden tables and bentwood chairs in place. At one end of the pub is sat a couple and their toddler. We catch a seat at the other end, which is conveniently near the bar.

It is a matter of coincidence entirely that I find myself in *The Russell Inn,* for its first landlady was none other than Jane Slade, in the 1800s. She was an unusual woman, by all accounts, involved as she was in the shipping business owned by her family. In Victorian society, it was completely unheard of for a woman to take care of any business, let alone own it, expand it, and build it into a thriving venture at a time when women did not have the right to vote. No wonder Daphne found herself enamoured of Landlady Slade, who she described in *The Loving Spirit* thus: "Like a lad she grew, tall and straight, with steady hands and fearless eyes, and a love of the sea in her blood." Only in the novel, Slade is renamed Janet Coombe, and Polruan is transformed into the fictional fishing village of Plyn.

Soon we are faced with our individual meals of fish & chips and a large pint, when through the squat, wooden door of the pub, a man enters. His hair is a longish mop of salt-and-pepper streaks, round glasses perched upon a well-formed nose. I notice him, despite being in the throes of my lunch, tucking in wordlessly with the kind of sincerity that the hungry reserve for food (remarkable, how the period between early morning to noon stretches thin when one is constantly on one's feet).

At the bar, he asks for a half-pint of ale, nattering with the barmaid as she pours him a glass. Must be a local, I think to myself. The man turns around to scout the other occupants of the pub as the barmaid turns away to attend to a trickle of customers. The family of three elicits a quick hello from him. At the other end is us. And at us, he lobs the question: "So, are you here from London then?"

"No, that would be Northampton," I say in reply. The exchange of a few words leads to more. It happens organically that he pops over to our table with his pint and a story that catches the imagination. First his name. "It's Alastair," he offers. We shake hands, introduce ourselves, and I watch with a bit of amusement as he stumbles over my name. It throws most people into a tizzy. Blame it on my parents who decided to name me for a star.

I don't know if you have noticed. But life is chock full of prosaic individuals. There are more people in this world who make you yawn with just a "hello", than there are those who turn out to be storytellers. For all the reasons that make me travel, meeting people who can weave a good story is my weakness.

If you are a worthy storyteller, I will give you the time of day. As for the kind of stories that people have to tell - they never cease to amaze me. Alastair is a born storyteller.

Before we hear his story though, we share thoughts on the common elements of life that thread each of ours, the thirst for places unknown, and at the end of our journeys, the eternal search for a place we want to call home. In my head runs a parallel thread of thought. Hesse's *Siddhartha*. The premise of life as an endless quest for illumination of the spirit.

"What is your story?" Adi asks Alastair. He is an intriguing individual.

Three years before this afternoon is to take place in the spring of 2017, Alastair arrived in Polruan, for a weekend away from his life in London City. "I was introduced to Cornwall early you see, by my parents who were keen travellers," he says. Upon his arrival in Polruan, the City worker found himself out of luck. No bed & breakfast accommodations were available for the night. A bench in the village served as his bed. His rucksack, his pillow. The next morning, ambling around, Alastair was captivated. He recalls: "Was it the tranquillity of Polruan, the atmospheric nature of it…I cannot tell, but whatever it was, I knew this was home."

Having had this epiphany, he looked up an estate agent and scoured the village for a house he could buy. Eventually, he purchased a cottage in Polruan. And the next time he returned to the village, it was with the bulk of his material possessions: two bags and a rucksack. It was the beginning of a new life, one that was to be sustained by a modest pension. Yet, Alastair was in Polruan, about to live the life that he had chosen. Before he takes leave of us, he says: "I have had to let go of a fair bit of what I had been used to. But it is what I dreamt of during my growing years. You see, I have roamed the world and never found anything like Cornwall."

Strange as it is, we find ourselves sharing our deep-abiding love for the Cornish countryside with a stranger. He nods, saying he has the measure of us. This after all is the great beauty of life. That you shall be understood out-and-out by a stranger than your closest family and friends. Then, as if realising with a start that he has been at our table for a fair length of time, Alastair mutters a dozen "sorry's" (what would the Englishman be without his army of apologies). Before he leaves, he invites us for a pint another day, adding, "My cottage is right at the top of this hill".

All along our journey through Cornwall, we are to meet people like Fellows and Alastair, strangers who have quit their former city lives to lead a rural existence, to live life on their own terms. So what, if one has to give up a few things along the way? I find them inspiring. "Maybe, one day, we too can take a page from their lives. Maybe, we too can give in to the magic of Cornwall," I say to Adi. My husband, the eternally pragmatic person that he is, indulges me with a smile, and says: "Maybe."

***

The satisfaction of a good walk and lunch over, we get back on the cobbled thoroughfare and end up at the quay. The sheltered sandy patch of the bay is bathed golden in the dying rays of the early evening sun. An assortment of fishing trawlers, dinghies and kayaks float in the shallow aquamarine waters, beneath the boatyard of C. Toms & Sons. People idle here while waiting for the ferry to Fowey.

We too want to get on the ferry, but not before we have a gander at the bits and bobs that make up this village, a humble outpost that once teemed with ships sailing in with their cargoes of china clay. In the Victorian era, Polruan was doing well for itself, the legacy of which are the houses that cropped up atop the hill. They look austere and proper as opposed to the quaint cottages of the fishermen that huddle around the harbour.

I let du Maurier's description of the villagers in *The Loving Spirit* be my imaginary guide. "… when the men came back from their fishing or down from their work in the fields, they would lean over the wall by the slip of Coombe's yard, and gossip over their pipes, the nets spread out to dry on the cobbled stones, and naught to watch save the gulls diving for fish in the water, and the smoke curling from their cottage chimneys, with the womenfolk at their doors."

The only other pub in the village, *The Lugger Inn*, is stood along the quay with its balustrade of ornamental wrought iron, and adjoining it is a convenience store-cum-post-office, *The Winkle Picker*. A quiet little frontier, shored up by a miscellaneous collection of surfboards, fishing nets, spades and plastic buckets, its name a legacy of its former owners. Ms. Joan Winkle and Ms. Joanne Pickering. In my mind, they show up, these two misses. Plump white-haired ladies with creases bunching up around twinkling eyes and flushed cheeks. In this, the village of the steep street that was home to the Winkle Picker women; the one that lured du Maurier to buy its boatyard; and made Alastair give up his busy life in London, it is not entirely inconceivable that I should fall under its spell too.

In my travel journal, I find my notes from the day. It reads thus: "I am knackered, but I cannot escape the feeling that I might be going the way of a plump Cornish cow. Fuelled by a steady two-day diet of scones, pasties, tarts, full-fat ice creams, butter biscuits, and onion rings, is it possible that the waistband of my jeans are screaming out for temperance? These are grave times. The scoffing has been going strong, especially after steep climbs through woods in the heart of Daphne's country. Now, I can barely keep my eyes open, but before I go, I must note that the dirty grey clouds of the morning scudded to give way to a sky so clear that the stars have reclaimed the inky dome for tonight. Life should be just so. Lived beneath vast swathes of sky, unfettered, away from the city lights, busy thoughts, and the worry about what tomorrow shall bring."

XV

Unlikely Dons of a Port Town

The sea gulls rule Padstow.

Here one may point out that they rule the roost in most coastal villages in this part of the country. But I will have you know that in the north Cornish outpost of Padstow, the gulls are your quintessential bandits. They are not satisfied with simply stomping across the road and staking their claim on food (with a certain insouciance), but they also stand guard above your head, swooping up and down, showing up everywhere, till they have lifted a few scalps, or some chips, please.

In Padstow of the whitewashed stone houses with roofs of slate and cottages with names such as "Miss Mopsy's", making you wonder if you have inadvertently stepped into a Blyton-esque world, I saunter along the inner harbour arm in arm with the husband. We watch young boys and girls trawl the waters for crabs, when I am stopped short outside of a chippy.

A scene is in the process of unfolding before the eyes.

A gull walks up to a man busy tucking into his box of fish and chips. The bird's beady stare is fixated on some chips scattered on the pavement near the man's feet. The man has the option of turning a blind eye to it, just let the bird have it. But does he take a step back? Dear god, no. He casts gimlet eyes upon this fearless creature, and extending one hirsute leg, places his foot firmly upon the chips. "Come mess with me if you will, you numpty!" I think I almost hear him grind his teeth and challenge the bird, except for the fact that all of this takes place wordlessly.

Thwarted, the gull turns around and struts across the road to the quay, its body language of supreme nonchalance. It does not give a toss for measly spuds removed from its reach by some tosser — that is if you are bent upon deconstructing the mannerisms of said bird. Now if your aching little heart is swelling with indignation at the thought of a poor creature being denied scraps of food, remember the one cardinal rule that holds strong in Cornwall. You do not feed the gulls.

Now that you have been introduced to the fowl category of dons that rule the roost in Padstow, we will get to the human variety by and by. It is difficult to steer clear of both in this fishing town that sits beatifically on the estuary of the River Camel.

From the top of a hill, a set of stairs passing through dry-stone walls and then a maze of narrow roads takes us to the nerve-centre of Padstow, the harbour. Which bifurcates into an inner and an outer harbour. This core part of it vibrates with life. Clusters of boats and faded buoys float in its shallow waters. These add splotches of colour to the general scene that is made up of loads of people and medieval stone houses with mullioned windows.

Ambling through, we spot tots fishing with their parents, crabbing nets and plastic buckets in tow. An ice-cream van sits on standby, cleverly positioned. The point is to get to 'em little ones after they have had their fill of plucking crabs out of the waters. The parents are a bonus. No one ever said no to ice cream, particularly in a seaside town.

At any given moment, there are so many scenes playing out at tandem in town that my head swivels as much as it can in the attempt not to lose out on anything. Notice the portly golden retriever sat by his roly-poly human? He gazes mournfully as the man sitting next to him scarfs down a takeaway meal of fish and chips; a boy focuses on his fast-melting cone of ice cream beneath the ardour of the not-too gentle April sun, while herds of families trail in and out of shops, picking up souvenirs that will be inevitably be relegated to drawers full of tchotchkes. The squawking of the gulls gliding in the air above our heads adds to the general hubbub.

It is the kind of chaos I find curiously comforting because I can sense that time too is ambling with us, as if it needs a hiatus from the hectic pace of life.

In the outer part of the harbour, a boatman with his voice booming across the quay, announces timings for the ferry that arrives and leaves for The Rock, the village across the estuary. Because posh Londoners troop into The Rock every summer, it transforms into 'Kensington-by-the-Sea' as locals mockingly call it. Hen's teeth and horse's toes if you find a local here who is not cross about this turn of affairs. They find it hard-pressed to be impressed by the number of luminaries who patronise the village across the water seasonally. For one, the trend has sent real-estate prices in and around it skyrocketing.

On Padstow's lively quay, we join a group of people around a busker who croons. A little girl with ringlets in her hair starts dancing, no cares resting upon those tiny shoulders.

Beyond the outer harbour, in the tidal part is a bank of yellow sand, stretched out to form a line of defence between the estuary and the sea. The Doom Bar, a deceptive strand of nature's art. It looks innocuous, yet it must have sealed the fate of many a ship and sailor for over hundreds of years. In this land of ancient legends, filled to the brim with tales of fairy folk, illusive piskies, goblins and elves, it comes as no surprise that there is a story associated with the Doom Bar. Local lore talks of the Mermaid of Padstow, a siren with flowing golden locks and the tendency to break into plaintive singing. She lured seafaring men, who disappointed her. The mermaid cursed Padstow and conjured up a storm that left behind the sand bar. You might be tempted to diss it as spliff talk, but I believe, happy are the folk who are blessed with such a blooming imagination.

I have to slip it in though that I have tasted the Doom. By which I mean the ale named after the Doom Bar. And it is hardly reminiscent of gloom. Try distinctly malty notes, perfect to wind up with after long hot walks on summer days in the West Country; simply flop down at a pub and ask the barkeep for a pint of Doom.

If Padstow is a happy amalgam of bookshops, cafés and pasty shops, old brick almshouses and charming pubs, on this sunny day, we find the town heaving with a mix of locals and tourists, and more than its average share of dogs ranging from the tallest to the tiniest. A melee is out and about, people stopping outside display windows of bakeries to stare at baked goodies, others weaving in and out of cafés. It is one heck of a hungry town, I think to myself. Everyone is on the hunt for good food. Adi and I included. We are ferreting about town till we find the perfect place to rest our feet and grab a bite.

The mention of food brings me to the other don in town. Rick Stein. The affable celebrity chef on telly, the one who goes around cooking curries in Asia, has woven his name into the streets of Padstow through the presence of a restaurant, a café, a deli, gift shop, hotel, a posh chippy and a cookery school in town. Having read Stein's memoir, *Under a Mackerel Sky,* I know that he began his career with a mobile disco in Padstow, and that his name is synonymous with the town, but nothing quite prepares me for Padstein, the locals' not-too-affectionate nickname for Padstow.

A bartender we meet at an old pub in nearby Tintagel, speaks in injured tones about Padstein. "What business does he 'ave to take over Padstow, eh? He is not even there 'alf the time. He's forev-ah travelling in foreign places cooking up foreign food." And so he says to a foreigner. Hah.

However, his point is noted, but I can only speak for the blooming goodness of Stein's chippy on the quayside. We make a stop during our wanderings to queue up for a takeaway lunch of fish and chips in Steinland.

The choice is tough in Padstow, I must add here, for the pasties that wink back at you from the pasty shops in town are beautifully plump, waiting to be devoured. But no sir, Stein's chippy it is because I overhear a man telling his son to hold onto his ravenous appetite for the real deal. It is a pity that we have but one stomach – it often makes me think that if there were a lottery for extra stomachs, I would be right up front. Imagine the sensory pleasures of devouring both pasties and fish & chips for lunch. Would it not be marvellous?

We demolish the contents of our takeaway boxes by the quay where we are joined by ranks of other fish & chips lovers. Beneath a sky swollen with heavy clouds and hesitant sunshine, we have the undivided attention of a couple of gulls. I keep a constant check on the two. And each time, they squawk, as if in rebuke: "Share some, you greedy gits!" But can we, will we indeed, part with any part of the cod fried to crisp perfection within its coat of fried batter? *Non.*

Fish & chips over? Time for Kelly's full-fat ice cream and a saunter through town.

A stone's throw from the harbour are Lanadwell and Middle Streets with their paraphernalia of old cottages, plaques announcing them to be "Cwtch Cottage" and the like. There are also enough drinking holes in town.

You can never go hungry or thirsty in Padstow.

There is something curious written outside one of the inns, *The Golden Lion* — that it is the stable of Padstow's Original 'Oss. It turns out that Padstow has an annual costume festival every May Day, associated with fertility rites, possibly harking back to the pagan times.

Thousands cram themselves into its narrow lanes festooned with cowslips, forget-me-nots, bluebells and sycamore twigs. Two 'osses' (horses) in hues of red and blue, show up from their stables, dancing their way through town, prodded on by a teaser. The young and the old join the retinue, gyrating in full faith. It is an affair that has to be experienced, locals say.

Stein's patisserie and café pop up in quick succession, and it occurs to me that "Padstein" is a neat fit alright. We wander in and out of interesting antique shops, passing slobbery Great Danes loping alongside white-haired humans. We stare at the facades of brick alms houses which look old and take us back to the Begijnhof of the Belgian towns of Bruges and Leuven, where once Catholic women lived a monastic life, but without taking any vows; they remind me of a cold winter's afternoon of pottering in the winding alleyways of the medieval German town of Lübeck, peeking into the *Stiftshöf*, similar accommodations for widows of merchants and sailors. In Amsterdam's Jordaan quarter, they call these former homes for the elderly widows *Hofjes*.

Padstow's almshouses with their roofs of rag slate (in line with traditional North Cornish architecture) and gable ends have the year 1875 inscribed upon them. There's a dedication too, to the memory of John Tredwin. My research upon him gets me nowhere. I can only let the imagination run amok. Could he have been the son of a pirate, who in his advanced years decided to appease his conscience, by parting with the family money for a charitable cause?

We leave it reluctantly, this coastal town that derives its name from St. Petroc, a peripatetic soul who had travelled around Cornwall, Wales, and Brittany, establishing churches and monasteries. The saint would be hard pressed to recognise the little settlement he had founded in the 5th century, now home to celebrity chefs, rambunctious gulls and a grand Elizabethan-era manor.

***

Thirty-five miles from Padstow, we drive to the moors of Bodmin next, to see a place I have long wondered about. *Jamaica Inn*, the coaching inn made famous by du Maurier. The precursors to this are the black caverns and the sandy stretches of beaches near Padstow that we happen upon. These natural features would have abetted the cause of smugglers, who landed on the beaches with boatloads of tea and spices in times bygone. Revenue officers, who dared to get in the way suffered, and the story goes that smugglers cheekily tied up one such officer to a rock at Porthcothan Bay. He survived the unfortunate incident, but the question is, did he carry on with his job?

At Jamaica Inn, I clap eyes on the ingenious schemes hatched by the lot of these smugglers.

But first let me tell you about the location of the inn, the moors. For it is an atmospheric place. Anything can happen on the moors, I think. The imagination is stoked by its desolate nature. I see why the place has been associated with stories of ghosts and strange beasts, but in reality, it is a granite moorland, wild and windswept, and the careful preserver of Bronze Age stone huts and Neolithic tors.

Jamaica Inn stands high and sprawling upon these moors. It is an old building, dating back to the mid-1700s. At the entrance, as if to conjure an ambience of intrigue, a plaque reads: "Through these portals passed smugglers, wreckers, villains and murderers but rest easy…I' was many years ago".

Eighty-seven years before Adi and I walk into its whitewashed, wooden-beamed interiors, du Maurier had stopped at the inn with her friend, Foy Quiller-Couch. They were taking shelter from a fog that had led them astray on the moors. The year was 1930, and they met a rector inside. He was full of stories of smuggling, shipwrecking and the supernatural. A writer is perpetually on the lookout for tales that trigger the imagination. Here was fodder for du Maurier's first book that apart from jump-starting her writing career had captured the fancy of many, leading them (the likes of me) to the black wooden door of the old inn.

"On either side of the road, the country stretched interminably into space. No trees, no lanes, no cluster of cottages or hamlet, but mile upon mile of bleak moorland, dark and untraversed, rolling like a desert land to some unseen horizon." Du Maurier's evocative description holds well even today for the inn that covers a cobbled stretch of courtyard in an L shape. Its original purpose, as a coach house with stables and tack room, has been tweaked to recreate an alternate world that smacks of a dodgy association with smugglers and shipwreckers.

I cannot believe that I am finally at *Jamaica Inn*, standing at a place I have only read about in a novel so far. But here I am, really.

Inside the inn is a museum showcasing smuggling curios. My eyes goggle at a bag of 10 pounds of Jamaican *ganja*, a 17th century Armada chest, some 18th century 'Wanted' posters and opium pipes. I stare wonderingly at du Maurier's typewriter and writing desk that are on display alongside. Adi is amused by my reactions, but even he is captivated by these relics. That I can tell.

At "Joss's Bar", a dark bar corner heavy with wood and decorated with a paraphernalia of antiquated tankards, bottles and kegs, I am startled to see replicas of Mary Yellan and Francis Davey (remember the heroine and the albino vicar of Altarnun from *Jamaica Inn*?) behind the counter. The figure of Davey is unsettling, as intended.

Later, Adi and I marvel about the ingenuity that the common folk showed in times of desperation. They were uncommonly canny in the art of concealment and thorough in their craft, as we have found at the museum. Villagers created false horseshoe prints in the sand to confuse followers; hollowed out books to make way for hidden chambers; and, stowed away jewels in corsets. A wanted poster from the 18th century, and the skull of a poor smuggler discovered in the cellars of an old house, are reminders of times which have been imparted a sheen of romance and bravado by modern minds, but on the whole, must have been a rather bleak era.

For us, these things seen and learnt of during our travels is part of a constant education. I might have known about it through my world of books, but for Adi, who is not an avid reader and knows about certain books through sessions of his wife reading out passages to him, this world of atmospheric coaching inns, smugglers and wreckers is all too heady.

***

Puttering down the A-roads from Padstow that eventually spill onto B-roads, we almost miss the village of Port Isaac. It is as if hidden from the prying eyes of the world altogether. I would have been sorry to have missed it and our path to it is more circumstantial than intentional. I need a loo break quite so desperately and the toilet at the large carpark in Port Isaac sits conveniently atop the village, with a view of the sea.

As I emerge from the toilet, I spot Adi devouring an ice cream cone. The sneak. What's more, his "do you want one" is tossed out half-heartedly. I decide to wait till I reach the village because his ice cream supplier is the ubiquitous Mr. Whippy, and I am an ice cream snob. I will have them full fat, so much so that for a magazine I wrote a piece for a while ago, I was a tad devious. I concocted an angle that would allow me to interview ice cream makers in the West Country and the Cotswolds. The focus of the story was traditional, farm-fresh ice creams. More to the point of it all, the interviews were followed by generous dollops of full-fat ice creams. So, one spoon, and I can discern if your cup of ice cream merits my time of day.

Anyway. The thing with having ice cream on the sly is that you've got to pay for it later when your wife goes into an artisan fudge confectionery and arms herself with a gourmet cone, studded with moreish caramel bits.

Providence is a sweet woman. She takes me by the hand and leads me to a confectionery in the village. Behind the till is sat a kindly old man. Has he played a part in the telly drama, *Doc Martin*? If you have no idea what I am on about, the show follows the goings-on in the surgery of a socially challenged doctor from London, Dr. Martin Ellingham, who arrives in the fictional village of Port Wenn (actually, Port Isaac) as the general physician. If you think of it, no one puts Doc Martin in a corner when in Port Isaac.

At this confectionery, which is called *Buttermilk,* and has the figurehead of an admiral jutting above its entrance as a nod to Port Isaac's marine heritage, I see apothecary goods have been replaced by the pleasing sight of fudges and ice creams. Temptation finds an easy friend in the elderly man behind the till. He urges us to "go on then, grab a few fudges".

I take my time to mull over the display of fudges and ice creams at hand, per usual. To procrastinate habitually when faced with a menu, to go back and forth between available options, is a strength of mine. A trait that manages to pickle the husband's nerves without fail. His face turns a few shades of purple by the time I arrive upon a decision. To mess with him, I throw in an additional few seconds of dithering.

The important business of ice cream sorted — a cone in one hand and a husband in the other looking at me from time to time to remind me that love means having to share ice cream more than other earthly goods — we weave our way through the narrow country lanes. I find that the locals have a term for these lanes that climb up from the harbour. *Opes.* These dialect-based words are curiously charming. I am chuffed to find out that there are more such interesting words to tuck into my bag of words unknown.

The alleys through which we meander, flanked by period houses that date back to the 18th-19th century, for instance, are *drangs* in local-speak. The houses in the *drangs* are packed together tightly enough that they shut out sounds from the harbour, cocooning our surroundings in a veil of tranquillity. Then, the slimmest of brooks gurgling through the lanes, past the old fishermen's cottages, we find, is called a *leat* here.

Discovering words like opes, drangs and leats, I feel like I am in the pages of a book in which people have the time and sensibility to invent terms, which might sound strange to us as outsiders, but they are splashes of local colour, organic to the villages we come across on our travels.

A signpost warns bulky vehicles from barging into the drangs. If you have harboured thoughts of squeezing a car that is not the tiniest of hatchbacks into them, you deserve to sit inside, while the rest of the world passes you by with cones of ice cream held aloft as beacons of goodness. We notice this at the outset when we realise that carrying on in a car down the lane leading to the village is a dreadful idea. Be warned in big, bold letters. Even if you do risk it and park the car on the beach, then forget about it, you might not have a car the next day. There is the distinct possibility that the sea shall claim it for its own (and it might just wash up in another continent altogether, like it did with a signboard from New Jersey which after three years of going missing, surfaced on a beach in France).

***

Beyond the obsession with artisanal ice creams and colourful local words, let me give you a broader picture of Port Isaac. The village is situated along the SWCP and deserves more than a passing mention.

A short distance from the carpark at the top, is a country lane that descends into the village. A granite church dedicated to St. Peter is perched upon the hill. From its purely functional but attractive grey exterior, the church seems to have Methodist leanings, a reminder of the faith that had won over the Cornish population during the 18th century by dint of its appeal as a religion for the masses.

The outside world is screened out by the time we reach the foot of the lane where *The Old School Hotel* is stood, silhouetted against the sun, as if brooding with its aged façade of stone, its roofs of slate. The hotel once was an old school, as its name suggests. Perched upon a clifftop, it has a smashing view of the cove. The salty tang of the ocean bathes our senses as we catch a moment of repose along the hotel's walls, watching the harbour. There's its old pier and breakwater along with a paraphernalia of boats, boys, and dogs, upon the shingle beach. Clusters of stone houses huddle around the harbour and the surrounding green cliffs complete this engaging picture.

The main thoroughfare is flanked by rows of fisherman's cottages, some whitewashed, others clad in fronts of dark slate. Twists and turns along the street drop us at the harbour where an elderly man is sunbathing with his Old English bulldog, but not before we have spotted evocative names like Squeeze-ee-Belly Alley (at the mouth of a superbly narrow alley), *Krab Pot Café and Crab & Lobster*. Notes of fried fish hang in the air outside these establishments, introducing us to the thought that we might be in the home of fresh seafood.

Its cosy vibes apart, there are three things going for Port Isaac. Location, location, and location. People have lived here by the Atlantic for centuries, since the mid-1300s. They called it 'Portusek' then. During the 1500s, pilchard fishing picked up in the village and fish cellars sprung up around Roscarrock Hill, right above the harbour.

The old-world atmosphere that hangs athwart the village in the present day, paves the way for the imagination to cadge up a scene from the medieval ages: men occupied with the task of unloading fish on the beach, above their heads, the wheeling of seagulls, and then the carting of fish to the cellars where women and children wait to salt them, before pressing them into barrels for export.

In the present hour, in one of Port Isaac's former pilchard-curing cellars by the harbour, a fish merchant is winding up his business of selling freshly caught shellfish. The cloud of fishy odour hanging in the air makes that part of me, not overtly fond of malodorous spaces, a bit glad that the fishermen are shutting shop. I scuttle out of the cellars for great gulps of fresh air. Well, there goes my lofty ambitions of learning to live off the sea when someday we have a sweet little cottage in the village (by now, you must have figured that I want a cottage in nearly every Cornish village we end up in).

Life in Port Isaac, as it is in the month of April, is sleepy what with its laidback community of a few hundred residents. Come summer, it will heave with tourists when the Fisherman's Friends, a group of fishermen-singers gather to chant sea shanties on the beach and wet parched throats with free beer. Naturally, *emmets* like myself fall prey to Port Isaac's charms all too often.

It seems it has had renown as a "a pretty fisher village" since the 16th century when an antiquarian by the name of John Leland described it so. In his days though, Port Isaac was called 'Porthissek', meaning "port of corn".

The harbour, which the locals refer to as the Platt. is the hub of the village. In the 1800s, the Platt served as a platform for the passage of consignments of Delabole slate, coal (from the quarries of Delabole nearby), timber, pilchards and herrings. Pilchard oil was one of the regular export items to Europe, and naturally, you can picture the harbour as a place of action. At the Platt, our senses are engaged pleasantly, roving eyes taking it all in. The surrounding hills are dotted with houses that stand heads above the village, and beyond the harbour, the bluish grey Atlantic is conscientiously contained by the breakwater. Within the cove is stood a Georgian pub overlooking the sea, through its interiors a smuggler's tunnel leading to the causeway, which in turn spills on to the beach. Meanwhile, an all-important 100-year-old lifeboat waits inside the lifeboat station. Necessary as a lifeboat is along these treacherous coasts, hopefully, it won't be called out to work today.

The fishing boats upon the slipway are waiting patiently too, and the large anchor which would pose a serious challenge to a gang of 40 beefy men asked to merely lift it, looks like it has been rusting away at leisure and has nothing more to do than rust some more.

Beyond all of these, our gazes are pulled back to the moody blue waters, the breakwater and the old Tudor pier inching towards each other at odd angles, working hand in hand to keep the town safe during stormy weather.

On our way to the other end of the village, Roscarrock Hill, we walk up the road that leads out of Port Isaac. We pass Fern Cottage, "Doc Martin's surgery". On the cliffs, below the road we are on, is "Bert Large's whitewashed restaurant". You will pardon these references, but the village is awash with them.

Curiously enough, all along the climb we hear baritone barks. Not your average smattering of barks, no, this being a remarkable volley of baritone woofs which refuse to cease. Curiosity overcomes us. We peek at the beach through a gap between the houses. A podgy basset hound materialises in our line of sight.

We get back on the climb and soon we are sat on the hill waffling about nothing of import. Swept up in the flow of the good mood prevailing on us, Adi starts adventuring down the hill which slopes into the sea. And he accompanies it with singing so bad that I get up and leave the spot all to him. He must do without an audience.

Gradually we start making our way down to the sandy-shingled beach riddled with rockpools. Here, we make a proper acquaintance of the mouthy basset we had sighted earlier. He continues to voice his list of grievances against the world at large. He is not alone. In his august company is another basset hound, who has admittedly less fat and gives lesser lip. I fancy that the other hound is intimidated by his mate's capacity for verbal outpourings. A few Labradors prance around on the beach, but let's not quibble about who steals the show. To agitate the excitable sausage of a hound, his human stoops to say a few things in his ears, which sets him off again.

This is how the coin drops. With the baritone barks of a basset hound. And this is how we take leave of the 700-year-old village, trudging up its main thoroughfare, ears ringing with the basset's booming barks, the sight of his droopy face, tubby body and pendulous ears carved into our memories, wondering wistfully if any other village shall woo us as Port Isaac has.

XVI

The Lizard's Salty Secrets

Having been to the Lizard Peninsula previously, we are not inured to its charms, especially Kynance Cove, which merits repeated visits by dint of its spectacular stacks. This time around we make our way to two lovely villages there along the SWCP.

From Kynance Cove we take a detour and come upon a hamlet that seems like the Lizard's little hideout. Church Cove, tucked away neatly into the parish of Landewednack, has chocolate-box charm. It is also important to note right at the outset that this is not Church Cove of Gunwalloe fame, where *Poldark* has been filmed in parts.

When we follow the country lane that leads toward *this* Church Cove, I have no blooming idea of what shall turn up. A church first (don't know why I was surprised), its tower standing prominent with a chequered façade of blocks of local granite and serpentine. The most southerly church in mainland Britain, St. Wynwallow's, named after Saint Winwaloe. Here is a hint that Wennec (Landewednack) might be a variation of Winwaloe.

As you must know by now, Cornwall is full of 'em saints. But why the church should be dedicated to a saint, who founded an abbey across the Channel in Brittany, is perplexing. Maybe it has something to do with it that Saint Winwaloe was the son of a Cornish prince and his three-breasted wife, both of whom had fled to Brittany to escape the plague. Or, it could be that one of Winwaloe's disciples from the abbey at Landévennec (in Brittany) established the original church of St. Wynwallow's.

In the old days, Landewednack served as the church town for the entire peninsula of the Lizard and was connected via motor buses that plied from Helston. According to author Arthur L. Salmon, Landewednack laid claims to being the last place from where a sermon was preached in the Cornish language in 1678. The tongue is said to have survived in the remote landscape of the Lizard longer than other places in the duchy. Its isolation must have played a viable part. In his book, *The Cornwall Coast*, Salmon quoted a loyal Cornishman, "…who bewailed 'our Cornish tongue has been so long on the wane that we can hardly hope to see it increase again; for, as English first confined it within this narrow country, so it still presses on, leaving it no place but about the cliffs and sea, it being now almost only spoken from the Land's End to the Mount, and again from the Lizard towards Helston and Falmouth.'"

Dawdling in the churchyard, in the shadow of its imposing tower of chequered granite and serpentine, affords us the serene experience of reading epitaphs. Some recall lighthouse keepers and lifeboat crew members; others reminisce about people who died of a plague that swept through the parish in the 17th century. Is a section of the burial ground roped off? It escapes my notice, but the story goes that when part of the churchyard was dug up, where the plague victims had been buried so as to inter the remains of shipwrecked sailors, the plague made a return. Hence, the fencing off, of a portion of the churchyard.

The travails of the past are a thing of the past. The present is suffused with tranquillity, the silence of the morning broken by the chittering of birds.

From St. Wynwallow's Church, where a reverend is said to have delivered his last sermon in the old Cornish language during the late 1600s, we carry on down a lane that threads through a charming profusion of flowers and shrubs on either side of it. And is followed up soon by houses with porches that look like they are fading away bit by bit, and, twee cottages with thatched eaves. The house names are evocative. "Grandad's Cottage" probably does have a grandfather with his pipe inside, whipping up a batch of pancakes for the kids, served up with tiny pots of fruit jams and drizzles of honey. Alternatively, he is a surly codger who wants to do nothing much but teach the grandchildren carpentry from time to time, when he is in the mood. The other cottages are atmospheric too. The Mariners, Cove Cottage, Church Cottage — they all look homey and inviting.

Of this attractive appearance of the Church Cove cottages, art historian and journalist Charles Lewis Hind observed in his notes after a walking tour through Cornwall undertaken in 1906. Hind was bound seawards, his mission to take a crabber to Cadgwith from Church Cove. While waiting for the boat to arrive at the slipway, he decided to take a quick walk about the hamlet. He wrote: "… I ascended to Landewednack, passing a charming group of Cornish cottages. Whitewashed walls with trailing roses and thatched roofs. Two girls were seated on camping stools in the lane producing watercolours of the cottages. It was a miniature Surrey in Cornwall."

Of the handful, the 17th century cottage of The Mariners stands out by dint of its size and its traditional thatched eaves. It is said to have been cobbled together from three separate cottages. The cottage has the sort of history that you associate the area with – of smuggling or free trading. The Mariners served as a "kiddlywink" during the 18th century. Kiddlywinks were beer houses, licensed by Customs & Excise to sell beer/cider, as opposed to traditional pubs and inns that required a magistrate's license. These establishments came up as response to the Beerhouse Act of 1830 that aimed at dissuading people from drinking stronger spirits like gin, directing them towards beer instead — here you have another arm of the Temperance Movement.

Given the contempt that the average Cornishman and woman held for the authorities, kiddlywinks were popular with smugglers. They met up at these pubs and I imagine them talking in hushed tones about elaborate plots, arrangements for storage, distribution of illicit liquor and the likes of that. Meanwhile, landlords and landladies kept kettles ready with smuggled brandy in way of concealment from the authorities. When a visitor winked at the kettle, it was a sign that they wanted more than beer.

With its trove of stories, it is not surprising that The Mariners drew the likes of English playwright and musician, Noël Coward. His room with a view of the sea inspired him to sing the classic number, *A Room with a View*. And some of his happiest days, it is said, were spent in the cottage, staring at the vista that lay before him, the verdure valley dipping into the hauntingly quiet cove.

***

The old moniker for Church Cove is "Parnvose," which means "fortified cove" and reminds me of the cottage found along the way to the beach with a similar name. Must be a shout out to the hamlet's original name.

The solitude that the place has to offer is remarkable. It is probably quieter now than it would have been in the 19th century when day-trippers arrived at this charmed village by boat. I do prefer the serenity of the present day to the incessant chatter of tourists from the yesteryears.

In her book, *An Unsentimental Journey Through Cornwall*, novelist Dinah Mariah Craik wrote of the sheer terror that ran through her when with her two children she arrived at the cove, for a boat ride into some sea caves in the area. "But between us and him (John, the boatman) lay a sort of causeway, of the very roughest rocks, slippery with sea-weed, and beat upon by waves— such waves! Yet clearly, if we meant to get into the boat at all, we must seize our opportunity and jump in between the flux and reflux of that advancing tide," noted Craik. To her credit, she did get into the boat. Having seen that causeway, I can assure you, I would not have been as brave.

Adi and I cross a construction site, the rough frame of a cottage evident beneath shrouds of plastic cover. From somewhere within we hear muted sounds of woodwork and the low-pitched chatter of men. There is minimal clatter, and a few yards away, I can barely hear them. I observe to Adi, construction workers worldwide should be sent over to Church Cove for training in the art of working quietly.

Before we know it, we have ascended a cliff with a fingerpost and are stood at the edge of it. Looking back for a proper view of the hamlet, we are faced by a narrow cove framed by black jagged rocks, which contrast startlingly with the aquamarine sea.

As at Kynance Cove and the Lizard, the cliffs here are a geologist's dream, sculpted from grey schist and greenish serpentine rocks. Rills of water run down fissures in the cliffs and empty into the sea. Above the cove is a gaggle of cottages. These comprise a former lifeboat station which was built in the late 1800s for the grand sum of £300 and sold a century later for £40 (talk about depreciation); some 18th century pilchard cellars; a winch house; and a round house. All are listed properties and have been converted into holiday lets. A slipway slopes down steeply from the foot of the boathouse. A cluster of colourful boats wait at the top of the slipway, biding time till they are taken into the waters by local fishermen.

The mouth of the cove is littered with shards of black rock layered beneath the clear waters, like monsters lying in deep slumber. Being already acquainted with Madam Craik's written account of skirting the rocks, an involuntary shudder runs through me.

We continue along the cliff for a while in the other direction from the cove, along the SWCP that snakes around the cliffs on either side of the cove, leading to Cadgwith in one direction and Kynance Cove in the other. But our aim is to reach the fishing village of Cadgwith with plenty of time in hand to explore it, so we make an about-turn.

We notice that there are no shops in this settlement. The nearest store, the butcher's shop, the post office, and the pub, are all to be found in Lizard village. A family of walkers turn up as we get ready to leave. We pass on the baton of seclusion and move on.

On the walk back up, we notice a new arrival at the construction site. A pick-up truck is positioned outside it and out of its window staring at us is the nonchalant face of a Labrador pup. With his solemn whiskered face, he ignores my baby talk for the longest time. But as we leave him behind, we have his attention. I turn back and see him leaning out of the window as far as he can, staring at our receding backs, possibly wondering at the daftness of the people who can bring themselves to walk away from this perfect little hideaway.

***

Four miles by road, we come upon the village where they say you work, if you don't know how to fish. More succinctly called Cadgwith. From the car park at the top of the hill, we pick our way down a narrow trail to the village. It feels intimate, this path, meandering as it does through a higgledy-piggledy row of cottages, past a small chapel painted in vivid shades of blue. Most who drive into this fishing village on the Lizard Peninsula would follow the same path as ours into its interiors. Only residents are allowed into the heart of the village with their cars.

Most people do not arrive upon Cadgwith. This is not by any devious design. It is just that it remains hidden from prying eyes, cocooned within a cove, and dotted with clusters of the most winsome chocolate-box cottages you will have laid eyes on. The oldest of these would have been built during the 16th century.

The other way of arriving in Cadgwith is via the SWCP from Church Cove, the advantage of which is the sight of *Hugga Dridgee*. This Cornish name might sound like it's Hagrid's hangout but it is a collapsed sea cave, a 200-feet-deep chasm in the cliffs through which the sea has forged a gaping hole. On stormy days, the waves crash against a boulder beneath this archway in the cliffs, making the fervid imagination think of the scene as of an egg in the process of being fried in a pan. The clue is in the name. *Hugga Dridgee* translated, means the Devil's Frying Pan.

The devil, along with giants and piskies, makes frequent appearances in Cornish folklore. According to Esquiros, he is the hero of most adventures in folk stories. "If his visits to the interior of the county are at the present day much less frequent than formerly," Esquiros notes, "he is restrained, so it is said, by the very legitimate fear of being eaten. The Cornish people are so greedy for pastry that they would catch him and put him in a pie."

At the time, Adi and I are the only two on the path into the village, and we wonder if there are curtain twitchers, old biddies behind lace curtains in these weathered cottages. At one point on the trail, we are perched above a plethora of roofs, some thatched and whitewashed, others fashioned out of slate, with walls of serpentine stone.

The thatched eaves are fishermen's cottages typical of the village. Cadgwith is far removed from the slate-producing region of Cornwall. Wildflowers abound on patches of green along the path, and as the road dips into the village, we have a clear view of the startling blue of the sea before us. It is utterly quiet in this stretch and we can hear the calling of some bird. Stout gulls have settled contentedly upon chimney tops to roost and this entire arrangement is a preview of what lies ahead.

The entrance itself is so enchanting that I wonder if the rest of the village will live up to this suggestive stretch. There's anticipation in the salty air, and it is with an inadvertent sigh of relief that we enter the square of the village to find that Cadgwith improves upon acquaintance.

Here is a small shop housed within a building of serpentine stone where they sell freshly caught fish. It looks like a small fish cave. Above the shop sits the *Crow's Nest*, a boutique-cum-gallery of handmade nautical-themed gifts and paintings sold by a local woman. She is chatty. There's time for a chinwag before we take leave of her to walk through the village by the sea.

Its maritime links are present everywhere we turn. The Cadgwith Gig Club announces the importance of cleaving to traditions in this part of the world where every summer there are bouts of gig racing. Towards the end of the 18th century, narrow six-oared boats known as gigs were a customary fixture in Cornish coastal villages where harbours were not big enough to accommodate ships. The function of the gig was to take the pilot out to the anchored ship. The gig that reached first received the money. It led to the practice of gig racing, which is a beloved fixture in most coastal villages.

The gig club at Cadgwith is housed in the former lifeboat club, another integral feature of a seaside village where lifeboats were a necessity, since shipwrecks were a common feature in this part of the country owing to the jagged Lizard coastline.

We drift into a couple of shops including the post office, where we take stock of bunches of postcards, candies, and thingamabobs of seaside villages — plastic spades and buckets, in blinding neon colours.

The doors of a van open before him, a fisherman is stood in the middle of the street that opens onto the fishermen's beach, in his well-worn yellow overalls. He is in the process of emptying crab pots. Witnessing a fisherman at work makes for a brief interjection in our walk, but it reveals the inner workings of a fully functional fishing village that still relies on a medieval trade for a living. From pilchards, the enterprising fisherfolk have shifted their attention to other creatures of the sea. Crabs and eels, sharks, monkfish, mackerel and mullet. As-fresh-as-it-gets seafood is what you expect on your plate when you sit down for a meal in the village.

We find two coves in Cadgwith. A patch of a beach is sprinkled with pebbles and boulders, and it is clearly the bathing beach where a boy and a girl play, their guardian sitting on the rocks nearby. This beach is separated from a bigger cove of slipway and shingles, that is the fisherman's bastion, by a finger of rocky land jutting into the shadowy green waters of the sea. Locals have a name for the promontory — The Todden. It is a neat vantage point. It makes me dream of a picnic hamper, chilled champers and sandwiches, followed by a brief snooze.

The people put The Todden to use alright. As of the noon, we are loitering around it, they seem to have transformed it into a fine sunbathing spot. A couple of old men and women are sprawled out in chairs on the promontory. Beneath in the cove, a flotilla of fishing boats splashes the shingled stretch of it with colours, catching some respite from the early hours of the morning when they are taken out to sea by the hardy fisherfolk. We spend time on this fishing beach, hypnotised by the relentless arrival of wave upon wave upon dark rocks with notes of sibilant shh, before dissolving into flecks of foam.

The cliffs above us hold a promise of spectacular views. When there is a good climb thrown in, one cannot resist the temptation. We ascend the road that leads us past the fish cellars on the beach, where they pressed and pickled herring in the old days, and then, a 300-year-old pub where libations in a sunny courtyard are for the few who are sat soaking in the idyllic beauty of a Cadgwith noon. If it had been a Friday evening, we would have caught the strains of music wafting from the pub. The Cadgwith Singers are somewhat of a local treasure who belt out old sea shanties at the pub on Fridays.

Turning right into the coastal path towards Kennack Sands, we trudge past a line-up of whitewashed cottages, and find ourselves alone again. In some time, a wooden bench materialises. On it is sat a middle-aged woman with the wind in her hair, her face reflecting serenity, and a glimmer of a smile.

"Look at this view. Isn't it something?" she asks, as we pass by. "I could sit here all day."

I think to myself, "I have a suspicion that you do exactly that, lady."

"This, right here, is the raison d'être of why we keep coming back to Cornwall. We cannot get enough of its beauty,' remarks Adi.

"And, exactly why I moved to Cornwall," adds the woman.

We do not know who she is, what her story is, or, where she has moved from to this part of the British Isles, but what shines through is her love for the unaffected glory of nature. And that she sits on this cliff every day with the wind in her hair and the sea in front of her. Sometimes, it is all that matters. A few words exchanged with a stranger. For, it is in the briefest of exchanges, we often find everything we want to know, where entire chapters may fail. Over and over again, during the course of our travels through Cornwall, we meet people who were outsiders, but they made it their business to become a part of the Cornish community.

We carry on, on a path tread by generations of walkers, and reach a compact outpost of dark grey stone. The huer's hut. I get excited. It is the first of the huts I have seen during our travels. The lookout spot is boarded up now, but back in the old days, it was the station of the huer who spent his time here watching out for shoals of pilchards and signalling to fishermen when he spotted them. Fishing fleets would head then out into the sea in seine boats to net their share of pilchards, and when the huer cried "hevva, hevva", the fisherwomen knew that their husbands were on their way back to the shore. They started the process of baking the preferred tea-time treat — the Hevva. Having had a taste of the dense Cornish cake in the café at Kynance Cove, I can see how it should sustain a hungry fisherman.

During my research later, while in the process of reading up literature on the village, I come upon an account of a Cornish local whose grandfather was a huer. Avice Etchells was born in 1920 in Cadgwith. Life was idyllic in summer when the crabbers left for the sea. She wrote that there was plenty to eat. Sunshine was abundant and the locals spent time on the beach and sunbathed on the Todden. The halcyon days of summer however were matched by the harshness of winter. It is most vivid in Etchells' notes, in which she described the howling of the wind under the eaves of her thatched cottage, as the cold months set in, and the pounding of the waves on the beach. There were no benefits to fall back upon then as it is now in modern Britain, and Etchells reminds us, "if you didn't work you couldn't eat".

From the huer's hut, we turn around and drink in the view of the village laid out beneath us, with its thatched roofs, boats and shingled beaches. The people are matchstick figures from our perch. The hut could have easily been a portal into another time when smuggling was a way of life in the community. Peeping over the edge of cliffs, beneath the lookout hut, we sight another kind of lookout spot. The Gull Rock, on which gulls and cormorants are assembled to spot their own cache of fish.

Upon retracing our steps back to the village square, on its fishing beach we catch sight of a fetching golden retriever who drools and stares with singular intensity at his silver-haired mistress as she scoffs a generously topped off cone of ice cream. He is eventually rewarded with the butt end of it. Inspired by this scene, we head for *The Watch House*, the former Customs Office and lock-up, where we get our own cones of divinely creamy treats and leave behind the cares of our modern life in sweet ol' Cadgwith.

XVII

Mount's Bay

On the sixth day of our travels, we get out late in the day and head to Mount's Bay, the stretch of the Cornish coast that is laid along the English Channel. Masses of billowing clouds tail us into the ancient market town of Marazion. The sun is blotted out and the clouds take over the formerly fizzy fields of blue that the sky was, with such determination that a dark, silvery sheen coats the seascape. There is enchantment in the air. The intangible feeling intensified as I set eyes upon the silhouette of the tidal island jutting out from the Celtic Sea, across Marazion.

St. Michael's Mount has that certain something, *je ne sais quois,* in the parlance of the French. Stood on the causeway that shoots off the small beach of Marazion, at first sight it is a rocky outcrop emerging from the sea, crowned by a turreted castle. As the tide pulls back, it transforms into a peninsula linked to the mainland by a causeway of granite.

Drawn to it involuntarily, I cross the causeway speedily, leaving behind a knackered husband at the car park on the beach in Marazion. He insists he needs sleep, so I leave him to the pleasure of an hour's kip. "Take your time," he adds. I need no prodding. The tide is low, the timing perfect as I set off across large cobbles. Sea water has collected in mysterious little rockpools, but not deep enough to submerge the barnacle and lichen-coated rocks.

It takes me a few minutes of leisurely pace to follow in the path of medieval pilgrims who would have trod this path to reach the church on the island. It's not a taxing walk by any measure. St. Michael's Mount is a half mile away from the mainland.

Bells toll in the old priory. Apart from the cawing of a few seagulls, the island is deserted. It must be a Saturday. It is the one day of the week when the castle is off bounds to the public. Of course, I had to arrive on a Saturday. I walk past stone cottages and tip my head back to survey the 12th century affair of a castle that towers above me. The St. Aubyn family has been living in the castle since the mid-1600s. Curiously enough, it is registered as a National Trust property. The family struck a deal with the trust, which takes care of the upkeep of heritage properties and woods around the British Isles. The clause states that the St. Aubyns shall live in the castle for 999 years. The deal having been struck in 1954, it means that they can live on St. Michael's Mount till the year 2953. From where I stand, it sounds lengthy enough.

Of the lonely nature of the castle, the 19th century English novelist Craik had commented on, after she climbed it during her trip to the rock. "How in the world do the St. Aubyns manage when they go out to dinner?" wondered Craik in her book, *An Unsentimental Journey Through Cornwall* (1884). The climb must be arduous, you think.

About thirty people live on St. Michael's Mount, but they are nowhere to be seen. I wonder where they might have disappeared to. Perchance they are on the mainland, enjoying the social rites that come with being confined to an island (isn't it human to yearn for what's on the other side?). Or I tell myself, they might be pecking daintily on tiny tea sandwiches along with a cuppa inside their twee cottages.

Either way, I am left to my own devices on the island, to explore it as I see fit. No one to nudge me along. I tread through the alleys of which there are not enough to get lost in. The tidal flats around the pier have a few boats sat on them, resting before they are called to duty, when the sea comes calling.

Diodorus Siculus, a Greek historian, wrote of an island called Ictis during the first century BCE. An outpost frequented by the Phoenicians for the trading of tin.

"The inhabitants of that part of Britain which is called Belerion are very fond of strangers and from their intercourse with foreign merchants are civilized in their manner of life. They prepare the tin, working very carefully the earth in which it is produced. The ground is rocky, but it contains earthy veins, the produce of which is ground down, smelted and purified. They beat the metal into masses shaped like knuckle-bones and carry it off to a certain island off Britain called Iktis," noted Siculus in his series of books, *Bibliotheca Historica*. Historians have deduced that Ictis could easily be ancient St. Michael's Mount.

As far back as the 5th century, sailors carried tales. Of a saint who had appeared to them on a small island and guided them to safety during terrible storms, warning them about treacherous rocks lurking beneath the waters, while also rescuing them from mermaids' intrigues. Meet the archangel St. Michael.

Across the English Channel, St. Michael's Mount has a twin in Normandy. St. Mont Michel could be mistaken for the Cornish island, unless you consider the fact that the French tidal island has an edge on its British counterpart. The spires of Mont Michel's Benedictine abbey shooting for the skies make for a slightly more glamorous picture. Two islands that mirror each other across the channel. What are the chances that they are not connected?

Lore has it that the archangel appeared on Mont Saint Michel, too. He commanded a bishop there to build a church for him. Now, the story of Michael the archangel maybe drawn from someone's flights of fantasy, but written records state that the abbot of Mont Saint Michel had ordered the construction of a priory on St. Michael's Mount in the 12th century. The Cornish priory is recorded to have sent a sum of 16 marks to the priory at Mont Saint Michel.

It took time before St. Michael's Mount came into its own. Sometime during the Middle Ages, the island became a centre of pilgrimage for travellers who travelled all around Europe visiting religious houses that contained relics of saints, in search for absolution. If relations were peaceful between the two tidal islands during the 12th century, it was because the kings of England were also dukes of Normandy, in control of their ancestral properties. The Hundred Years' War changed everything.

Relations between England and France soured and the proper break between the two priories took place in the 15th century when King Henry V confiscated St. Michael's. After him, King Henry VI snipped off the final tie with Mont Saint Michel and made over St. Michael's to the Bridgettine convent of Syon in Middlesex. The irony in all of it is that the St. Aubyns trace their lineage back to Normandy.

The thread between the two ancient islands is tenuous, but what's interesting to note is that it remains. Their fortunes changed with the passage of time. Henry VIII had already dissolved most monasteries and religious houses in England. The priory at St. Michael's Mount also met the same fate. It was transformed into a manorial house which eventually became home for the St. Aubyn family from the 1600s.

Standing on the pier of this small patch of land surrounded by the waters, it is difficult to believe that it could have been home to 300 residents when the island traded in copper and tin. I can barely visualise thirty people fitting in.

But oh, the narratives around the island. They must be as tall as the giant who lived on St. Michael's Mount many moons ago. Cormoran, an 18-feet-tall fellow, whose girth spanned a width of three yards, is a familiar figure in fairy tales. Think back to your reading of Jack the Giant-Killer.

"You must look out over the sea, too, which surrounds the giant's Mount, and try to picture to yourself a large forest in the place of it, and the sea six long miles away, for that was how it was in Cormoran's time, until one day the sea rose quite suddenly, a huge mountain of water, and rushing over the six miles of land, covered it and the forests too, even above the tops of the tallest trees," wrote Mabel Quiller-Couch, Daphne du Maurier's great friend and daughter of Arthur Quiller-Couch. Mabel put out a book titled *Cornwall's Wonderland,* recounting the strange romantic legends surrounding Cornwall.

Cormoran must have painstakingly moved rocks on the island, you would imagine, but then you have another think coming. His wife, Cornelian, did the muscular job in his stead. When the giant felt hungry, he hopped across the causeway for the cattle of Marazion. What a nuisance he must have been! Of literally giant proportions. To the rescue of the people of Marazion came Jack, who not only killed Cormoran, but went on to slay many more giants.

There are stories aplenty, but all I experience at St. Michael's Mount is calmness. I think of it as an oasis in the sea. One that I walk away from without sightings of giants, saints and spirits. I am the happier for it, and when I am upon the shores of Marazion again, I turn back for a ringside view of this fairy-tale island that looks like it may dissolve any second into a fantastic figment, a dream conjured up in one's fevered imagination.

***

The town of Marazion is a few miles from Mousehole. Located within Mount's Bay and reached via the A-road between Penzance and Helston, the place is bustling with the flavour of a small seaside village, when I awaken Adi. We sit by the beach watching dogs chase frisbees and each other, and children play in the sand, before we get off our backs to amble through its galleries and shops. Victorian houses line the main street of town. They have flawless views across Mount's Bay. The chapel in town is particularly pretty with its small bell tower as is the town hall with its startling red pipings.

We are peckish. Beer, fries, onion rings… just anything will do. The kind of devourables you can safely tuck into and yet keep space for a hearty dinner later on. Our pitstop is at *The King's Arms*, your atypical pub housed in an old property, made up of red carpeted floors, beers on tap, bentwood chairs, and neat wooden tables. From our cosy perch inside the pub, we espy a mournful spaniel sat at the window of a whitewashed cottage on the opposite side of the road, brown nose pressed to the glass. The signage on the cottage reads: *The Rigging*. Stocks of a nautical nature.

The waitress arrives at our table with a plate that has everyone's attention. Giant onion rings threaten to spill over the plate. I sense that this is tough on our neighbours, who are trying hard to look away nonchalantly, and failing a hundred per cent. There is no significant wait on our part. We fall upon the plate like gluttonous children who cannot keep their grubby hands off what they have been told that they cannot have. But we have the memo. We can have the forbidden plate of goodies. Ah, the unadulterated joy of being a grown-up.

Guilt is oceans away as we scoff perfectly batter-smothered rings of onion, the oil dribbling down our throats, and inviting generous swigs of the pints we have ordered to offer the onion rings emotional support. We have grown to favour these local ales that leave in their wake a fresh and bitter aftertaste.

Beyond an hour, the larger part of which one spends on St. Michael's Mount, there is not much to do in Marazion. I picture Craik's ill-concealed dismay when she arrived by boat to Marazion to stay at an old-fashioned inn. The Victorian traveller found only its name picturesque. As for the place itself, she described it as "the most commonplace little town imaginable" and its beach "small ugly fish-smelling". I suspect she would have found present-day Marazion more to her liking.

Craik was not alone in her disapproval of Marazion. During the early part of the 19th century, an English man of letter, W.H. Hudson, followed suit. He too wrote of it in less exalted tones in his book, *The Land's End*. Hudson observed: "Streets narrow and others narrower still, some straight, some very crooked, with houses on either side, mostly modern, all more or less commonplace in appearance."

Marghas Yow, the old name of Marazion, means 'Thursday Market'. It conjures up images of an awfully busy town that was furnished the status of market town by a royal charter as early as the 1200s.

I imagine life as it might have been in ancient Marazion. Tradespeople going about their daily work and the busy fisherfolk; pilgrims arriving in town and bound for the abbey, the Ultima Thule of their journeys; ancient Phoenicians arriving in town to buy ingots of tin (though some say that Phoenicians in Cornwall is a figment of some febrile imagination). Victorian holidaymakers who brought in the early crowds into town. A Nazi foreign minister travelling through town and losing his head over St. Michael's Mount. Joachim von Ribbentrop, Hitler's aide, had travelled through Cornwall in the '30s and envisioned living on the rock after the Nazis were done with mastering the world. And I come to the conclusion that Marazion remains a sort of a footnote in the chapter of St. Michael's Mount, of middling stature, yet not to be totally dismissed at any rate.

***

At the edge of St. Mount's Bay, the biggest of all bays in Cornwall, is the fishing village of Mousehole. Tiny it might be, but on no count should we miss out on its existence even though it foxes us on a couple of counts. To begin with, there's its name. It is a puzzle. Secondly, there is the business of locating it, tucked away as it is into a sheltered harbour below a hill. The road passing through the village of Paul dips into Mousehole. So, if perchance we did not know of its existence, and therefore had not gone looking for it, we should have surely passed by it without a thought.

But here I am, the queen of research. Intent on collecting bits and bobs of info about places before we even get there. I have to confess: I find it difficult to pull back. To know when to stop ferreting for particulars. Too much research can be a hindrance to the cause of travel, to the cause of being struck by wonder at discovering things for oneself, instead of muttering "I know" every time I spot something that I've already read about. Yet, the sole reason we are in Mousehole is because of this penchant of mine.

Parking is conveniently at the top of the village, at the parish church that serves the villages of Paul and Mousehole. St. Pol de Léon looks ancient. The churchyard surrounding its 15th century edifice is dotted with granite gravestones and cloaked in serenity. Resting below the plain gravestones are the skeletal shells of those who once lived. People who must have walked the streets we are about to venture down, who would have experienced love, hatred, jealousy, envy, happiness, bitterness. Yet when the time was ripe, they cast off the gamut of emotions that consume the frail human soul, along with their earthly bodies. Now, all that remains of them are headstones inscribed by loved ones. They are remembered.

I scour the names and the epitaphs on these headstones. Mute as they are, they tell stories of lives lived to the fullest, of some cut short by illness and by war, and of those who never got a chance to take the first steps of their mortal life. Some stones date back to WWII, others are older memorials, recalling those who died in the earlier centuries. They look the part; the inscriptions worn down by the passing years. Are there any graves here of the old smugglers of Mousehole, I wonder.

Customs books from Penzance, dating back to the period when smuggling peaked in Cornwall, refer to the fair number of smugglers who belonged to Mousehole and the neighbouring village of Newlyn. Most of them were fishermen by profession, in need of a side hustle to make a decent living. That smuggling was not just a figment of one's fancy is proven by the discovery of a tunnel in a 300-year-old cottage in Mousehole. It is presumed to have led to the harbour from where smugglers sneaked in contraband goods, hidden from the prying eyes of the revenue men.

I have no luck with spotting the graves of the free traders of Mousehole, but that would also be because their stones would have hardly declared them as smugglers (how daft of me!). I must have come upon them unwittingly. Easy to spot, however, outside the church is a tall granite memorial to a former village icon. The epitaph on it reads so.

> *"Here Lieth Interred Dorothy Pentreath who Died in 1777.*
> *Said to have been the last person who conversed in the ancient*
> *Cornish. The regular language of this county from the earliest records*
> *till it expired in the eighteenth century in this Parish of Saint Paul.*
> *This stone is erected by the Prince Louis Lucien Bonaparte in Union*
> *with the Revd. John Garret Vicar of St Paul.*
> *June 1860*
> *Honour thy Father and thy Mother that thy days may be long upon*
> *the land which the lord thy god giveth thee Exod. xx,12*
> *Gwra perthi de taz na mam de dythiow bethenz hyr war an tyr neb*
> *arleth de dew ryes dees. Exod. xx,12"*

Here we find whole sentences in Cornish. The tongue tangles and trips over these unfamiliar words. Yet for a philologist such as the French emperor's cousin, Prince Louis Lucien Bonaparte, on the lookout for dying languages, this must have been enchanting. His tribute was allegedly placed over the wrong grave in 1860. The error was corrected twenty-two years later when it was moved to its current location.

Such pother about a fisherwoman (who you have already been introduced to in the early chapters). I was curious. Turns out, Dolly was a fishwife from the village of Paul, who lived in Mousehole. Her fame came around the time that a British antiquarian and philologist by the name of Daines Barrington was touring the duchy. His quest was for a speaker of the Cornish tongue.

The year was 1768, and Barrington happened to meet a couple of biddies who informed him that their neighbour, Dolly Pentreath, was the woman he was looking for. In his letter to the Society of Antiquaries in London, Barrington revealed the particulars of his meeting with the 82-year-old Dolly. As a fisherwoman who sold her wares in nearby Penwith and Penzance, she was a colourful character. Dolly smoked a pipe and guzzled pints at the old Keigwin Arms in Mousehole. In fact, she lived in a small cottage near the pub. A former Mousehole resident, Bernard Victor, described Dolly Pentreath in his letters to an author from Plymouth who was compiling a glossary of Cornish words.

Victor wrote: "Though there were several of Dolly's neighbours who had an acquaintance with the old Cornish, she became more generally known as a living repository of the almost defunct language from her occupation as a fish-seller, or back-jouster, her particular vocation calling her to nearly all parts of the surrounding country, where the good, but perhaps parsimonious housewives, declining her terms, and refusing the fish, often drew from the ancient dame, in choicest Celtic, the outpourings of her wrath; for Dolly was a woman of spirit, and had a sharp tongue."

With this little backstory, it is easy to imagine the part of their conversation when Barrington questioned the authenticity of her claim. Was she really well-versed in Cornish? To Barrington's ears, she sounded so very Welsh. Dolly was cross. She swore, calling him *kronek hager du!* ("an ugly black toad").

Eventually, the antiquarian was convinced that Dolly had indeed been bred to the Cornish tongue. He proclaimed her to be the last speaker of Cornish. After Dolly's death, a fisherman from Mousehole called William Bodener wrote to Barrington about his knowledge of Cornish. Bodener penned a few sentences in Cornish to make good on his claim. He mentioned others he knew of, in Mousehole, who could converse in the old language.

But then, languages are that way. Born of the land, they tend to stick. Old Cornish itself is one of two branches of the Celtic language, one of which includes Irish and Gaelic of North Scotland, called Goidelic or Gaelic. The other branch, known as Brythonic, comprises Welsh, Breton and Cornish. Knowing this gives us perception about Barrington's confusion when Dolly sounded almost Welsh to his ears.

Legends grew around Dolly after her death at the age of 102. Of her hard face and her voice that rang as far as Newlyn. Her heart of lion that made her fight a press-gang that had arrived in Mousehole to recruit men for the navy with a hatchet and rain curses upon their heads with her remarkable Cornish vocabulary. And, of course, her famous last words of not wanting to speak the English tongue.

***

We descend into the village of the formidable old fisherwoman, through Mousehole Lane. The descent is steep, marked by hedges and granite cottages with grainy textured walls. The house fronts are trellised with plants and decorated with sprigs of bluebells and blooming roses. Planter pots hang off the eaves of cottages. Rustic garden sheds with signages ask the onlooker to give a wide berth to "grandad's shed".

The cottages are straight out of an artist's dream. I fall a little in love with Mousehole straightaway. Some of the house names allude to foxes. It makes me imagine the wily creatures sneaking around the narrow lanes of Mousehole, foraging around human establishments for food, messing with humans in their endeavours for survival.

Arriving upon the harbour is like stumbling upon a postcard-perfect scene. A live canvas an artist would be hard-pressed to replicate on paper. When we clap eyes upon it, the April sun is shining benign and a charming tableau is laid out before our eyes. Families sun themselves on the sandy strip of beach that runs alongside the inner harbour; tots build sandcastles; some splash in the startlingly clear waters that sparkle like jewels in palest hues of blues and greens. Simultaneously, as if to balance it out, there are serious conversations taking place nearby. A girl in pigtails is being told off by her father in a grown-up voice – no baby talk here. I can imagine her tiny lips quivering with indignation and eyes welling up with hot tears. I don't hang around to catch the after-effects of the scene.

In the shallow waters, small boats slumber. Two breakwaters keep the sea out; they are sturdy protectors separated by a small gap. The gap between the two is the mouse hole. But call it Mousehole, exactly as it is written, and you are rewarded with blank stares. I make the gaffe in a shop, which is suffused with the mixed aromas of too many candles. The woman behind the till looks bewildered when I say Mousehole (as it is spelt). I ask her, "Am I saying it wrong?"

At this tentative query, her face breaks into a grin and she replies, "Oh, but it is 'Mauzle'." "Mau-zle?" I repeat after her stupidly. I mull over it and decide that Mauzle certainly scores over the old name of the village, Porth Enys, meaning island port. I tide over the bemusement by way of gobbling down a fat cheese and onion pasty from one of the lichen-splotched houses that huddle around the harbour. The buttery shortbread crust of the pasty crumbles in my mouth delightfully as I watch the lone seagull standing upon an upturned boat. It too seems contemplative as it struts up and down, turns around, and resumes the course of strutting thoughtfully. An unlikely mendicant. Or should it be mafia? Probably devising ways of stealing the pasty from my clutches.

It is refreshingly tranquil in this working harbour from where men still set out to fish in the waters for their livelihood. Mousehole is almost entirely free of the crowds, which can be a tad stifling in towns like St. Ives at the peak of summer. It is part of the Cornish AONB zone. Once you walk into it, you will not be driven to ask why.

It is noon as my mister and I dawdle by the harbour. About a hundred and fifty odd years ago, Esquiros may have sat at the harbour as we do now and let his gaze glide over it. The workings of the harbour commanded his attention. He noticed fishermen lumbering over to the quay, with fishing nets hanging over their backs, and eventually spreading them out to dry. A woman in a light cotton dress and bonnet washed linen... The scenes have changed, with people basking in the sun for the most part, but the serenity remains intact in the middle of this unhurried pace of life, the kind you stumble upon only in a quaint village by the sea.

***

A certain kind of deception is at work in Mousehole. It is easy to be fooled by its present unassuming self where life is idyllic and a handful of eateries shares the harbour with *The Ship Inn* and *The Old Coastguard*, the two pubs in the village (its third pub, *The Kings Arms*, sits high above the village, but don't let that little fact distract you).

However, during the Anglo-Spanish war of 1585-1604, a 400-strong band of Spanish men arrived in the village. They did not bother to colonise it. Oh no, they decided to keep things simple. They razed it down.

Between the 14th and 16th century, before the Spanish marauders descended upon it in droves, Mousehole had enjoyed a position of distinction as a port in cohorts with its Mount's Bay neighbour, Marazion. At Mousehole's granite pier, French and Spanish ships were known to flock for pilchard oil and cured pilchards, but the destruction wrought by the Spanish was intense. Only one house was left standing in the entire village, *The Keigwin Arms*, which was then a pub. A plaque on its walls stays as a reminder. It states: *"Squire Jenkyn Keigwin was killed here 23rd July 1595 defending this house against the Spaniards."*

Legacies of its pilchard fishery days are preserved too. *The Old Pilchard Works* in the village is a luxury B&B in the present day. It is a spiffier avatar of the pilchard press that it served as in the old days. The original version would have been a tottering shed. Picture a roof held together by solid beams of wood, balanced upon crudely cobbled-together stone walls, where women would have pressed pilchards onto beds of coarse salt lining the cellar floors, before washing them and packing the lot into barrels called hogsheads.

Netting the pilchards was a game honed to perfection by the fishermen. The fish required careful attendance. The Cornish naturalist Jonathan Couch, a grandfather of writer Arthur Quiller Couch, had written a book titled *A History of the Fishes of the British Islands*, considered to be unparalleled in its genre and time. Couch had studied the migration pattern of the pilchards. According to him, they travelled west of the Isles of Scilly in winter, nestling in the depths of the ocean there. By summer they started moving in massive shoals, splitting up in places, with schools of pilchards migrating towards the Cape of Cornwall and other schools reaching Land's End from where they drifted into the English Channel.

Off the Channel, the fishermen of Mousehole and Newlyn lay in wait. When they spotted the colour of the water changing to a reddish hue – in shoals, the pilchards were phosphorescent – on the darkest of nights, the fishermen would set off in their boats.

The return of the men at dawn marked a change of personality in this otherwise calm village. The bustle of the fish market in the early hours of the morning must have been a sight to behold. The fishermen in their sturdy sea boots and oilskin waterproofs, the women ferrying loads of fish from the boats to the beach, fish buyers elbowing each other. With the arrival of the last fishing boat and the exit of the hawkers, the village would have returned to its former mood of quietude.

Since the mid-20th century, pilchard fishing has dwindled, with lesser demand for the fish. Nowadays, the fishermen net catches of mackerel, pollack, bass and conger.

Come December 23, a curious pie is baked in the ovens of Mousehole. Fish heads poke out of the crust of this custard pie, their inert eyes gaping at the stars. Stargazy Pie. Your first reaction, naturally, would be baulk at this strange dish. "What a spectacle!" you exclaim. And it is that. A spectacle alright. But it is a pie beloved of locals, enriched with bacon, potatoes, and hard-boiled eggs.

The backstory here is a famine that the village was threatened with in the past. No one can tell the exact date and year, but the story has been handed down the generations that a villager called Tom Bawcock braved the stormy seas to bring back a catch of sardines, in order to help tide the famine. In celebration, his catch was baked into one pie with the upturned pilchards sticking out of the dish. The occasion, Tom Bawcock's Eve, is so well entrenched in local memory that it continues to be celebrated in the present day.

In a way, there's honesty baked into the Stargazy Pie, along with flamboyance. You know you will be eating fish – and with it, plenty of pints of beer. We want to eat this pie (despite the fish heads) and return to this ancient place, but for now our part is to trudge up the hill back to the car park and try not to grow wistful. For who knows when we shall find ourselves in this oddball of a village again.

XVIII

A Georgian Port Town

One of the days, we take it quite so slow. We spend time, resting our feet in the byre, barbecuing meats on the grill outside and walk around the farm. It is nice to take a break from all the information that jostles for space in the brain, when one is constantly making mental notes of sights gathered on one's travels. But as I rifle idly through the pages of brochures collected earlier, I see photos of the nearby town of Charlestown. Some connection with *Poldark* and all that, it states. I am in. Adi gives in too, once he realises that the driving time should be minimal. Charlestown is only seven miles away from Lostwithiel.

The midday sun beats down upon us by the time we get into Charlestown. For respite from it, we nose around the musty corridors of the antique stores. Not many people are to be spotted in this old port establishment near the market town of St. Austell. Have we been transported back in time to the late 1700s when just about 9 people resided in this quiet village? I would have no quibbles about it. The lack of the early spring crowds is a welcome note and I take to Charlestown quite easily.

Our first sight, as we near its inner harbour, are of a couple of square-riggers. The tall ships are not rigged up, but they make for a dramatic picture nonetheless. They speak volumes of solid craftsmanship, built as they were to work the open seas, carry cargo and sailors, battle stormy weather. And here they are now, post-retirement period pieces, enjoying their time under the sun.

The celebrity of the lot docked in Charleston is *The Phoenix*, built in the late '20s in Denmark. From offering passage to missionaries and transporting cargo, she has made the jump to films, her vintage charm pegging her as a favourite with those in the business of making cinema.

In the backdrop of the harbour are historic Georgian properties and pretty fishermen's cottages. I see why Charlestown is a popular filming town. Indeed, I cannot shake off the feeling that I have stumbled into a perfectly togged-up film set.

If the past is a big part of the present, it is particularly so in Charlestown. It was a humble fishing village to start with, comprising two farms known as Higher and Lower Polmear. There were all of three cottages here. The harbour that we see today came later and it had a different name then too. Pilchards were its mainstay (no surprises). The nine-odd residents of the village had to be fishermen you think.

Charlestown's days in the sun began when a Menabilly-born Rashleigh, Charles Rashleigh – who belonged to a line of entrepreneurial men – decided to develop the village as a port town. He teamed up with a renowned civil engineer of his day, John Smeaton. It is Smeaton who hit upon the idea of a deep-water harbour. When the port town was done up to his satisfaction, Rashleigh arranged for the export of copper from the local mines, of which there were a few around. Naturally, the village was referred to as Charles's Town, before villagers decided to call it Charlestown.

Wandering around town, we spot the local pub, *The Rashleigh Arms*, which does its bit in harking back to the founder of Charlestown. What better way to have your name remembered than when it adorns a pub sign!

Now, given its history as a look-out point for invaders from the days of the Napoleonic wars, Rashleigh had a cliff-top gun battery installed above Charlestown. But it turned to be more of a huer's hangout. He used the spot for his customary job of alerting fishermen to the presence of shoals of pilchards.

The fortunes of Charlestown were closely tied to the discovery of china clay in the St. Austell area, by a chemist from Devon, William Cookworthy. As mining dwindled, the town turned to the export of china clay, essentially a form of decomposed granite and used in the production of porcelain, paper, textiles, and other industries. China clay brought prosperity to Charlestown, allowing affiliated businesses to crop up alongside. Shipbuilding, brickmaking, rope making, pilchard curing. By the early 20th century, the number of residents in Charlestown had peaked to a count of 3,000 and above. The business of exporting china clay eventually petered out in Charlestown, but its legacy is a network of tunnels that transported clay to the harbour and have recently been discovered beneath the Shipwreck Museum in town.

The bustle of its china clay trading days now relegated to the past, there is not much happening in Charlestown nowadays than when film crews swing into town. The coverage in shows like *Poldark* and its UNESCO world heritage site status means that tourists do throng it, however locals have not taken kindly to the idea of fishing out drunks who have been known to plop into the harbour.

The wrap-up note for me in Charlestown is not up to my taste. Before we take off, I nip into the public toilet for a wee. While I am in the midst of it, a woman flings open the door and walks in – just like that. A door that I have surely locked. Hot flushes wash over my body in waves, and oh, I want to disappear. Every atom of energy in my body is focussed on taking flight, but it turns out to be bit of a challenge when caught in a toilet with your pants down.

I cannot even begin to think of an incident that can topple this one from the top spot in a list of things that are bound to leave me cringing every time I think of them. For the sake of hypothesis, let me have a quick think. There was that time when I decried the parquet flooring of an apartment to a friend who lived in a similar flat, and did my best to babble about what I Really meant; another time, I stood at a bar in Oxford, tipsy, brimming with love for my fellow human beings, and I said to a bartender, who happened to be easy on the eye, 'I love your man' (the unhappy coincidence was that this was witnessed by my husband who never fails to snicker at the memory); the most potent one though might be that time when I laid out a paper filled with cuss words to dry on the dining table of my childhood home, so that my father eventually picked it up and realised that his 14-year-old daughter was prolific in more ways than he had given her credit for. Which meant that my father roared, carried on with tearing up the precious list, and, right after, gave me a solid whopping. In my father's defence, he has hardly ever slapped me. That was my mother's department.

I have a long list (for your sake, I had to put the brakes on it before it got out of hand) to fall back upon for the sake of comparison. But this event being heart-stopping, both of us scream. The girl who has walked in on me, runs out as quickly. The only good news for me in all of this is that the episode occurs as we are about to take our leave of Charlestown. I escape it without meeting the girl again. A stranger who shall at best remain that. A stranger.

Goodbye Charlestown, you lovely old Georgian town. I don't think I can forget you even if I tried to.

XIX

The Old Mines and the Sea

One morning, we arrive at Botallack, in the far west of the county. The best of all the mines was once to be found here. It is a spectacular spot still.

Empty shells of former engine houses have endured the lengthy strides of time at Botallack. It has been a while since they have been productive, but they continue to cling to the sides of steep cliffs that rise stridently above the Atlantic. And even as they crumble away, the ruins serve as relics attesting to man's industry, harking to a time when he eked bread from the bowels of the earth.

Mining can be traced back to the Bronze Ages in this part of the country. The Cornish have always been people of the earth, mining for tin and copper being an ancient vocation in the south west of Britain, dating back to 2000 BC in counties like Devon and Cornwall. By the 18th and 19th centuries, Cornwall was producing millions of tons of copper and tin. At the peak of the mining industry during the 19th century, Cornwall had 2,000 working mines. They employed entire families. The men worked underground, while the women who were called Bal Maidens, worked above the ground. They were accompanied by young girls and boys, some of whom swept arsenic from the calciner flues. The boys, when considered old enough, were dispatched to the mines to work alongside the men.

The seriousness afforded to the profession was such that as early as 1201, the Charter of Liberties ceded the right to the tinners of Devon and Cornwall to scour for tin in any open land. The charter also exempted them from military service and certain laws of the land, while allowing them the privilege of paying lower taxes.

We already know that this age-old profession of the Cornish was important enough to be captured in St. Piran's banner, or the flag of Cornwall. St. Piran, the patron saint of miners, is said to have rediscovered tin smelting by virtue of a chance incident when his black hearth stone, which contained tin ore, got so hot that tin spurted from it. A feast is held annually in the saint's honour. And as you would imagine, wine flows at this even because …oh well, you have got this one.

In Botallack, the day is turning out to be glorious. The sun is shining lustily from skies that look freshly washed. Salty ocean air saturates our senses, as Adi and I explore an ancient landscape made of stone and furze. A land marked by chimneys, scarred by rubble, that men have gouged for underground treasures of copper, tin and lead, for thousands of years before economic depression set in. The land that in the present is the haunt of the peregrine falcon and the chough.

Of its 400-mile long coastline, the tin coast in Cornwall occupies a seven-mile stretch, which in a manner serves as a conduit for dialogues with the past as it throws up remnants of the industrial era. Engine houses and chimneys turn up along the walk, arsenic calciners and stamps dot the coastal landscape. For the most part they look dilapidated. Their cultural significance however is not lost upon anybody who recognises the hold that the past exerts upon the human mind. This part of the coast has been classified as a UNESCO World Heritage Site.

Alongside, it has been accorded the Coastal Community Status. This means that local communities care for the ruins. Maybe that is way to go for preservation of old monuments. Get locals involved.

Our explorations begin at the car park itself, where there is a Count House workshop. In it, during the 19th century a carpenter would have worked, before the mine shut shop in 1895 (following a terrible accident in which twenty miners perished). Next to the carpenter's workshop, at the Count House, miners would have queued up to collect their pay, and here sumptuous dinners would have been laid out for shareholders on days when accounts had to be browsed and approved. Nowadays, people rent the Count House for a few nights as a base from which one may potter about the beautiful tin coastline.

In the workshop, currently a National Trust property, one can stop for a quick bathroom stop and a cream tea. Relief and delight at a go. Beneath the wooden rafters of the stone building that houses the workshop, there is a small exhibit of photographs from yesteryears. Grimy faces of miners stare back at us, their eyes shining through faces darkened with soot, others less smutty, some with pipes jammed in their mouths. Would they have imagined that cream tea would be sold here – here, where they were used to the sounds of wood being hacked and sawed?

Leaving the Count House behind, we sight a series of chambers upon the cliffs, adjoining which a chimney stack aims for the sky. Being creatures of visual pleasure, I believe you would like to see the weather-beaten structures with your own two eyes, to get the true measure of the landscape. What I can do however is concoct for you a visual through the workings of my imagination. That in the past the chimney belted out fumes of sulphur and arsenic into the open skies, and below it in the chambers, arsenic was extracted in labyrinths. The deadly poison was a by-product of tin extraction from its ore and was sold as an insecticide. It was especially exported to North America, where it was used against boll weevil that afflicts cotton production.

The part which tantalises us is the neck of land that projects from the cliffs and dips into a headland below. This strip of land, which shoots into the Atlantic before joining up with the headland, looks too narrow for comfort from where I am on the cliffs. Almost instantly, I want to go ahead with it no more. But Adi will not be deterred. He starts descending the strip, and naturally, I follow in his steps, a lamb to the slaughter. Gusts of wind as if favour his decision and push us onward.

As we near the narrow neck of the promontory, it starts to appear less intimidating. But the trail is still remarkably narrow, with a sheer drop on both sides. I peek down one side of this strip and see ocean waves surging against the rocks, regurgitating flecks of foam like a frothing sea creature. It is a magnificent sight, but it is easier to pull back and not look down twice. We carry on and find ourselves at the tip of the promontory.

Before us is the ocean, poetically blue. On the right-hand side, it cuts into a deep gully. The wind rips through my hair, leaving it in tangles, and I feel like a wild child standing at the edge of land, hypnotised by the view that has surfaced before the eyes. The uncontained wildness of nature is alluring and intimidating simultaneously.

Across us are the two engine houses, clinging to the adjacent cliffs on different levels. The electric blue waters of the ocean churn endlessly beneath dark boulders and the waves are tempestuous as they slap the rocks endlessly, disappearing in curls of white foam. The contrast between the colours of the ocean and the dark rocks coated with yellow lichen is most pleasing to the eyes.

The Crowns Engine Houses, formerly of the mines at Botallack, are ours for the noon. There is no one around. The husband declares it to be one for the books. He proceeds to hoist himself upon an outcrop of rock that juts out at an odd angle from the edge of the headland we are on. It is an endearing (and annoying) quality of his to push the boundaries of my comfort zone. After a few customary protests, I give in, my outlook being this that we might as well tip over together than one left behind to mourn the loss of the other. It is not uncommon in the south west for entire sections of cliffs to fall into the ocean.

Sat upon our precarious perch, we wonder at the sheer ingenuity of man, his genius at figuring out a way of exploiting treasures lodged deep within the earth, to as if make nature count. Was it an element of hubris that led miners to soldier on in the face of the harshness of his environment? Maybe the ancient Athenians had a point about this flaw born of the intrepidity of man.

"So, this is Grambler," I murmur. The mind is wandering to Winston Graham's *Poldark*, envisioning another time and place when the landscape would not have worn this air of tranquillity. When the scene would have been grimy and thick with industrial activity. In my mind's eye, I see a trail of carts proceeding to and from the paths skirting the cliffs, the air rent by the deafening sounds of blasting, the crushing of ore. The general chaos is intensified by the clanging of pumping engines as they lift water from great depths to prevent waterlogging in the mines. These are melded with the sounds from the mills working nearby; of smiths hammering metal; even as the engines and the arsenic chambers belch smoke furiously. There, do you hear the bell announcing the change of the shifts? Do you see them now, the row of men in sooty clothes making their way down to the mines, in hand candles (to be stuck with clay upon their hard hats) and bagged pasties for lunch?

In his novel, *Ross Poldark,* Graham wove into the narrative the plight of the miners who climbed "ant-like a hundred fathoms of rickety ladders, sweat-covered and stained with rusty markings of the mineral rock or the black fumes of blasting powder". The workers, he pointed out, would take half an hour or more to come to the surface carrying their tools, and on the way up, they would inevitably be drenched with water spewing from leaky pumps. After this exhausting exercise of reaching the surface of the earth, they had before them a further three to four-mile walk through the wind and rain to their dwellings.

I am fascinated by the zeal of the Victorians. Spurred by curiosity, they made the effort of exploring these mines. Even the Prince and Princess of Wales at the time is recorded to have undertaken a journey down the shafts of Botallack. You could almost say that the mines had celebrity status, for the who's who of the times had mine trips chalked up on their been-there-done-that list. To achieve a visit to the mines then would have been say the equivalent of trotting into the Met Gala. Only in the case of mine visits, the gear required getting used to.

Of those who ventured into the underbelly of the earth, some wrote about their experiences prolifically. Wilkie Collins preceded me by a hundred and sixty-seven years, having visited Botallack in the year 1850. His Cornish friends had described it to him as the most extraordinary mine in Cornwall. He reached Botallack with great expectations, and an artist friend in tow, their first view of it, as noted by Collins being "as striking and extraordinary as the first view of the Cheese-Wring (a granite tor in Liskeard) itself".

Collins' was the view of nature tamed by man. In his book, *Rambles Beyond Railways*, he wrote: "Chains, pipes, conduits, protruded in all directions from the precipice; rotten-looking wooden platforms, running over deep chasms … There did not appear to be a foot of level space anywhere…"

Mine is free of the industry of man, but for the crumbling remnants of his design on nature.

***

The most scenic of all the mines in Cornwall must be at Botallack. There are two engine houses here located along the sides of a headland that has been chiselled by the ocean over a narrow sea-inlet, referred to as *zawn* in West Country lingo. These zawns reveal vertiginous cliff sides, streaked with veins of mineral reserves. Once, zawns served as identification points for miners, giving them an idea about rock faces that were potential sites for "streaming", for the acquisition of ore. As much as these zawns of granite would have excited miners, today they fire up the imagination of climbers seeking rushes of adrenalin.

As with most good things in life, the engine houses are best appreciated from afar.

When we have had our fill of the headland views, we start back toward the cliffs and aim for the engine houses, following a winding path that hugs the side of the cliffs. The Lower Engine House is in close quarters of the ocean. It was economical for mine shafts to be sunk as close as possible to mineral lodes. Thus, pumping engines were propped nearer sea level to reduce the distance over which water had to be pumped out. But to breach the Lower Engine House is tough, so we climb back up the trail and carry on to the Upper Engine House where I fancy myself as an agile goat and walk along its ledges, peeking into its granite interiors. The insides quail at the thought of plumbing its inky black depths — I cannot even spot a ladder plumbing its depths. Yet men did it every day of their lives in fair and foul weather. They went down this very inclined shaft that plummeted below the sea.

At this submarine mine of Botallack, the tunnels covered a distance spanning 2,500 feet. Ponies were sent down the shafts too. Only unlike men, the poor creatures stayed on for months at a time below the earth. As man and animal worked hard on extracting metal from the underground, the sea, ever present, pounded above their heads.

Collins had descended the ladders inside this very shaft. Accompanied by his friend and a miner guide, the author explored the galleries that ran below the sea, in miner's clothing that he declared as "Brobdingnagian" on his five-feet-six-inch body. They journey through surroundings slippery with water and copper-ooze, "the voice of the miner below, rumbling away in dull echoes lower and lower into the bowels of the earth — the consciousness that if the rounds of the ladder broke, you might fall down a thousand feet or so of narrow tunnel in a moment…". Eventually, they were a hundred and twenty feet below sea level, conscious of the fact that trading vessels sailed above their heads. Two hundred and forty feet beneath them, men were at work. Beneath those men were embedded even deeper galleries. You would be hard pressed not to be filled with disquiet at the description of the sounds that the subterranean explorers described, as "unlike anything that is heard on the upper ground, in the free air of heaven; so sublimely mournful and still;" And the fact that all that kept the sea out was a knob of wood "as thick as a man's leg" jammed into a hole.

Our own dilemma centres around finding access to the Lower Engine House, the purpose of which was to pump up water out of the shaft. There is no way of going down these engine houses in the present time. The shortest way from the Upper Engine House is surely to slide down the craggy rocks that tumble into its lower counterpart, but this not being the equivalent of taking a joyride, we forego the option. Broken necks, with no hope of rescue, teamed with tempestuous waves and only the red-billed choughs for company, do not make for an attractive incentive. The husband decides that he has got to make one final effort to reach it.

When you have lived long enough with your partner, you know the way the strings work. I do not waste breath dissuading him. I let him go down that ribbon of a path twirling around the cliffs, before it disappears around the edge. A path that is horribly slippery with mud. I know because I have tried walking up and down it and turned back for the sake of avoiding foolhardy actions. Before Adi leaves, I simply ask him to leave the car keys behind. That's all.

***

From the Crowns Engine Houses, if you carry on walking south, you pass by Wheal Owles, Ross Poldark's "Wheal Leisure" and some others, before reaching the mining town of St. Just with its huddle of workers' weathered granite cottages and charming market square. But we – Adi having decided not to go down the tricky bend in the cliffs (aha) - take the coastal path north, past the Levant and Geevor Mines. Stony tracks lead us through miles of furze, remnants of old mine workings, and abandoned shafts. The calling of the chough accentuates the solitary aspect of our environment. The startling blue of the North Atlantic alongside adding character to our meanderings as we press on through a bleak landscape of rubble and rough vegetation. Only once, do we sight someone. A photographer with his tripod setting up a vantage point among the rocks.

The Levant and Geevor mines are educative stops for insights into the lives of miners who worked in cramped conditions, into the kind of awful accidents that took place in the shafts in which men perched themselves upon ledges to work man engines. The engines carried men up and down the shafts - instead of the ladders that Collins had climbed earlier in the day. The shafts made it easier for workers to return quickly to the surface. Their pay was calculated based upon the time at which they emerged. Lives were often hinged upon the fate of an iron cap or a bolt. If there was a malfunction in the engine, columns of men stood at risk of being crushed to death. An example of it was the dreadful accident that took place in the Levant mines in 1919.

In an issue of the *Cornishman And Cornish Telegraph,* a miner from St. Just narrated his experienced from the day when 31 miners were killed, as the connecting link between the beam and the wooden rod of the shaft of the man-engine broke. He was one of the 120 men who were making their way up from a day shift. The miner recalled: "When the engine broke it was a tremendous crash for in dropping she knocked away timber and everything else in her path. The engine rod on which we were traveling shook violently…The screams of some of the men were awful, as they gripped the rod like grim death…I wouldn't go through an experience like that again for the world." To his credit, the miner had hauled himself and a 25-year-old friend, who had fainted on one of the platforms below him, to safety.

Life for the miners would have been hazardous, not entirely unimaginable given that their job involved descending into the belly of the earth, working all the while in dusty, damp and humid conditions. Many died from wasting diseases. Silicosis, tuberculosis and rheumatism were common afflictions. Others suffered from deafness. There were injuries from rockfall and falls down the ladder. Arsenic poisoning would have been a serious concern for those working in calciners, poorly protected as they were by lengths of cloth roughly wrapped around their heads, not unlike mummies with bandages shrouding their faces. The men were not alone in their endeavour. They were supported by their families and worked 10-hour days, except on Sundays. Their incentive was the pay, which is said to have been good for the times.

A mile and a half from Geevor, where the last of the mines in the region ceased operations in the '90s, is stood a fetching white lighthouse near the village of Pendeen. It is said to have stood for over a hundred years along the inhospitable coastline, steering many a ship to safety with its oil lamp, and steep our senses in the remoteness of the landscape around us. For miles, chimney stacks stick out from the craggy landscape. And around us are the vast moors; their only residents, a herd of wild ponies. Curious shaggy fellows, who come by for a spot of conversation.

***

There are plenty of tin mines dotting the far west in Cornwall with names that ring with character and hope. Wheal Prosper, Wheal Harmony, Wheal Fortune are just a few, the word 'Wheal' implying 'place of work' in Cornish, but Wheal Coates in St. Agnes captures our attention.

Its location is possessed of inexplicable beauty. At the time we reach the car park at Chapel Porth, careful not to step into an adjacent field that harbours an angry bull within its perimeters, or so a plaque warns us at any rate, the sun is dissolving into the sea in a burst of orange and pink. We are on a steep slope athwart cliffs which swoop into the ocean below. Sandwiched between the ocean and this rugged descent is an engine house.

Privy as I am to the inner workings of my husband, it should come as no surprise that he figures a faster way down to the engine house. "Let's cut across the slope. Come now," he urges. Then he looks at my expression and figures he needs to belt out words of reassurance. "It's not too bad, come hold my hand," he adds, as one would to an addled child. Be it upon my head for taking his words at face value.

Halfway down the slope, I start wailing like a banshee, my feet unsure of conquering crumbly stones. I sit down, refusing to budge until Adi convinces me that the only way is to get it over with. He pulls me to my feet, but I break out on my own, determined to find a safer path down to the engine house. Which I achieve, but not before I have zig-zagged all along the trail, taking many a detour till I find my feet on reliable ground. I do not think I have ever felt more relief at reaching any other engine house than I do Wheal Coates.

The Towanroath Shaft engine house is silent this evening, bathed in the golden glow of sunset. It is a lonely outpost on the cliffs, just as its many counterparts, serving as quiet sentinels in the vast loneliness of a melancholic landscape. One can imagine the spirits of miners, some of whom died in the mines more than 200 years ago, trapped by the very tranquillity of this place. How do you leave such impossible beauty behind? Anyway, superstition has always been a way of life in Cornwall.

Miners were wary of 'knockers', spirits of dead tinners that lived in the galleries underground. According to local lore, they looked like goblins, these knockers, and were kitted up as miners. They made knocking sounds in the mines, which led some to consider them as warnings before things went south as it was not uncommon for walls and timber to cave in upon workers. As a reward for their services, miners tossed the last bits of their pasties to the knockers.

There are conflicting legends about the little folk of Cornwall, but they travelled with miners when large numbers of the community migrated to the New World, as mining lost value in these parts of the Old World that had once supplied the world with tin and copper.

Roughly 49,421 acres of the tin coast have been accorded World Heritage Site status and it is not difficult to believe there were once 2,000 tin mines strewn around the coast of Cornwall. Plummeting prices of tin, and mass migration of miners (called "Cousin Jacks") to other countries, led to the last of the mines shutting operations in the late '90s. The door was closed. Upon a way of life that had sustained the Cornish for generations, a dangerous way of life in which men habitually, almost contemptuously, tested their mettle against the steely resolve of nature.

XX

The Lighthouse on Trevose Head

Lighthouses are by nature hauntingly lonely. I would not be alone in finding them arresting; neither would I be alone in romanticising about living in one of those statuesque, albeit solitary structures that hug perfidious coastlines. Built to be independent, built to battle the bluster of sea winds and wild waves on their own, built to guide sailors to safety, the sole purpose of a lighthouse is to show up as a beacon of hope on nights when hope is the last thing in the minds of sea voyagers, caught unawares by the vastness of water. I find a strange kinship with lighthouses. Maybe because I find more pleasure in my reclusive life as a writer as opposed to my erstwhile life of attending news events and interviewing celebrities.

The loneliest of lighthouses in the British Isles is the South Stack Lighthouse at Anglesey in Wales. It might have something to do with its location, perched as it is upon a small islet off the cliffs of Anglesey. The islet is connected to the mainland by a bridge. At South Stack, we met more puffins, guillemots, choughs and kittiwake than we sighted humans. There was the matter of the lighthouse caretaker telling us about things she had seen at the lighthouse, phenomena she could not explain. But less of the beguiling Welsh lighthouse and more of its Cornish counterpart that we are off to.

Five miles west of Padstow, we pootle down the B3276 through farming country, networked by grids of fallow land. Vast serrated slabs of chocolate interspersed with green pastures. The colours of nature come together to sing to the senses. There is such goodness in it. Nothing is contrived. Thoughts flow and the mind floats free in the middle of such unfettered beauty.

On days when the sky is a dome of sparkling blue, clear of passing clouds, the countryside as if reaches out to the horizon to get a measure of its loveliness. After a point of time, when this scenic display starts to lose its edge and the mind begins to wander, beyond the edges of cliffs that roll off into golden bays with their outcrops of dark volcanic rocks, the Atlantic shows up. An infinite stretch of cobalt blue.

Enough bays and coves are left along the way so that we began to lose count. Trevone, Newtrain, Harlyn. The names fly at us, fingerposts marking the lanes winding into each bay. The arterial B-road that we are on has nothing much going on in the way of habitation, except for the scant presence of an inn and a holiday park hosting very few caravans. All along we have been skirting the SWCP. It really is a most marvellous trail, inspiring one to dream of walking along its entire length through four counties. Some day.

Soon after Trevose headland and somewhere near Polventon Bay, also called Mother Ivy's Bay after a local white witch, we traverse a bylane and find ourselves at the entrance to a large-ish house constructed in the Art Deco style. It is white and modern and stands out fairly in this part of the country where most cottages are built along traditional design aesthetics. Its view of the cove and ocean is mesmerising. Then, realising that we are trespassing for this is private property, we turn around, keen not to incur the wrath of a stranger. Later, I find out that the house belongs to Rick Stein. His father had built it before the onset of WWII as a holiday home for the family. Nowadays, it serves as a holiday let.

In the matter of a few minutes we are on the road back towards Trevose headland and faced by the tell-tale signs of a lighthouse, its lantern room glinting in the sunlight and emerging above the hump of a green hill. Trevose Head Lighthouse, a glimmer of hope during the 19th century for sea-borne men sailing the waters between Land's End and Lundy, off the coast of North Devon.

It is less isolated than the other lighthouses I have set eyes upon. It being imperative that we examine it up close – both of us cannot leave anything unseen, unless caves are in question, for then Adi will bow out — we amble over to the north-west tip of the headland that sits above cliffs of dark granite, to have a better look at the lighthouse. A few whitewashed cottages squat around its foot, the former offices, storerooms and living quarters of its lighthouse keepers; in present times, rented out as self-catered holiday units.

I am curious about the stories associated with it, but there is no way of rooting them out. We see no one at the lighthouse. No keepers, no visitors. The lighthouse turns out to be off limits for the general public, but the landscape around it, gently sloping off into the ocean are not off bounds. We plant ourselves on the green cover, dawdling and staring at the waterscape, wondering why the bay beneath carries the strange moniker of 'Stinking Cove'. Push the imagination and you will find it plausible to picture the lighthouse as it must be inside. A winding staircase, the ascent of steep steps taking you past the machinery room, the dwelling room and ancillary rooms, to the watch room right at the top the tower. A chamber sheathed in glass. The centre-stage of it being a lantern that is magnified so many times over that its light reaches those adrift on sea. Beckoning them to terra firma.

Imagine a sea mist creeping in wraithlike over a darkened coastline. On certain nights of the year, impenetrable fog descends like a pall of gloom upon the ocean just off Cornwall. On such grim occasions, and on wild stormy nights, sailors would be pressed to give these craggy shores a wide berth. And it is on nights like these that even a glimmer of light emanating from the lighthouse or the sound of gunfire would have been crucial to the survival of countless mariners.

Laid on our backs on the slopes of Trevose, we fantasise about living in a lighthouse. How would we deal with it? Thoughts are kicked back and forth. Adi easily opts out. It is not for him and he does not need to give it a second thought, he says. I mull. The job of a lighthouse keeper would have involved hardships in the old days when oil lanterns were in use. I think of the plight of the keeper, that state of constant alert, the responsibility to keep the flame stoked in the lantern, to snuff it on time. Oh, the monotonous nature of his life.

To give you an example, I would have to channel Esquiros, who recounted in his book a story he had heard about a lighthouse keeper. The man had lived for forty years in Eddystone Lighthouse. And he had spent most of his leaves at the lighthouse off Plymouth in the English Channel, so when the time came for him to live on the mainland, he had little idea on how to go about it. "As long as he had been on the rock and in his stone dungeon, he had behaved well – ashore he found himself in a strange land, and doubtless, to drown his grief, gave way to habits of intoxication. He was taken back in that state to Eddystone Lighthouse, in the hope that he would recover his senses and temperate habits there. After languishing for some days he died," noted Esquiros.

Despite all my romantic notions of it, the life of a lighthouse keeper - just as for my husband - is not for me too.

The wind is naughty, rather blustery above this isolated patch of land. It makes us get off our backs, but not before we have taken a good look at the landscape around. Adjacent to Trevose Head is a promontory covered with a vegetation of wild asparagus and gorse. Dinas Head. Beyond it, rocks and islets jut out from the ocean, with curious names such as 'The Bull' and 'The Quies', and their vast potential to rip out bottoms of unfortunate ships. They have fulfilled this potential, alright.

Later, while scouring the BBC's archival records on the Second World War, I come upon a random piece of information related to The Bull and The Quies that makes me smile. A man on leave from a naval training ship narrates the story of his having witnessed the spraying of bullets on the waters between The Bull and The Quies by a Luftwaffe plane, sometime in 1941. In the days that followed, shoals of dead fish washed up ashore. These were promptly sourced by the RAF messes for a fishy kinda feast.

**

Twenty minutes by car from Trevose Head, something astonishing comes our way. Bedruthan Steps.

The mythic stomping grounds of the giant Bedruthan who jumped from stack to stack in a hurry to get somewhere; probably, an outcome of the fantastic imagination of some Victorian advertiser who wanted to draw the crowds to the spot, at a time when the railways had connected London to the duchy. The site of a working mine in the 1800s. Of all these bits of information, I can say little with authority. In the moment, it is a place where magic takes place as we climb the cliffs and our eyes rest upon stately stacks of granite, rising like devilishly dark figures from a golden beach. This spectacular landscape lies within the ancient parish of St. Eval. In the earliest written records dating back to the 14th century, it was known as Bodruthyn, or 'Ruthyn's dwelling'. Its present name can be traced to a local weekly newspaper, *The West Briton*, which in 1847 mentioned the "steps" for the first time.

The cove at Bedruthan was privately owned. Now it is a National Trust property. A 19th century book, *Complete Parochial History of the County of Cornwall,* authored by William Lake, named the former owners as Mr. Humphrey Williams, Esq of Carnanton and Mr. Drew of Canhewas. The latter had started a clifftop mine that was called Carnewas Mine. It is said to have yielded a blend of silver and copper, along with iron, lead and antimony. And it is to make way for the miners to reach the beach — these mining sites being near the low water mark — that staircases were cut into the rock.

Hence, Bedruthan Steps.

We find the way down from the cliffs to the beach below. A few hundred steps teetering down to the sands. Oh, but they look alarming. A perpendicular drop of steps that is sandwiched between mesh-netted, sheer cliff faces. Feeling wildly adventurous, we take it upon ourselves to descend them. Utter tomfoolery because the steps plunge to the bottom. Also, they are wet and slippery. Anyone with half a brain shall not take them on. Our two halves at work here, almost halfway down, we turn tail and climb back to the clifftop. Clumps of pink thrift sway in the wind, welcoming us back from a horrid fate.

The tide sweeps in fast here and when it does, getting stuck on the steps is not an adventure you want to be caught in the middle of. Or, lying at the bottom of the steps with broken necks. What unappetising thoughts, but you see, it takes a moment for things to go awry. I quail to think of miners hurrying up and down the steps. There must have been bad accidents here.

The preservation of the steps itself is a tale of man's constant tussle with nature. The steps have often been barred for public use over the years because they tend to crumble in the face of the elements. During the '90s, about twenty feet of the stairs was washed away by the waters. I believe we are fortunate to have gone down even a portion of them because they have been roped off again due to a cliff fall in February 2020.

Others before me have been overwhelmed by the steps. Take a London-born traveller from the 19th century, Charles G. Harper. In his book *The Cornish Coast*, Harper wrote: "Rude flights of steps, cut into the profile of the cliffs, and fortified here and there by a crazy iron or timber hand rail." Harper was a true son of his age. The Victorians made a beeline for the nearby resort town of New Quay, when passenger trains started bringing Londoners into this part of Cornwall. Naturally, they chanced upon the landscape at Bedruthan comprising the astonishing rock stacks and began arriving in droves. An astute local farmer decided to capitalise on the curiosity of the Londoners. He charged toll and provided stalls for the horses.

(Nowadays, New Quay has a different sort of clientele. The town brims with raucous revellers on summer weekends. We keep going back to it time and again, but our reason is more to do with a certain restaurant, Lenny Leong's Malay Chinese at Shanghai Express, than party with the laddies.)

At Bedruthan Steps, we have codged up a couple of quid for two hours' parking at the National Trust car park near Bedruthan Steps. If you are a National Trust member, you pay nothing. The National Trust shop and the Carnewas tearooms have both winded up for the day. They are all that remains of the mines that existed here. The mine's former counting room has been converted into the National Trust shop and its former stables for ponies serve as the tearoom. The word *Carnewas* is Cornish for "rock pile of the summer dwelling". It refers to an ancient settlement in the area. There are barrows, ancient burial mounds, and a menhir of white quartz nearby as proof of habitation.

A few steps from where we are sat is the location of a former promontory castle. Redcliff Castle is thought to be an Iron Age structure, though most of it, along with part of the headland it was erected on, has been lost to erosion.

Not a single soul is to be spotted in the waters below. Bedruthan — you rapidly arrive at the conclusion — is not a bathing beach. The waters around it are deceptive. The area is known for its rip tides. "It is best to come during the ebb of a spring tide, when the coves and caves may safely be explored; at other times there is grave peril," warned the author Arthur L. Salmon in his book, *The Cornwall Coast*, that was published in 1910. The landscape must have been always forbidding, even though it is jaw-droppingly picturesque. The gnarled, volcanic pillars at Bedruthan Steps have been whittled from the cliffs by the wild waves of the Atlantic. Something of the scenery, the isolated nature of it, those stacks, put me in mind of Kynance Cove and its startling stacks.

At Bedruthan, you feel like you are part of a primeval landscape that has been traced back to the Devonian period and that existed between 416 to 359 million years ago. Such a long time ago indeed that the mind cannot even wrap itself around those figures. A period marked by the formation of new supercontinents and recorded as the age of fish when strange creatures would have swum in the waters. These prehistoric inhabitants of the watery world have left their stamp on the rocks, it is said, around this wild landscape dotted with brooding, everchanging rocks that come with odd names. Some are referred to as islands for when the tidal waters sweep in, these rocks transform into cloistered outcrops. Queen Bess, Samaritan Island, Redcove Island, Pendarves Island, Carnewas Island. Their names are intriguing – some, repository of stories.

We play spot-the-rock and find it easy to identify Queen Bess, a stack named for the Virgin Queen, Elizabeth I. In 1897, an English author from Somerset, John Lloyd Warden Page had made notes on Queen Bess, on her "ample skirts from the base of the crag", "the figure and face, aquiline nose, and all on the top of the head, eighty feet above the water, a tiny crown." But our queen is headless. Sepia-tinted photos of Queen Bess reveal that the top portion of the rock has been lopped off with the passage of the years.

Then there's Samaritan Island, which carries in its name, the hints of a scandalous past. It recalls the fate of a ship that was wrecked at the rock in 1846. That same year, *The West Briton* carried a reportage of the wrecking of the East India Company ship called *The Samaritan*. The backstory being the Hungry Forties — that infamous period in European history when potato blight led to a famine — the ship is said to have been divested of its cargo of barrelled beef and bales of cottons silks and calicos by locals. There is no proof, however, of rumours making the rounds that the ship was deliberately wrecked.

In his book, Salmon had made observations on the not-so-apt name of Samaritan Island. "… because it proved the destruction of an East Indiaman, the "Good Samaritan", many years since; but as it is an ill wind that blows no one any good, so it is certain that the wreck of this richly-cargoed vessel provided the woman folk of the district with fine silks and satins for many years after. You thus understand the point of the local saying, 'It is time for a Good Samaritan to come'."

A popular song is known around these parts.

"The Good Samaritan came ashore
To feed the hungry and clothe the poor,
Barrels of beef and bales of linen,
No poor man shall want a shillin'."

Not even the wreck was spared. Remember, these were desperate times. According to a report carried by *The West Briton* in 1847, the remaining wreck *"with 2,000 lbs of bolt and sheet copper, 10 tons of casement, nail rod and other iron, and about 50 boxes of tinplate"* was slated to be auctioned off at Bedruthan Steps on February 19th. Toward the latter half of the 19th century, the newspaper made a supposition. Maybe, the steps were not built to be a passage for miners. Instead, it may have been a conduit for smugglers and shipwreckers.

Dark and thrilling stories aside, your own instinct warns you. You are not to mess with nature at Bedruthan Steps. You know it has served you well when you come upon a tablet of granite on the cliffs dedicated to the memory of Alex Laurie from Derby who had drowned in the waters, off the beach, in 1903. Laurie's friends, who were with him had survived. They wanted the piece of stone recalling his fate to serve as a deterrent to others. It is a sober reminder of man's puniness in the face of relentless old nature.

There is no scope for our green-eyed friend *ennui* to invade the moment, even as we gather a seat on the cliffs for a prolonged while. Lounging upon our rough bed of greenery, we gawp at the scenery spread out lavishly before our eyes and find that we are bewitched by the beauty of this coastal landscape that certainly has no parallel in the south west.

XXI

Where Hardy Came Across a Pair of Blue Eyes

"I found her out there
On a slope few see,
That falls westwardly
To the salt-edged air,
Where the ocean breaks
On the purple strand,
And the hurricane shakes
The solid land."

The water in the harbour glistens an iridescent blue, turning inky in places where smudges of seaweed undulate upon the bed. Black craggy cliffs stand guard above this scene. Cliffs where the devil bellows; in Boscastle Harbour. At a certain spot in the cliffs is a sea cave that nurses a blowhole. During mid-tide, water is spouted from the blowhole with a boom with the kind of sonic impact that has earned it the label *Devil's Bellows*.

But tide has set in on the noon we reach the harbour on the penultimate day of our holiday and we find ourselves conveniently conned of the marvellous sight of jets of water spraying mist into the air. The devil is not going to bellow for us today. We are not on time. Punctuality as always is the deal breaker, even with nature.

The land-and-waterscape of the village of Boscastle is transfixing. In April 2017, I am stood with my husband under the fury of the midday sun, gazing at the harbour and wondering about Thomas Hardy, his chance meeting with the love of his life in this North Cornish village tucked comfortably into a ravine. A dramatic landscape such as this laid out before the eyes must surely have been an elixir for young love.

The opening lines of this chapter are culled from Hardy. In the late 1800s, he wrote *Tess of the D'urbervilles*, challenging the stodgy notions of morality in Victorian England. After I finished reading it for the first time, I remember being baffled by the empathy Hardy shows with his heroine. Hardy gave Tess a soul, a feat not achieved by many worthy writers of his time and whose characters risked the tag of caricatures. But here was a writer far ahead of the times that he was a product of. The world has needed and will continue to need such writers. I fancy, Hardy might echo Paul Newman in the classic film, *Butch Cassidy and the Sundance Kid*, when he remarked: 'Boy, I got vision, and the rest of the world wears bifocals.'

But this chapter is not on Hardy (here you might interject 'really' with disbelief, eyebrows touching your scalp, given that I have waxed upon his love for two paragraphs and shall devote more to it), neither is it on the strain of realism that pervades his writing. The whole exercise of it is to teleport you into the quaint fishing village of Boscastle.

It is in Boscastle that Hardy had arrived as a young architect in 1870 to work on the restoration of the Church of St. Juliot. What was his prize in this village of the ravine and eye-catching harbour, you might ask? But the possessor of a pair of blue eyes (you know who the novel derived its title from) and a swathe of blonde hair. The owner of those attributes, Emma Gifford, would have his heart for a long time even after she died, and even when Hardy had married a second time. Their life together was a strange, troubled one, yet Hardy's heart is buried with Gifford at her grave in Dorset. His ashes are buried in Westminster Abbey, in keeping with the country's tradition of honouring its literary geniuses.

The heart being buried on its own was not an uncommon funereal practice amongst the medieval elite in Europe. In an exhibition of romance, the heart considered to be the source of all emotions, was carved out of corpses and left to rest at a place beloved of the deceased person. It continued well into the future, from say the 12-13th century, when during military campaigns people died overseas and had their hearts preserved and transported in boxes. Percy Bysshe Shelley's heart — though some quibble, it was his liver — was scooped out of his body by his friends who gave him an ad hoc funeral pyre, after he drowned accidentally. It is said that Mary Shelley had custody of the heart, and to her dying day, the author of *Frankenstein* kept it in a silk bag upon her desk. Not entirely unbelievable since Mrs. Shelley had a tendency towards challenging social mores.

As for Hardy's heart, for this entirely odd and macabre topic had its beginning there, a surgeon is supposed to have carved it out after his death and kept it in a cookie tin. A cat is supposed to have stolen and devoured it. Now this story has all the potential of being dismissed as cockamamie because who would like to believe that a feline heart lies buried at St. Michael's churchyard in Dorset?

Back to when Hardy was alive and had arrived in Boscastle as a 30-year-old, he would have come upon three pubs in the village, a lime kiln and stonewashed cottages said to have been built with stones sourced from the ruins of Botreaux Castle. A Norman family by the name of Botreaux built a stone motte and bailey fortress between mid-to-late 12th century in the village, off the B1345 road. The castle was described as a manor house by an English chronicler in 1478, and a couple of hundred years later, a Cornish antiquary mentioned the use of it as a prison.

Botreaux's Castle no longer exists, having given way to a cottage, but from it the village derives its present name, Boscastle.

We passed a few times through Boscastle on the way to Tintagel during our earlier breaks in Cornwall, but had yet to stop until this spring. Firstly, I want you to know this that Boscastle is one of the most picturesque villages in North Cornwall. The kinds that lure artists to splash canvases with brilliant paints to capture the ridiculous beauty of the landscape and inspire poets to compose odes. It is the kind of place that makes you want to build a tiny cottage high up on the blustery cliffs, to grow old here, to fade away with the elements and the auks.

A B-road winds past the Cobweb Inn into the village. If you have been puttering around the countryside in Britain, you have a handle upon it that monikers here are literal. Naturally, when you come upon a Cobweb Inn, you can safely expect cobwebs hanging from its eaves and ceilings. In the early '90s, health & safety inspectors happened to the inn. Why, they said, swathes of cobwebs to keep flies away from wine? So, I would imagine, they stomped their feet and declared that it would not cut the mustard. These inspectors must have had enough cheek to question the wisdom of men who had run the pub as a wine cellar and flour store since the 1700s, men who had specialized in the mastery of cobwebs.

Those were grave times in the history of the village, but the crux of the matter is that the inn lost its cobwebs — to the tyranny of the health and safety brigade. The passing years have meant that squeamish modern-day travelers, such as you and me, have little to do with such charming extras but there is enough to keep the attention engaged in Boscastle.

There are charming boutiques to potter about in and dilly-dally over beach ornaments. A tearoom run by the National Trust means that you can make life-altering decisions revolving around the choice of the right wedge of cake. Later perhaps, when you have nattered to your heart's content and scoffed enough cake, you might find yourself waddling over to the museum on witchcraft. At the entrance to it is the grave of a 'witch' called Joan Wytte. This 18th-century woman's skeleton hung for years at the museum till one fine day some benevolent person decided it was not okay and that Wytte demanded a burial.

The River Valency passing beneath old and new bridges, gushes along the sprinkling of cottages, shops and museum that are all couched in the bowl of green that is the Valency Valley.

We decide to follow the path that runs parallel to the river up to the cliffs and above the harbour because we want to set out on the SWCP, but not before we have had tea and grazed on cake at the National Trust tearoom. This is followed up by a chance meeting with a pair of Leonberger dogs, Remus and Luna, who have deigned to dip their feet in the Valency because that is the most that this giant breed can and will do in the name of a walk. Next to them is stood a mangy dog, some breed of pooch suitably overshadowed by their presence. The point of standing next to a Leonberger is that no one knows you exist. I doubt even the pooch knows of its existence. But herein is the supreme contradiction. Remus and Luna, their human informs us, are intimidated by the pooch which is his mother's pet.

We meander up the cliffs, where we are stood awhile above the Elizabethan harbour, a powerful reminder of times when privateers, wreckers and smugglers carried on thriving business. We find it easy to cast our minds back in time. Bung in a gale, a stormy sky, and turbulent waters lashing against the cliffs, maybe even the Devil's Bellows at half-tide spouting below, and yes, we could have been in another time and age with the necessary ingredient that is the essence of every wild imagination, a 'willing suspension of disbelief'.

How quiet and serene the village seems at the time with its handful of inland tourists, but in times past, Boscastle would have look vastly different given its renown as a big port. The harbour handled a large proportion of the trade between Bristol and the south western ports. Historians maintain that since pre-Celtic times ships have sailed into the cove of the village.

The nearby villages and towns of Tintagel, Camelford, and Delabole, were all rather dependent on Boscastle's harbour for their supplies of coal and imported goods.

During my research, I happen upon a book by Mr. William Francis Allen Burnard of Bridge House in Boscastle. In his book, *History of Boscastle and Trevalga*, published in 1962, Burnard had noted: "...I hope that, as they peruse its pages, it may add to the interest of the place with its living memories. Also, to the visitor and tourist it is the sincere wish of the writer that their visit to the village may be the best holiday of their lives."

If only I could, I would let Mr. Burnard of Boscastle know this that some of the best memories my husband and I have made, belong in this beloved village that he proudly called home.

***

The path of less resistance can lead to legs that shake like The King's.

This is how.

My husband was never one for walking-hiking holidays, even though I am informed (and thereafter reminded, time and again) with a degree of ill-concealed pride that he used to be an amateur mountaineer in his teens. I was perturbed and surprised in equal measures when I arrived upon the fact with certainty that Adi's idea of a good holiday hovered somewhere between the realms of lazing around and noshing. Then, I happened to him. The day that took place, unknowingly he had signed himself up for more, way more than he had bargained for. But, as you know, a person who reckons with the forces of nature, adapts. It's as simple as that.

The passage of nine odd years has done the job and I can now tell you with some measure of relief that the husband of mine is a convert, and boy, he tends to get attached to things in a solid way. A trait which can be traced back all the way to his childhood days when the story goes that he had to change from one classroom to another, but he turned the prospect down flat on its sorry face. He would have none of it. Leave Claudette behind? Why, it was unthinkable. Claudette was his teacher, you see, and young Adi had a crush on the pretty mademoiselle.

It took my husband all of three months to get used to the idea before he grudgingly agreed to leave her behind and move on. From Claudette to Cornwall is a leap alright, but pray indulge me.

We have chosen the hottest day of the week in April to set out on a hike, which translates into four hours of dawdling under a sun that first threatens us with dire consequences and then delivers on it. By the end of the trip, the skin has started to peel off our napes in strong protest. Not a fetching sight. The payoff is the landscape, sprinkled generously with Red Devon and Friesian cows, stretches of wild gorse bushes, fragrant with heady notes of vanilla, and meadows dotted with daisies, nodding bluebells, and purple saw-wort.

Climbing the cliffs above Boscastle past its sheltered harbour, we leave behind kissing-gates and fields with dry-stone walls, all of which make up Forrabury Stitches, a medieval concept of open-field farming that lingers on in Cornish country. We turn back frequently to let our gazes rest upon this green maze of fields stitched up by tall rows of grass. It is easily the largest patchwork quilt I have ever seen.

A whitewashed tower resembling a folly crops up upon a promontory. Lonely and high, it overlooks the protected harbour fronting Boscastle. Willapark as it is known materialises in our field of view first as a white speck upon the cliffs. It starts growing bigger and bigger as we keep climbing past Boscastle's harbour. Its views across the infinite stretch of the sea and the rugged coastline ahead must have been reason enough for a local landowner to build it as a summer house in the 1800s. He would have never wanted to leave this pleasure nest of his. I certainly wouldn't.

Willapark was leased out eventually to the Board of Trade. Revenue men started using it to keep a close watch on smugglers. The coastguard service had been started in 1822 along cliff tops to allow revenue men to peer into hidden coves and nooks, in their effort to smoke out the wily "free-traders".

Right below the southern cliffs upon which Willapark stands is Western Blackapit, a spot where many a ship is known to have been wrecked. It is now a lookout point for the Boscastle National Coastwatch. The signage at the tower warns us about the strong winds that sweep across the bluff, and that one should keep one's dog on a lead here because it could lead to a 318 ft. fall into the depths. We peek over the edge at Western Blackapit, realise how easy it would be to wind up with broken necks at the bottom of the cliff, and we continue the walk, deciding that the warning for canines holds good for humans too.

Descending the promontory, on the way back to the trail, we happen upon a couple splayed upon the slopes, having a spot of picnic under the robust watch of the morning sun. We pass through pastures, keeping in mind the unstated but important manual that ramblers like us should keep in mind while charting cattle territory. The calm cud-chewing lot can turn on one quite out of the blue.

Salient pointers from the manual include the following clauses:

a) That we do not exhibit threatening behaviour towards calves, which constitutes approaching them in close quarters, talking loudly and being generally noisy, or getting in the way of a calf and its mother. One does not want to provoke a mother's wrath. The best plan is to keep a distance from the bovines and walk along the hedges.

b) If cows do approach, we are not to run away as this would only encourage them to give chase. In which case, we are to stand our ground and stretch our arms wide to appear bigger and intimidating. I have received this kind of advice for bear encounters too. I have however not had the opportunity of testing out the strength of the counsel on either animal. As you can well imagine, I would lean in favour of trying it out on a cow than a bear.

c) The last of the clauses warns walkers from taking their dogs into fields with cows, particularly when calves are in attendance. But if one must, and the cows charge, one might as well use the dog to his own advantage and distract the cow. Release the dog from its lead, as it shall outrun a cow, which in turn might prefer to chase the dog than you. In any case, the dog would be more agile than you.

The animal conversationalist in me has a tough time keeping a fair distance from the bovines that turn up by and by. I cannot resist a wave and mouthing cheery hellos to the tawny cattle lazing along the ridges. Few of them glance our way, but we are far enough for them to resume the idle pursuit of chewing cud. Others are sat staring contemplatively at the idyllic view presented by the shimmering sea. Do they appreciate the view that they have? The one that they soak up every morning of their lives, without realising the privilege they have been born to.

A couple of pastures later, when we have covered the length of the lush meadows, meandering up and down the cliffs bordering the Celtic Sea, I strike gold. A bunch of Friesian calves in a field without watchful mothers in tow. Curious faces, yellow tags sticking out of the ears like showy earrings — how on earth does one resist such a sight? Adi does. He is wary ever since a whole herd of cows, threat radiating off their big beautiful bodies, descended upon us during a random stop at a pasture on our way to the Lake District. Five years have passed, but Adi cannot bring himself to shake off the terror of this memory.

If you choose to walk the South West Coastal Path from Boscastle to Tintagel, the pleasurable news is that for the most part it is of moderate intensity. Each stitched-up pasture is crossed via stone steps and the occasional nimble leap across dry-stone walls that network the length and breadth of the trail. Serious climbing is thrown in too, in bits and bobs.

Expect to saunter through meadows brimming with wildflowers and prickly gorse which burst into bright yellow clumps of flowers once spring arrives, suffusing the air with a vanilla-coconut fragrance. But here I repeat myself. The gorse though is absolutely a thing of wild beauty. Some locals use its blossoms to make cordial.

Meanwhile, all along on our right, the changing hues are hypnotic. Where the sea meets the horizon, it is icy blue. Nearer the coast, deep blue currents hypnotically swirl in and out of the pale waters. The waters below the cliffs gleam in shades of sapphire blue and turquoise, and when we peer down, tendrils of turquoise waves flecked with white foam curl around the shores.

***

We opt for a lunch break at a bench, sheltered from the scorching sun by overgrown plants and hedges. The view with its roll call of blues is exquisite. As we nibble on sandwiches, an elderly couple pass us by, commenting upon the irrefutable beauty of the spot. Eventually, we fall back upon the path. We pass by the hamlet of Trevalga. The length of the walk and the intensity of the midday heat conspiring to make us fantasise about tubs of chilled beer. I do not know why, but it never occurs to us to stop at the inn at Trevalga for a pint, as in the past drivers of horse carriages carrying slate would have, before carrying on to Boscastle with their goods. We press on, relentless in our aim to reach Tintagel, observing along the way dark islets that are home to colonies of seabirds.

Midway between Boscastle and Tintagel is Rocky Valley, a sylvan landscape dramatically framed by a canyon that is for the most part composed of piles of slate, stacked together by some unseen hand. The walking trail plunges into a gorge. We cautiously tread the descent. Wet slate is a notoriously slippery customer. A river cascades alongside us into rock pools before making its way to the sea. Meanwhile, a sign shows the walker the path to an old mill in the area. We leave it behind, and a wooden footbridge later, we are on our way up the cliffs.

"What a beautiful spot you have!" I call out involuntarily to a woman with a shock of white hair who we meet along the way. She is sat on a boulder at the edge of the cliff top with a frisky pooch for company. The little fellow prances around us for a bit as we exchange the customary pleasantries. Strangers bound together by a common appreciation of the land they find themselves in.

At this point, we espy the sheltered beach at Bossiney Haven, and Hotel Camelot silhouetted against the afternoon sun, a few cliffs away. Our first reaction? Whoops of glee. Succour lies ahead of us, in the shape of pasties and beer. And at this moment, the thought of draining pints is as alluring to us as the singing of mythic sirens to lovelorn seafarers.

Finally, the moment arrives when we find ourselves dragging our tired bodies through the well-loved lanes of Tintagel. An antiquated scene plays out before our eyes. A girl is stood outside a pasty shop, announcing to all and sundry that pasties and pies are going at half price because it's closing time. They do things the old way here in North Cornwall. In a heartbeat, we feel the trappings of the modern age fall away. We buy pasties for a few quid. As we are leaving, a couple of old men walk into the shop, wondering aloud, "How on earth is it any good if it is so cheap?"

"Oh, ye of little faith," I think to myself. Something tells me that they do take the leap of faith.

A few steps down the road we enter *The Cornishman Inn* and order pints of Doom. As is normal in this part of the country, the bartender is up for a natter. Hearing of our travels, he wonders, "Did you know that your drink is named after the Doom Bar in Padstow?" And then, the topic shifts to food. Rick Stein being synonymous with Padstow, it is natural that the conversation embraces him. The bartender nurses a strong opinion on Rick Stein. Are there any merits to the chef? If you listen to the man behind the bar, you shall make that a thumping no. He expresses in as many words as possible, his disgust at the thought of the celebrity chef transforming Padstow into his fiefdom.

You know how beer flames the fumes of hunger, and anyway we are knackered after our walk, so we wolf down the half-price pasties, which taste twice as good (don't most things, when acquired on the cheap?). This is before we realise with a start that a long wait lies ahead of us if we are to take the bus that will take us back to Boscastle. It is not a frequent service, something that we failed to check before undertaking the walk. Thus, you have two chumps left with the prospect of a solid three more hours of walking. I have never felt more shattered; if only for a cloud to descend and offer us a comfy ride back to Boscastle, allowing our worn-out limbs much-needed rest.

We pass by hamlets, woody paths leading down to the river, and in the village of Bossiney we see asymmetrical stone cottages built with stacked shards of slate. They look the part of modest fisherman's' hutches. I am quite in two minds about knocking on the door of a quaint cottage that is surrounded by straggling plants, wildflowers, and bushes, but Adi refuses to have any of my impulsiveness at a moment when all he dreams of is a pub and glasses brimming with ale.

We plod on for what seems like eternity before we walk past St. Juliot's Church and reach *The Wellington Arms* in Boscastle. Not a person is to be seen on the country lanes. Adi and I are the only two people in the village who happen to be outside. Soon I realise why. The roads might be empty, but the pub is comfortably full. Everyone has the customary pint on their tables. The fire is on, the cosiness of it lulling, and I cannot express in words the sheer relief we feel at sinking into cushy armchairs and letting our legs off the hook.

"What, another pub already?" I hear you say. To that I will have you walk 10 interminable miles, so that your legs declare that they do not belong to you – they might as well be columns of wobbly jelly — then perhaps you will see that there is no path but one to bliss. To be had within the cosy portals of a pub.

The tiredness starts seeping out and we feel as happy as clams.

After a stretch of quiet in which we chug on our beer with great focus and love, we compare notes. We agree that the landscape all along has gone down a treat. One simply cannot tire of views of rolling pastures, bands of cows and sheep, the sea, that church spire in the distance. The English countryside exudes the kind of serene beauty, the likes of which you would not find anywhere else in the world. And, I have been around a bit.

There is a photograph that I have of Adi, at the entrance to Boscastle on the evening. In it, he is stood behind a big tablet of stone inscribed with the name of the village, throwing his hands up in the air for the moment, a shark-y grin pasted upon his face. It is the unrestrained triumph of the victor, his cheeks shining in the delicate salmon rays of a dying sun. At one point, he even hugs the stone with gratitude – for just turning up and signalling an end to our walking adventures for the day.

XXII

Of Twin Seaside Villages and a Farewell

The sky is flawlessly blue when we begin our journey to the "forgotten corner" of Cornwall on the last morning of our ten-day holiday, but as the morning progresses, clouds appear and curdle into a fine buttermilk consistency; the sun has his hat on. The Rame Peninsula in South East Cornwall, near the border with Devon, is a designated area of outstanding natural beauty and strangely often skipped by travellers. Like we have a few times, mostly because we were not aware of it. This time we find photos of it in the pages of the same brochure in which we had discovered Charlestown and make it a point to touch upon its pastoral set-up.

On the way to the Rame, a viaduct is thrown up in the distance. St. Germans Viaduct. What a man-made spectacle a viaduct is with its row of perfect arches, an example of a fine feat of Roman engineering from another age yet look at the timelessness of their sensibility. This one spans the width of the dried-up bed of River Tiddy. Gazing at the symmetry of the arches which are seventeen in number, I can imagine the way Jean-Jacques Rousseau felt when he first clapped eyes upon the Pont du Gard, a limestone aqueduct in the south of France. The 18th century philosopher had observed: "The echo of my footsteps under these immense vaults made me imagine that I heard the strong voices of those who had built them. I felt myself lost like an insect in that immensity… and, I said to myself with a sigh, 'Why was I not born a Roman?'"

St. Germans Viaduct is however not the brainchild of the Romans. It was designed by Isambard Kingdom Brunel in 1855. You know him from before, as the iconic British civil engineer behind the conception of the Royal Albert Bridge over River Tamar. Brunel's original viaduct was built in timber but reworked in stone in the early part of the next century. Stone is long lasting after all. The run of the bridge is impressive. It goes on and on, and when I look up the details, I am impressed to see that it measures 945 feet in length, carrying as it does the main rail line from Plymouth to Penzance.

Fertile pastures roll by in shades of light and spirulina green (in case you have never had spirulina, it is algae packed with nutrients and I bung it into my fruit smoothies, hence the re). In just such a serene state of mind, we are introduced to the twin fishing villages of the Rame: Kingsand and Cawsand. They are positioned right across the border from the neighbouring county of Devon.

In the village of Kingsand we spot a house, on the pastel blue walls of which are the words "Devon Corn" carved in iron. You might think one of two things. That the house hoards corn from Devon. Or, that the house has been built with money made from rich harvests of Devon-grown corn. In either scenario, you would be overthinking it. It is a symbol of the past. You see, the villages of Cawsand and Kingsand have not always been part of the same county. While Cawsand was Cornish, Kingsand used to be a part of Devon. This was before the year 1844 when the border line was shifted, so now the above-mentioned house straddles the old border between the two counties.

A maze of narrow streets run the length and breadth of Kingsand. On these streets, the houses are tightly knit together, which to me occurs to be a clever way of providing shelter from inclement coastal weather. The house fronts are painted in soothing whites and pastels, the occasional purple door peeping out from an otherwise muted façade to shake things up a bit. There is no uniformity in architectural styles on the streets of Kingsand. In fact, the difference in textures and details of the various house fronts is engaging, allowing little scope for the mind to zone out. I love the sight of the fishermen's lime-washed cottages built with stone rubble, their roofs sheathed in slate. They look more a part of the landscape than the eighteenth and nineteenth century townhouses of red sandstone. But I do eye elements of elegance in them. The sash windows of the townhouses are altogether fetching. Before we exit the network of houses that gradually spills over into an open space by the beach called The Cleave, I dawdle in a tiny shop and exchange notes on the weather with the woman at the till. If you have met a Brit who does not spend the first five minutes of the conversation talking about the sun or lack thereof, something must be terribly off with him/her.

When we make our way to the beachfront, we see rows of lobster pots and fishing nets plopped in front of houses in soft pastels and bright window trims. There's a pub and a café for refreshments, of which we make immediate use of the latter and coffee cups in hand, check out the clock tower that seems to occupy pride of place on the beach. Clad in reddish stone and built to commemorate the coronation of King George V, I take a shine to it.

Looking up from where we are on the sun-drenched shingle beach, I like the look of the dark green woods that billow in the backdrop of the village. It looks like the settlement has been tucked into its surroundings rather than the other way around.

That we are in traditional fishing villages is reinforced by the sight of the 18th century seafront pilchard cellars, outhouses and net huts built in the locally quarried, red volcanic stone. The pilchard palaces, roofed courtyards where pilchards were traditionally pressed with salt, must have come handy in the great Cornish occupation of smuggling during the 17th and 18th centuries. Many a free-trading vessel is said to have passed through Cawsand Bay. The alternate calling of the Cornish people in "Kings Sand and Causam Bay" finds mention in the records of historian Richard Carew in the *Survey of Cornwall* (1769). "I have heard the Inhabitants thereabouts to report, that the Earl of Richmond (afterwards Henry the seventh) while hee hovered upon the coast, here by stealth refreshed himselfe; but being advertised of streight watch, kept for his surprising at Plymouth, he richly rewarded his hoste, hyed sppedily a shipboord, and escaped happily to a better fortune," wrote Carew.

We are in the former headquarters of the West Country Free Trade movement - that was stymied by the mid-1800s. There are plenty of hidden coves and corners in both villages to encourage dubious, unsanctioned activities. What made it worth the while for smugglers in the Rame to risk their lives in ferrying contraband goods, is its proximity to Plymouth that was a booming market for goods acquired on the sly. The bluster of the band of night-time operators in the twin villages is revealed in a report carried by *The Times of London* in October 1785. It recalls an incident in which a couple of smuggling boats from Cawsand were spotted by naval officers. One of the officers was shot by the smugglers, subsequent to which the night sky is said to have rang with the smugglers' cries of, "kill them all, don't let one go ashore to tell their story". Then these intrepid smugglers went ahead and unloaded their cargoes. This sort of daredevilry must have been acquired through practice, of taking care of the authorities in like manner, over a prolonged stretch of time.

An 1804 survey of the revenue services estimates that the two villages had had landings of 17,000 kegs of spirits in just about a year. That these are not fanciful concoctions is evident through records left by a fair number of eyewitnesses. A Devon-based author, Laura Quigley, quotes an 18th century visitor to Cawsand in her book *Bloody British History*. In descending a "very steep hill", the visitor noted, "amidst the most fetid and disagreeable odour of stinking pilchards and train oil…we met several females, whose appearance was so grotesque and extraordinary, that I could not imagine in what manner they had contrived to alter their natural shapes so completely; till upon enquiry, we found they were smugglers of spiritual liquors."

Curious, later I do some more poking into the wide wild world of the Internet (along with packing for our impending Big move) and come across notes from excise officers logged in the journal of the National Maritime Museum of Cornwall. They state that midway through the month of January in 1801, five excise officers raided the house of a couple of fishermen in Cawsand. The party entered the house and mounted its stairs. While they had proof that there was contraband liquor stored inside — one of them having tasted the spirits too, the fishermen were enraged at the intrusion. One of them brandished a bayonet and "threatened in the most violent language that he would murder every Man who should attempt to approach the said Stairs". Petrified, the officers scuttled before the man made good on his word.

For all the stories you hear, there is disappointingly little that remains of the smuggling operations in the villages. The tunnels that were used at the time have been sealed up. Instead, we have innocuous beaches and rockpools to play with and bathe in the juicy sunshine of the noon.

Sauntering by the *Halfway House Inn*, a congregational church tucked in at the end of a passage, and a large mural titled *Plenty of Fish…?* on a house front (put up by Austrian artists using marine plastic litter), we do not even realise when we enter Cawsand. It is a seamless transition - as if it is normal for villages in this part of the country to meld so.

***

The road dips into Cawsand as we walk past quaint seaside cottages, down a hill. The bay surfaces into view. And a ball of fur comes charging towards us. A gregarious English Springer Spaniel for whom any amount of attention falls short. An elderly woman appears in the spaniel's wake and offers to rescue us from his exuberance. This opens up a window for a chinwag, while we lavish affection on our frisky friend.

After, we are stood awhile by the old stone walls perched above the bay, taking in the sight of houses and cottages huddled in a semi-circle around it. The shingle beach at Cawsand Bay is remarkably empty as it bakes beneath the stringent attention of the midday sun. Only kayak trolleys are to be found scattered on the beach. A few boats are out on the waters, now bewitchingly blue, across which is Plymouth Sound and a dark hump sticking out from the waters, The Great Mewstone. Further beyond is the coastline of Devon.

As felt and observed in Kingsand, I experience the same calming quality about the setting of Cawsand. Both coastal villages, built as they are into steep hillsides and sheathed in dense greenery, are located within a country park that once belonged to the estate of the Earls of Edgcumbe. Nothing feels contrived about the park even though part of it is. The woods were laid out sometime during the 18th and 19th centuries. This natural halo about the villages is stamped on most of its buildings. St. Andrew's Church in Cawsand, for instance, looks as if it has sprouted organically, an effect compounded by walls of sandstone rubble and roofs of slate. As we start climbing up and leaving the villages behind to work our way inland, the scenery is quilted with vast fields, creeks and valleys.

Keeping watch on the horizon above Cawsand is a 19th-century fortification that was built during Napoleonic times for protection from a French invasion, but that never took place, so it sits like a giant reminder of a time of political unrest when forts and batteries were natural responses to threats of attack from neighbours. Looking at the fort closely, we realise that it is an apartment building now. Vast residential quarters that resulted from a time when the fort was abandoned by the military in the late 1920s. I am green at the thought of the view that the fort residents are treated to on a daily basis. One could live with such an outlook for all of one's living years.

But why should we rush out of Cawsand, when there is time and intent to luxuriate in its tranquil alleys? The mood for ambling is cemented when we pick up Cornish ice creams and hang around the bay, thinking of different times. Cawsand under the cover of night, as a port-of-call for covert operations, dodgy operators and contraband cargoes. Of Harry Carter, the famous smuggler and brother of the King of Prussia (John Carter) who used this very bay as his one of his bases.

Cut. To a frigid January night in the late 1700s when Carter is working on the unloading of cargoes in the waters near the bay. He spots two men-of-war, from which officers board his lugger before he can escape. In the skirmish to follow, during which most of his men are laid low, he fights hand-to-hand with an officer. Carter receives the gravest of wounds from a cutlass and pretends to lay dead on deck while the officers examine him for signs of life. "I have thought hundreds of times since what a miracle it was I neither sneezed, coughed, nor drew breath …" writes Carter in *The Autobiography of a Cornish Smuggler*. He escapes from his lugger and manages to drag himself to the beach we are on. He's in luck. The fishermen of Cawsand are on the lookout for him — on the instructions of his brother Charles Carter. In one of these houses surrounding the beach, he finds refuge and a brother joyous to see him alive.

If I am questioned by the King's Men, I know better than to let my tongue run away, for if I pay heed I can hear them, "Five and twenty ponies,/Trotting through the dark". Them with their booties of brandy and tobacco. My job is simply to be the onlooker. Lay low, call upon St. Piran for deliverance and watch the wall while the Gentlemen go by.

Lingering comes easy, especially, when you are about to leave Cornwall. How do you leave a duchy that is so wrapped up in its own tranquillity that it does not need to look outwards?

Leave we must, but we do so with our heads saturated with memories of its wild, wild shores, the coastal paths running through meadows of bluebells and gorse, the dense woods, its crummy old mining towns and kebab houses, the many fishing villages and pasties and fish pies, the chatty Cornish, and those seriously tall tales of smuggling. There will come a time when these memories will start to fray at the edges and we will squint to remember the details, but both Adi and I know that we will always have Cornwall.

EPILOGUE

With the hope that you have read these essays at leisure, preferably with a cup of tea and a wedge of cake (mind, nothing good comes of not giving into cake), I shall confess to you that like Marco Polo I did not, indeed I could not, write half of what I saw. Some things, like the moment itself, the way you react and feel in the thick of it, or the way your relationship with your loved one changes over the course of this time, is often lost in the act of recalling details and putting words to paper. But having parsed the memories of our travels over the passage of the years and observing how we live and travel, I can fairly say that our Cornwall years have changed us for good.

As a couple we have calmed down. Which however does not mean that we have transformed into blooming saints, but we listen to the other, better than we did in our twenties. When you have grown together in a relationship and seen the world together alongside, really absorbed the fact that it is a beautiful, yet difficult place to trample through, I believe you lean into each other. And in doing so, it works towards healing the tears, big and small, in your partnership.

Also, I find that we are not in a hurry to rush through a place. We take the time to rummage through flea markets, have a cuppa even if we have to queue up for it (and really, if we did not learn the art of queueing in the UK, what would we be). We indulge in conversations with fellow diners, gather stories wherever we come by them, and take off on random rambles into the woods where (this did happen to me) a deer might creep up on us. As long as it's not a bear, a timber rattlesnake, or a mountain cat, there being more wildlife in the forests of the East Coast than we accounted for, I have no cause for complaint. We shall keep calm and carry on. A couple of additional elements from our Cornish travels that have followed us into our transatlantic home is the fact that we have swapped cosy pubs for small breweries in upstate New York — and, we still stalk dogs.

About the Author

Arundhati Basu is a former journalist from Calcutta, India. She studied English Literature at Presidency College, Calcutta, and followed it up with an MA Diploma in journalism studies from the Indian Institute of Mass Communication in New Delhi. Basu started her writing career in 2003, reporting for the leading dailies in Delhi, *The Times of India* and *The Telegraph*. In 2012, she quit journalism. In the same year, she relocated with her spouse, Aditya Varma, to the Midlands in the UK. She started working as a freelance writer. Alongside she travelled extensively with Varma and wrote about her travels in her popular travel blog, *The Travelling Diary of a Dippy Dotty Girl*. In 2017, she relocated with her husband to the United States. Now, she lives in Bayonne, a port town across from the Big Apple, where she spends her time reading, writing and painting. When ennui strikes, Basu dreams of life in a cosy cob cottage on the craggy cliffs of Cornwall, its walls blowsy with wild vines and roses, the high wind whistling around its roofs of thatched eave.

www.arundhatibasu.net

Printed in Great Britain
by Amazon

58748482R00151